The State and Local Government Political Dictionary

State governments are no longer sleepy backwater operations located in far-off capitals where few people know or care what they are doing. They are big-time organizations on a par with many "Fortune 500" companies.

—THAD L. BEYLE

THE
STATE AND
LOCAL GOVERNMENT
POLITICAL DICTIONARY

Jeffrey M. Elliot
Sheikh R. Ali
North Carolina Central University

ABC-CLIO

Santa Barbara, California
Oxford, England

Library of Congress Cataloging-in-Publication Data

Elliot, Jeffrey M.
   The state and local government political dictionary.

   (Clio dictionaries in political science)
   Includes index.
   1. State governments—Dictionaries. 2. Local
government—United States—Dictionaries. 3. Federal
government—United States—Dictionaries. 4. Municipal
government—United States—Dictionaries. 5. Local
finance—United States—Dictionaries. I. Ali, Sheikh
Rustum.   II. Title.   III. Series.
JK2408. E44   1987   353.9'03   87–18722
ISBN 0–87436–417–5 (alk. paper)
ISBN 0–87436–512–0 (pbk. : alk. paper)

10 9 8 7 6 5 4 3 2 1 (cloth)
10 9 8 7 6 5 4 3 2 1 (paper)

ABC-Clio, Inc.
Riviera Campus
2040 Alameda Padre Serra, Box 4397
Santa Barbara, California 93140–4397

Clio Press Ltd.
55 St. Thomas' Street
Oxford, OX1 1JG, England

This book is printed on acid-free paper ∞ .
Manufactured in the United States of America

*To Dr. Austin J. Lee, for his honesty,
sensitivity, and humility, this book,
with admiration and affection*

*To Dr. Helen G. Edmonds, a beacon,
a guru, and a treasured friend of the Alis*

Clio Dictionaries in Political Science

Clio Dictionaries in Political Science

SERIES STATEMENT

Language precision is the primary tool of every scientific discipline. That aphorism serves as the guideline for this series of political dictionaries. Although each book in the series relates to a specific topical or regional area in the discipline of political science, entries in the dictionaries also emphasize history, geography, economics, sociology, philosophy, and religion.

This dictionary series incorporates special features designed to help the reader overcome any language barriers that may impede a full understanding of the subject matter. For example, the concepts included in each volume were selected to complement the subject matter found in existing texts and other books. All but one volume utilize a subject matter chapter arrangement that is most useful for classroom and study purposes.

Entries in all volumes include an up-to-date definition plus a paragraph of *Significance* in which the authors discuss and analyze the term's historical and current relevance. Most entries are also cross-referenced, providing the reader an opportunity to seek additional information related to the subject of inquiry. A comprehensive index, found in both hard cover and paperback editions, allows the reader to locate major entries and other concepts, events, and institutions discussed within these entries.

The political and social sciences suffer more than most disciplines from semantic confusion. This is attributable, *inter alia*, to the popularization of the language, and to the focus on many diverse foreign political and social systems. This dictionary series is dedicated to overcoming some of this confusion through careful writing of thorough, accurate definitions for the central concepts, institutions, and events that comprise the basic knowledge of each of the subject fields. New titles in the series will be issued periodically, including some in related social science disciplines.

—Jack C. Plano
Series Editor

CONTENTS

A NOTE ON HOW TO USE THIS BOOK

The State and Local Government Political Dictionary is organized so that entries and supplementary data can be located easily and quickly. Items are arranged alphabetically within subject-matter chapters. For example, terms like *Gubernatorial Powers* or *Department of Human Resources* can be found in the chapter titled "The Executive Branch." When doubtful about which chapter to refer to, consult the general index. Entry numbers for terms appear in the index in heavy black type; subsidiary concepts discussed within entries can be found in the index identified by entry numbers in regular type. For study purposes, numerous entries have also been subsumed under major topical headings in the index, affording the reader access to broad classes of related information.

The reader can also more fully explore a topic by employing the extensive cross-references included in most entries. These may lead to materials included in the same chapter or may refer the reader to the subject matter of other chapters. Entry numbers have been included in all cross-references for the convenience of the reader. A few entries can be found as subsidiary concepts in more than one chapter, but in each case the concept is related to the subject of that chapter in which the entry appears.

The authors have adopted the format of this book to provide the reader a variety of useful applications. These include its use as (1) a *dictionary* and *reference guide* to the language of state and local government; (2) a *study guide* for the introductory course in intergovernmental relations, or for more specialized courses in the area; (3) a *supplement to a textbook* or a group of paperback monographs adopted for use in these courses; (4) a *source of review material* for the political science major enrolled in advanced courses; and (5) a *social science aid* for use in business, education, government, and journalism.

PREFACE

The State and Local Government Political Dictionary reflects the authors' combined total of more than 20 years of study, research, writing, and teaching state and local government courses at a variety of institutions to a variety of students. This breadth of experience has enabled us to produce what we hope will be an indispensable guide to the enormously rich lexicon of state and local government. We believe that knowledge about cities and states is vitally significant. Knowledge is understanding and appreciating what is important, not simply memorizing names, dates, and events. Yet the path to knowledge inevitably involves learning facts and gathering information. This volume includes myriad facts and information, but it also provides ample analysis and interpretation. In writing this book, we were motivated by two goals: first, to present factual information about state and local political institutions, processes, and policies, and, second, to encourage the interested reader to take a more active role in the day-to-day affairs of his or her city and state.

Although this volume employs the dictionary format, it includes several important variations. Entries are categorized into subject-matter chapters that parallel chapter topics in most leading textbooks in the field. In addition to a brief definition, each entry features a paragraph of *Significance* to assist the reader to better understand the historical roots and contemporary meaning of the concept. Furthermore, an extensive cross-reference system is used throughout the work, enabling the reader to seek additional information on desired topics.

These 290 entries have been systematically selected and organized to complement most standard works on the subject. Thus, the instructor or student can use this dictionary as a teaching/learning supplement to the core text or as a tool for unifying courses developed around individual readings. Throughout this volume, we have attempted to define and explain each term as authoritatively, succinctly, clearly, and readably as possible. Where we have failed, we would welcome comments from instructors and students as to any sins of commission or omission. Finally, please remember that, in selecting these entries, we have chosen to be discriminating rather than exhaustive; we included only those terms that we deem essential to a basic understanding of state and local government.

We wish to express our appreciation to the many students who, over the years, have stimulated our interest and excitement in the politics of grass-roots government. If we have done our job well—that is, written an informative and engaging work—then perhaps they, too, will experience a similar fascination. The authors deeply appreciate the assistance of the many people who helped to produce this book. To begin with, we would like to acknowledge the general support given by Cecelia A. Albert, associate editor, ABC-CLIO. Her encouragement was no small element in the overall success of this undertaking. We would also like to extend our gratitude to the staff of ABC-CLIO, with special thanks to Ronald J. Boehm, president; Marie S. Ensign, director of editorial operations; Ann L. Hartman, director of marketing and sales; and Terri MacRae, graphic production manager. Most of all, we are indebted to Jack C. Plano, series editor, who read the manuscript in its entirety and made many valuable comments and suggestions, and whose wise counsel and balanced judgment gave us the incentive to see it through to conclusion.

—Jeffrey M. Elliot
—Sheikh R. Ali
North Carolina Central University

The State and Local Government Political Dictionary

1. Federal and State Constitutions

Bill of Rights (1)

The first ten amendments to the United States Constitution or the provisions of state constitutions pertaining to individual liberties. The federal Bill of Rights specifies rights that the federal government cannot violate. These include substantive rights, such as freedom of speech, press, religion, and assembly, as well as procedural rights, such as the right to trial by jury, protection against self-incrimination, and protection against unreasonable search and seizure. The Bill of Rights was added to the United States Constitution in 1791. The Thirteenth, Fourteenth, Fifteenth, and Nineteenth Amendments to the Constitution, added later, are also part of the American system that protects individual rights. Every state's bill of rights places constraints on government's freedom to proceed against persons suspected of crimes. In addition, most of the rights protected from arbitrary violation by the federal government through the guarantees of the Bill of Rights are also safeguarded from arbitrary state actions by the due process clause of the Fourteenth Amendment. *See also* CIVIL LIBERTIES, 4; CIVIL RIGHTS, 5.

Significance   The Bill of Rights was introduced as a compromise between the Federalists and Anti-Federalists when the latter insisted on the inclusion of the Bill of Rights as a condition for ratification of the Constitution. The restraints contained in the Bill of Rights were imposed only upon the federal government, as the Supreme Court later decreed in the famous case *Barron v. Baltimore* (7 Pet. 243: 1833); the states and local governments for many years were untouched by the prohibitions contained in the Bill of Rights. Beginning with *Gitlow v. New York* (268 U.S. 652: 1925), the Supreme Court began a selective

3

incorporation of the rights specified in the Bill of Rights into the liberty clause of the Fourteenth Amendment, making them apply as limits on state and local governments. In addition, all state constitutions contain a list of individual rights to be protected through actions by state courts.

Charter   (2)

The basic law or constitution of a local government. A charter defines power, responsibilities, and organization of local governmental units. These units are cities, towns, townships, municipalities, special districts, multipurpose districts, and villages. There are four general types of charters. "Special act" charters are drawn specifically for a particular city, and these cities are completely under state legislative control. "General act" charters categorize cities by population and apply appropriate state law to all cities in each size category. These divisions may include cities with populations of less than 10,000, between 10,000 and 25,000, and so on. An "optional" charter law affords a city government more freedom of choice by permitting it to select the form of government it prefers from among several alternatives provided by state law. The "home rule" charter provides a city with the greatest degree of self-rule by permitting it to draft and change its charter and manage its affairs. *See also* CONSTITUTION, 8; STATE CONSTITUTIONS, 26.

Significance   A charter is granted to a local unit by the state; every local government is therefore a creature of the state. This subordinate status means that the local governments have a dual function. First, they must satisfy the demands of citizens for services, and second, they must carry out state policies and regulations, as set forth in their charters and in general state law. The charter has been the focal point of reform movements at the local governmental level. During President Andrew Jackson's administration (1828–1836), for example, the method of selecting a mayor was changed from appointment by the council to election by the people in most parts of the country. Many reformers prefer home rule charters, which allow cities to choose the form of government they prefer. Home rule tends to move the state-local relationship in the direction of federalism.

Checks and Balances   (3)

The constitutional principle that enables each branch of government to limit the powers of the others. The principle of checks and balances operates among the legislative, executive, and judicial branches, between the two houses of the United States Congress, between the two houses in state legislatures (except in Nebraska, which has one house), and between federal and state governments. The United States Congress investigates, appropriates funds for, and confirms appointments to the executive and judicial branches. Congress can override a presidential veto, impeach federal officials (executive and judicial), and give "advice and consent" in foreign policy matters. On the other hand, the president as chief executive can check Congress by using the veto power. The president may pardon persons convicted by the judiciary, and through selection of its personnel maintains checks on it. Congress has the impeachment power of members of the judiciary. The judiciary, by reviewing a law, may declare it unconstitutional. *See also* CONSTITUTION, 8; SEPARATION OF POWERS, 25.

Significance　　　The principle of checks and balances means that each branch of government not only has the authority to exercise its own powers, but to limit those of the others. This principle, devised by James Madison, the main architect of the United States Constitution, reflected his objective of setting power against power. Madison and the other founders were faced with a dilemma. The new nation needed strong leadership, yet tyranny was greatly feared. The answer for the founding fathers was to provide the essential powers, but to safeguard against misuse by a system of checks and balances, that would ensure moderation in the use of power. The United States Constitution and the state constitutions have made the various branches of government "co-equal" with a system of checks and balances that prevents tyranny and abuse of power.

Civil Liberties　　　　　(4)
Basic rights set forth in constitutional documents that safeguard individuals and groups from arbitrary and unjust actions by government. Civil liberties usually include freedom of speech, press, assembly, petition, association, and religion, together with procedural guarantees, such as freedom from unlawful searches and seizures and the guarantee of a full and speedy trial. In the United States, civil liberties are guaranteed by the Bill of Rights, by the Fourteenth Amendment, and by state constitutions. The First Amendment reads: "Congress shall make no law respecting an establishment of religion, or prohibiting the exercise thereof; or abridging the freedom of speech, or of the press; or the right of the people peaceably to assemble, and to petition the Government for a redress of grievances."

Along with the First, the Fourth, Fifth, Sixth, Seventh, and Eighth Amendments most directly seek to restrain the government from interfering with an individual's basic rights. Many state constiutions include civil liberties and civil rights. *See also* CIVIL RIGHTS, 5; DUE PROCESS OF LAW, 11.

Significance   Civil liberties are based on the sovereign role of the people as the source of governmental power in a democracy. These liberties are basic to a democratic society, and act as a restraint upon government power. The interpretation of civil liberties is an important function of the courts, especially the United States Supreme Court. Often, state courts overlook state constitutions in dealing with civil liberties because they base their rulings on decisions of the United States Supreme Court. Some state laws extend greater protection than federal laws, but the United States Constitution and the Bill of Rights incorporate many of the basic concepts of liberty. The United States Supreme Court has played a major role in upholding the constitutional right of citizens and limiting the power of government.

Civil Rights   (5)

Protections against discrimination or arbitrary treatment by government or by private groups or individuals. Civil rights safeguard individuals against discrimination on grounds of race, color, creed, sex, or national origin. Protected rights are grouped in a Bill of Rights, guaranteeing individuals freedom from interference in their private lives. Guarantees are also sometimes written into state constitutions but usually take the form of statutes guaranteeing fair trial and due process of law. The Fourteenth Amendment to the United States Constitution states that no state shall "deprive any person of life, liberty, or property without due process of law, nor deny to any person within its jurisdiction the equal protection of the laws." Civil rights safeguard against discrimination and are derived from the equal protection clause of the Fourteenth Amendment and from statutes passed by federal and state legislatures. *See also* CIVIL LIBERTIES, 4; DUE PROCESS OF LAW, 11.

Significance   Civil Rights belong to individuals as a result of their membership in an organized and civilized society. To a large extent, civil rights are nothing but natural rights that have been recognized and defined by the state. In the United States, the Congress passed the first Civil Rights Act in 1866, which for the first time defined citizens as all persons born in the United States except nontaxed Indians. The act became the Fourteenth Amendment to the Constitution on July 28, 1868. Since then there have been many attempts to promote the observance of civil rights. Many civil rights organizations have emerged, such as the National Association for the Advancement of Colored People (NAACP), which concerns itself mainly with legislative matters dealing with the rights of black Americans. The United States government has attempted to extend protection of individual rights to the nation's various minority groups and to women.

Concurrent Powers (6)

Authority that can be exercised by both the states and the federal government. Concurrent power involves the sharing of power between national, state, and local governments. Any power not exclusively conferred on the national government by the Constitution may be concurrently exercised by the national and state governments, if this is not in conflict with national law. Examples of concurrent power include the power to tax, spend, and borrow money, to enact federal and state criminal laws for the same crime, to take property after paying just compensation, to spend money for the general welfare, to establish courts, and to enforce laws. Article VI of the United States Constitution states that there can be no conflict between national and state law; national law takes precedence. Whenever action of the national and state governments conflict, the former prevails. *See also* CONSTITUTION, 8; EXCLUSIVE POWERS, 14.

Significance   Concurrent powers enable the states to function without undue dependence on the national government. The fact that certain powers have been delegated to the national government does not mean that this authority is exclusively possessed on that level. For example, Congress prohibits the states from exercising powers relating to treaty making; in this instance it is the nature of the power itself that determines its use by the national government alone. However, it is possible that certain phases of a treaty dealing with commercial intercourse may be validly the subject of state regulation so long as this does not conflict with national laws. In case of conflict the power of the national government is supreme. It is essential that both national and state governments possess powers necessary to enable them to function. The courts usually support the ability of the national government to meet changing expectations of the nation.

Confederation (7)
An association of independent states that possess a central government or administrative organ but maintain their individual sovereignty. Under a confederation—as distinct from a federation, where supreme authority is lodged in the central government—the central government is limited to that power delegated to it by the member states and has no autonomous power of its own. In addition, each member state has the freedom to withdraw or secede from the confederation if it so chooses. In a pure confederation, the representative body—if it has one—is chiefly concerned with diplomatic functions as opposed to legislative ones. Representatives are solely responsible to the member states and may not enact laws that are binding on the member states without their approval. Likewise, the executive and judicial branches have little if any authority over the member states. A confederation is often deemed desirable when the member states wish to achieve collective territorial integrity, as well as "institutionalized" political coordination without surrendering their individual sovereignty. *See also* FEDERALISM, 29; SOVEREIGNTY, 50; STATES' RIGHTS, 51; UNITARY STATE, 28.

Significance   A confederation was originally instituted in the United States under the Articles of Confederation. Drafted under the auspices of the Continental Congress in 1776, it was approved by the member states one year later. The Articles provided for a weak chief executive and weak congress, which was handicapped by its inability to tax. In 1789, the founding fathers replaced the Articles of Confederation with the United States Constitution. However, widespread concern for state sovereignty, as expressed in the Articles of Confederation, has continued to shape America's historical development. This was particularly evident in the Civil War era, when the Southern states voted to secede from the Union and to form the Confederate States of America.

Constitution (8)
The supreme law of the land that defines and limits the powers of government and sets forth the relationship between the government and the people. A constitution is usually a written document that incorporates the fundamental laws of the country. A constitution can be rigid or flexible. Rigid constitutions are typically long, specific, and require frequent amendment. The United States Constitution is rigid in form, but flexible in substance, which means that it is difficult to amend, but flexible enough to meet changing needs and times. The

Constitution, written in 1787 by a convention of 55 delegates, went into effect on March 4, 1789. The framers of the Constitution drew upon the various state constitutions, which were adopted immediately following the country's independence in 1776. The authors of the Constitution were also influenced by the Articles of Confederation. In general the Constitution established the governing rules and relationships and provided a means for enforcing them. Each state possesses its own constitution. In a conflict between the United States Constitution and a state constitution, the former, as the supreme law of the land, prevails. Most state constitutions are lengthy and filled with details. *See also* PREAMBLE TO THE CONSTITUTION, 20; STATE CONSTITUTIONS, 26.

Significance   A constitution, whether written or unwritten, attempts to reconcile liberty and security, freedom and order. Most countries boast constitutions, but many are not democratic in character. The U.S. Constitution provides certain generally understood powers that belong to government, as well as certain restrictions upon those powers. The Constitution guarantees, among other rights, freedom of speech, press, religion, and petition. The United States Constitution is the oldest written, living constitution in the world. It has survived remarkably well, with only 26 amendments in nearly 200 years. This is due to the wisdom of the framers, who wrote a document of barely 6,000 words that established the legal foundation of the nation.

Constitutional Amendment   (9)

An addition or alteration to a constitution. The process of constitutional amendment is essential to meet the changing needs of the nation. Article V of the United States Constitution provides for amendments to be adopted through a two-stage process of proposal and ratification. An amendment can be initiated by a vote of two-thirds of both houses of Congress, or by a national constitutional convention called by Congress upon application of two-thirds of the state legislatures. Only the first procedure has been used to date to propose amendments to the Constitution. The Constitution has been amended 26 times, with the first ten amendments, known as the Bill of Rights, adopted in 1791. All state constitutions contain provisions for proposing amendments by vote of the legislature, either by two-thirds or three-fifths of each house. All states, except Delaware, require that a proposed amendment be ratified by a majority vote in a general election, with some requiring an absolute majority of those participating in the election. Also, in a number of states, the people can propose a constitutional amendment through the initiative procedure. *See also* CONSTITUTION, 8; LEGISLATIVE BRANCH, 95.

Significance   A constitutional amendment provides for adjustment to new and changing conditions. Many sections of the United States Constitution have been changed through amendments, judicial review, and court decisions. If the American government is now more democratic than the framers of the Constitution intended it to be, it is because of amendments that provide for many more rights than contained in the original Constitution. No constitution can provide guidance for every situation. It must be amended as circumstances and times change. Through its various amendments, the Constitution of the United States has survived longer than any other constitution in the world. Unlike the United States Constitution, state constitutions have needed frequent changes because of their inflexibility.

Delegated Powers   **10**
The specific or express authority granted to the federal government by the United States Constitution. The delegated powers are, by and large, enumerated in the first three articles of the Constitution. They take two forms: express powers and implied powers. Express powers are explicitly stated and delegated to the legislative, executive, and judicial branches of government. Implied powers refer to those powers delegated to Congress "to make all Laws which shall be necessary and proper for carrying into Execution the foregoing Powers, and all other Powers vested by this Constitution in the Government of the United States, or in any Department or Officer thereof" (Article I, Section 8). *See also* RESERVED POWERS, 24.

Significance   The delegated powers granted to the national government under the United States Constitution are frequently referred to as "enumerated powers." These differ from the "reserved powers" granted to state governments and guaranteed under the Tenth Amendment. Specific powers delegated to Congress include, among others, the power to coin money; to borrow money on the credit of the United States; to lay and collect taxes; to declare war; to organize, arm, and discipline a militia; to establish courts inferior to the United States Supreme Court; and to regulate commerce with foreign nations. The Constitution grants the president the power to make treaties (with the advice and consent of the Senate); to appoint ambassadors, public ministers, and consuls, and judges of the

Supreme Court (with the consent of the Senate); to command the armed forces of the United States; to convene, on extraordinary occasions, one or both houses of Congress; and to grant reprieves and pardons for offenses against the United States (except in cases of impeachment). The Supreme Court possesses the express authority to hear cases affecting ambassadors, ministers, and consuls; to hear cases of admiralty and maritime jurisdiction; to hear controversies to which the United States shall be a party; to hear controversies between two or more states, and between a state, or the citizens thereof, and foreign states, citizens, or subjects. Together with the "reserved powers," the delegated powers provide the constitutional basis for dual sovereignty. Despite the fact that these powers are expressly delegated, they are not without controversy. For example, the necessary and proper clause has stirred considerable debate, particularly as it relates to states' rights. Currently, one of the most heated controversies surrounds representation for the District of Columbia. According to Article I, Section 8 of the Constitution, Congress has exclusive legislative authority over the District. On the other hand, District residents have voiced repeated concern over their lack of representation and power. These complaints have generated a broad-based movement in behalf of statehood for the nation's capital.

Due Process of Law   (11)
The fair administration of established procedures, regulations, and principles. The phrase—due process—is used in the Fifth and Fourteenth Amendments to the United States Constitution to protect individuals from arbitrary government action against their basic freedoms. These amendments forbid denial to any person of life, liberty, or property without due process of law. They protect persons from arbitrary treatment and entitle them to certain procedural rights, such as a hearing, trial by jury, the right to present witnesses and confront adversary witnesses, and protection against cruel and unusual punishment. These imply the right of an individual to be informed of the causes of deprivation of the due process of law and to have the opportunity to appeal in case of abridgement of any right or privilege. *See also* CIVIL LIBERTIES, 4; CIVIL RIGHTS, 5.

Significance   Due process of law has become a basic right of individuals and a key component of the American system of government. In numerous cases, the Supreme Court has defined due process as reasonableness, fairness, equity, and justice. Any unreasonable or arbitrary action by government is therefore in violation of the requirement of due process of law. Due process has at least three functions: (1) It serves as a limitation on public officials; (2) it gives power to judges, who have wide latitude in applying the law; and (3) it protects an individual against arbitrary treatment. The Fourteenth Amendment to the United States Constitution forbids states, but not the federal government, from denying any person the equal protection of the law. However, the Supreme Court has interpreted the Fourteenth Amendment's prohibition "nor shall any State deprive any person of life, liberty, or property without due process of law" to suggest that certain minimum standards of fairness must be maintained in all trials. If this minimum protection is not guaranteed a defendant, the conviction will, in all likelihood, be overturned as a violation of due process.

Emergency Clause   (12)

A provision written into the Constitution granting the federal government temporary powers during a crisis. The emergency clause refers to Article II, Sections 2 and 3 of the United States Constitution, which grant the president powers as commander-in-chief of the armed forces and, although the Constitution does not explicitly state it, enable him to function as a crisis manager by virtue of the vast array of powers accorded to him. As commander-in-chief, the president may take personal command of the armed forces, as George Washington did during the Whiskey Rebellion in 1794. During the Civil War (1861–1865), President Abraham Lincoln used the power of commander-in-chief to expand the size of the army and navy beyond congressional authorization, to expend funds without congressional approval, and to suspend the writ of *habeas corpus*. All governments, including state and local authorities, possess the means to suspend certain constitutional rights in times of emergency. *See also* CONSTITUTION, 8; STATE CONSTITUTIONS, 26.

Significance   The emergency clause of the Constitution may be invoked by the president to resolve national crises. After the Civil War, the Supreme Court declared that "the government, within the Constitution, has all the powers granted to it which are necessary to preserve its existence." In the landmark case of *Ex Parte Milligan* (4 Wallace 2: 1866), the Supreme Court held that the suspension of *habeas corpus* should be made by the president only with the approval of Congress. The Supreme Court, in light of the war emergency, found President Franklin D. Roosevelt's action in 1942 ordering large numbers of American citizens of Japanese origin into relocation camps a permissible exercise of his powers as commander-in-chief. Although the Court has upheld such emergency powers in wartime, in the case of *Youngstown Sheet and Tube Company v. Sawyer* (343 U.S. 579: 1952), the court denied President Harry S Truman's assertion that the inherent powers of the president justified the seizure of the steel mills without congressional approval.

Equal Protection of Law (13)

A requirement, set forth in the Fourteenth Amendment to the United States Constitution, which has served as the basis for overturning laws that unreasonably classify people. The equal protection clause prohibits states from classifying persons or businesses arbitrarily. The states are forbidden to discriminate against people or businesses unjustly. The relevant portion of the Fourteenth Amendment reads: "No State shall . . . deny to any person within its jurisdiction the equal protection of the laws." The applicability of the equal protection clause precludes unreasonable government classification, such as, for example, treating blacks differently from whites for voting purposes. The equal protection clause does not require identical treatment. For instance, taxation based on ability to pay is considered a reasonable classification. Men can be drafted into the armed forces, but not women. *See also* CIVIL LIBERTIES, 4; CIVIL RIGHTS, 5; DUE PROCESS OF LAW, 11.

Significance   Equal protection of law is an inherent obligation of the states. Inherent in due process, it is therefore binding on the federal government, too. The Civil Rights Act of 1875 prohibited discrimination in public conveyances, hotels, and theaters. But the United States Supreme Court held this law unconstitutional. The key Supreme Court ruling against racial discrimination in education was *Brown v. Board of Education of Topeka* (347 U.S. 483: 1954). In this case, the Court reversed its holding in *Plessy v. Ferguson* (163 U.S. 537: 1896), as applicable to public schools, and ruled that "separate but equal" is a contradiction in terms. This means that segregated educational facilities, even though equal in their physical aspects, are "inherently unequal" and deprive black children of equal educational opportunities. Since the *Brown* decision, many courts have struck down schemes designed to circumvent its implementation. Current interest in the application of the equal protection clause centers on economic, commercial, and legislative regulation such as equal justice for the poor, equal opportunity for minorities, and equality in state legislative apportionment.

Exclusive Powers   **(14)**
The sole authority of a government to perform certain duties and maintain control. Exclusive powers at the national level belong to the federal government, which controls foreign and defense policy, currency regulation, and the postal service. Unless limited by the United States Constitution, the states may exercise such powers as those relating to marriage and divorce, control over local government, and the general police powers to protect the health, safety, morals, and general well-being of their citizens. Article I, Section 8 of the United States Constitution enumerates 18 powers delegated to Congress. These include power over foreign affairs, power to conclude treaties and declare war, raise armies and navies, regulate interstate and foreign trade, make uniform rules for naturalization and immigration, issue currency and control its value, establish post offices, build roads, impose taxes, grant patents and copyrights, make laws on bankruptcy, pay government debts, and provide for the defense and general welfare of the people. Article II, Section 2 gives the president authority to formulate the defense and foreign policy of the nation. *See also* IMPLIED POWERS, 16.

Significance   Exclusive powers for the federal authorities underscore the need for a strong central government. The framers of the Constitution divided governmental control between the federal and state governments. The powers of the federal government are considerably broader than those of the state and local governments. Many areas once considered within the exclusive jurisdiction of the states have since fallen under national control. This has occurred, for the most part, because the states are unable to cope with the growing problems of economic depression, unemployment, and inflation. The public views the national government as the ultimate authority to meet their demands for social welfare, unemployment compensation, and medical care. The post–Civil War (1861–1865) generations think of themselves more as United States citizens than as Marylanders or Virginians.

Full Faith and Credit Clause   **(15)**
A provision in Article IV of the United States Constitution requiring each state to accept the laws, records, and court decisions of other states. The full faith and credit clause is applicable to noncriminal cases only. Article IV, Section 1 states: "Full Faith and Credit shall be given in each State to the public Acts, Records, and judicial Proceedings of every other State." This ensures that wills, property titles,

marriages, divorces, court awards, and other records listed in one state be honored in other states. Article IV, Section 2 provides that persons charged with a crime who flee to another state be returned to the state having jurisdiction over the crime. The clause ensures that one cannot escape legal opposition by moving to another state. If, for example, a person owes money to one state, the obligation remains even if the person moves to another state. Enforcement of Sections 1 and 2 of Article IV is not automatic and often may involve legal difficulties. *See also* INTERSTATE COMPACT, 48; INTERSTATE/INTRASTATE RELATIONS, 49.

Significance   Although the full faith and credit clause requires the states to honor the civil rulings of other states, differing marriage, divorce, and child support laws have been a source of conflict over the years. However, the general principles embodied in the clause are usually honored throughout the country. How much credit must a state give to a divorce granted by another state? A divorce granted by a state to two of its residents is recognized by other states despite the grounds for divorce. However, if divorce is granted by a court in another state with one of the parties not given an opportunity to contest the divorce proceeding, their divorce may not be recognized in their home state or other states. This problem has largely been mitigated by new liberal attitudes concerning marriage and divorce. In a mobile nation such as the United States, this clause promotes a sense of fairness, and lawbreakers are usually brought to task.

Implied Powers   (16)

Authority of the national government that can be inferred from the enumerated powers of the United States Constitution. Implied powers are derived from the necessary and proper clause in Article I, Section 8, which gives Congress the right "To make all Laws which shall be necessary and proper for carrying into Execution the foregoing Powers, and all other Powers vested by this Constitution in the Government of the United States, or in any Department or Officer thereof." Governmental powers may be broadly classified as enumerated and implied. The former are delegated or declared in specific words; the latter are logical deductions from the wording and purpose of the declaration (Constitution). For example, the congressional authority to incorporate a bank is inferred from such enumerated powers as the power to lay and collect taxes, to coin money, and to regulate the value thereof. *See also* DELEGATED POWERS, 10.

Significance   Implied powers have strengthened the authority of the federal government in resolving many problems of a vast country with a diverse population. Implied powers are assumed to exist to implement laws made under the enumerated powers. This assumption of implied powers was originally stated by the Supreme Court in the case of *McCulloch v. Maryland* (4 Wheat. 316: 1819). The case involved the Bank of the United States, which had been created to oversee the government's monetary and fiscal policies. In a landmark decision the Supreme Court upheld the power of the national government to establish a bank, and denied the state of Maryland the power to tax a branch of the bank. The Court held that it was not necessary for the Constitution expressly to authorize Congress to create a bank. In the opinion by Chief Justice John Marshall, the power to do so was implied from Congress' power over financial matters and from the necessary and proper clause of the Constitution.

Inherent Powers   (17)
Authority not expressly granted in the Constitution that flows from the fact that the United States exists as one nation among many. Inherent powers are assumed by virtue of the need to have authority to administer the affairs of the nation, particularly in its relations with other nations in peace and war. These powers derive from the fact that the United States is a sovereign nation and therefore must be able to meet its international responsibilities and obligations. Inherent power, it is maintained, is the authority to protect the country in times of national emergency by whatever means seem appropriate to achieve the end. Many presidents, including Washington, Lincoln, Roosevelt, and Truman have pursued unauthorized actions to meet emergency situations. Presidents have been challenged more for their emergency actions in internal matters than in external affairs. *See also* IMPLIED POWERS, 16.

Significance   Inherent powers are critical in times of emergency. This would seem to contradict the notion that government can only employ the powers given it explicitly by the Constitution. Nevertheless, presidents, with or without the support of the judiciary, invoke inherent powers in times of crisis. Whether or not this is legitimate depends on interpretation of the Constitution by the Supreme Court. Cases can be cited supporting both points of view. Two cases in which the president's inherent powers were put to the test were *United States v. Curtiss-Wright Export Corp.* (299 U.S. 304: 1936) and *Youngstown*

Sheet and Tube Co. v. Sawyer (343 U.S. 579: 1952). In the first case the Supreme Court recognized the full responsibility of the national government in foreign affairs and the importance of the president's role in this field. In the second case, the Court struck down the president's executive order that had authorized seizure of steel mills and their operation by the federal government so as to end a strike during the Korean War. Since emergencies will always occur, and presidents will be required to act, the debate surrounding inherent powers will continue.

Limited Government (18)

The restriction of national, state, and local authority in a democratic constitutional system. Limited government is a basic feature of the American constitutional system—national and state governments are limited to exercising only those powers authorized by their respective constitutions and are explictly forbidden certain powers. In addition, they are limited to what the Constitution permits in a positive sense (i.e., the enumerated, inherent, and implied powers). The national government is forbidden to abridge guarantees contained in the Bill of Rights (the first ten amendments to the United States Constitution containing individual rights). It cannot suspend the writ of *habeas corpus*, except in cases of rebellion or invasion. Neither the federal nor state governments can deprive any person of life, liberty, or property without due process of law. The national government cannot approve slavery nor grant titles of nobility. It may not use its taxing power to make it impossible for the states to function. *See also* BILL OF RIGHTS, 1; DUE PROCESS OF LAW, 11; EXCLUSIVE POWERS, 14.

Significance   Limited government is designed to prevent concentration of power into a single government. This helps to prevent the development of dictatorial tendencies in any one government. The judiciary acts as the guardian of the Constitution to void governmental actions that exceed the limitations prescribed by the law of the land. The Constitution, through a system of separation of powers and checks and balances, has restrained governmental authority and power. In a democratic society, like the United States, the government exists for the people and not vice versa. The framers of the Constitution provided adequate safeguards for the people by limiting the powers of the government. What is considered a proper exercise of authority by the federal government may be a limitation for the states, and a restriction on the liberty of the people.

Popular Sovereignty (19)

Legal authority ordained and established by the people. Popular sovereignty implies that, ultimately, the people can establish, alter, or abolish the government. The doctrine was set forth by British philosopher John Locke in his *Two Treatises on Government* (1689). It influenced many eighteenth-century thinkers in the United States, particularly Thomas Jefferson. The Declaration of Independence, written in 1776, affirmed this principle, stating, ". . . Governments are instituted among Men, deriving their just powers from the consent of the governed. That whenever any Form of Government becomes destructive of these ends, it is the Right of the People to alter or to abolish it, and to institute new Government." *See also* CONSTITUTION, 8; SOVEREIGNTY, 50.

Significance   Popular sovereignty is largely theoretical. No authority allows the people to abolish the government. The framers of the Constitution largely ignored the natural rights of the people in failing to include the lofty ideals of the Declaration of Independence, such as the principle that "All men are created equal." The people's abolishing a government is tantamount to revolution, and no government will permit people to take the law into their hands. However, in many countries, including the United States, people are permitted to change their governments through periodic elections. Many provisions of the United States Constitution and state constitutions come close to popular sovereignty by having the people actively engage in writing, amending, and revising federal and state constitutions. State governments go a step further to encourage citizen participation by holding elections for almost all public offices (the federal government appoints judges and cabinet officers). State governments seem to reflect the immediate wishes of the people more than the federal government does, and thus manifest popular sovereignty to a greater extent.

Preamble to the Constitution (20)

Prologue affixed to the document dealing with the fundamental law of the land. The preamble to the Constitution introduces the document. It reads: "We the People of the United States, in Order to form a more perfect Union, establish Justice, insure domestic Tranquility, provide for the common defence, promote the general Welfare, and secure the Blessings of Liberty to ourselves and our Posterity, do ordain and establish this Constitution for the United States of America." Most state constitutions also include preambles, which closely mirror the language of the federal Constitution. They indicate that the source of governmental authority is the people. The preamble stresses obedience to government, while at the same time it proclaims the supremacy of the people. Although part of the Constitution, the preamble is of no legal consequence but only serves as a guideline to the salient principles of government. *See also* CONSTITUTION, 8; STATE CONSTITUTIONS, 26.

Significance   The preamble to the Constitution contains a statement of the purpose of the Constitution as well as the government. The phrase "We the People of the United States" in the preamble to the Constitution is ambiguous but underscores the supremacy of the people and gives due importance to them. Since the adoption of the U.S. Constitution in 1789, the reference to "the People" in the preamble has become so much a part of the constitutional history of the world, that the United Nations incorporated in the preamble to its Charter in 1945 the words "We the peoples of the United Nations." Newer state constitutions also have adopted the phrase "We the people of the State." The preamble to the United States Constitution ordained and established a government by the people. Although the preamble to a constitution has no legal standing, it serves as a guiding principle. The image of the political system itself, the character of the people, and their ideas and ideals are reflected in the preamble to a constitution.

Privileges and Immunities   (21)

Advantages, benefits, and exemptions granted to citizens of each state. Privileges and immunities are special rights and opportunities provided by law to an individual or group to which they may not be otherwise entitled. Article IV, Section 2 of the United States Constitution provides that "The Citizens of each State shall be entitled to all Privileges and Immunities of Citizens in the several States." Also, the Fourteenth Amendment (Section 1) states that "No State shall make or enforce any law which shall abridge the privileges or immunities of citizens of the United States." These clauses are intended to prevent discrimination against citizens of other states. For example, a citizen of California is entitled to police protection, access to the courts, the right to own property, or to travel freely in North Carolina or any other state. Privileges and immunities do not extend to such political rights as voting and serving on a jury. A state may refuse a corporation the right to do business within its territory, but it cannot, with a view to diminishing competition, refuse to grant a trucking company a permit to use its highways for the interstate transportation of goods. *See also* FULL FAITH AND CREDIT CLAUSE, 15; UNIFORM STATE LAWS, 27.

Significance   Privileges and immunities are fraught with ambiguities and technicalities. Although Article IV has served to unite the people of the various states and strengthen their ties, the full and precise meaning of the language has never been established by the courts. Equally vague is the language of the Fourteenth Amendment, which places certain restrictions on the people concerning civil rights and civil liberties. In interpreting these clauses the courts usually take the view that the United States is a nation composed of individual states, which are permitted to distinguish between residents and nonresidents. Only with respect to characteristics considered vital to the unity and solidarity of the nation must all residents, nonresidents, and aliens be treated equally.

Rendition Clause   (22)

A constitutional provision that a state shall surrender a fugitive to the state within whose jurisdiction a crime was committed. The rendition clause is more commonly known as extradition, which is also the international legal procedure by which fugitives are rendered up by one country to another. Article IV, Section 2 of the United States Constitution states, "A person charged in any State with Treason, Felony, or other Crime, who shall flee from Justice, and be found in another State, shall on Demand of the executive Authority of the State from which he fled, be delivered up, to be removed to the State having jurisdiction of the Crime." Normally, governors comply with extradition requests from other states. Although there is a strong predisposition of governors to extradite, they cannot be compelled to do so. Congress has made it a federal crime to flee to another state or foreign country with the intent to avoid prosecution or confinement by a state. Still, many states receive 500 to 1,000 extradition requests every year. *See also* INTERSTATE RENDITION, 129.

Significance   The rendition clause would appear mandatory as it employs the phrase "shall . . . be delivered up." However, the United States Supreme Court, in *Kentucky v. Dennison* (24 Howard 66: 1861) ruled that this language was not intended as mandatory, but as declaratory of the moral duty the United States and the states bore to each other. Congress implemented this constitutional provision by outlining the procedure by which a governor could request the surrender of a fugitive, but did not provide a means to enforce the law. The law as interpreted does not oblige the governor to return the fugitive to the state in which the crime was committed, but makes this a matter of courtesy at his or her discretion. Many governors extradite with the knowledge that, if they do not, then others will not comply with their requests. When extradition is politically unpopular, a governor may not comply with a request to extradite.

Representative Government (23)

A system of government in which citizens elect representatives to enact and administer laws. The term, "representative government," is often used interchangeably with "representative democracy." The United States Constitution guarantees a representative government, both at the federal and state levels. Article IV, Section 4 of the Constitution states: "The United States shall guarantee to every State in this Union a Republican Form of Government." No additional requirements are placed on the design of state governments. A republican government can take one of two forms: direct or indirect. The indirect form is most common, and can be defined as one in which elected officials are delegated the authority to promulgate laws for the citizenry they govern. In a direct system, the laws are made by the voting populace, and the elected officials simply administer and enforce those laws. The referendum—which originated during the Progressive era and which exists in many states—is an example of representative government. *See also* HOME RULE, 47.

Significance The Constitution mandates a republican government, both for the federal government and the states. However, the characteristics of this system remain undefined. The United States Supreme Court has refused to adjudicate the specific requirements of a republican system, believing that such definition lies within the realm of Congress. In practice, the Supreme Court has held that a republican government is one in which legislative power flows directly or indirectly from the people. In 1912, the Supreme Court addressed the constitutionality of the initiative and referendum (procedures by which the voters can enact legislation or "veto" it at the ballot box). In *Pacific State Telephone and Telegraph Company v. Oregon* (223 U.S. 118), the Supreme Court ruled that provisions for direct legislation did not conflict with republican principles. This decision challenged the widely held belief that the referendum violated the principles of republican government. Although all state governments have adopted the representative model, variations can and do exist.

One such variation lies in the powers granted to the governor. In some states, such as North Carolina, the governor has minimal power, while in others, such as Maryland, the powers are considerably greater. Despite these variations, all state governments reflect the view that legislative power stems directly or indirectly from the electorate.

Reserved Powers (24)

That authority not granted to the federal government nor denied to the states by the United States Constitution. The reserved (also known as residuary) powers are expressly stated in the Tenth Amendment to the Constitution, which reads: "The powers not delegated to the United States by the Constitution, nor prohibited by it to the States, are reserved to the States respectively, or to the people." These powers typically include health, safety, morals, and welfare. Still, the powers of the states were, for the most part, left undefined, thereby affording the states significant control over their own domain and citizenry, and autonomy from the federal government. Under the reserved powers clause the nation's states have the authority to adopt their own constitutions and to legislate their own laws within the parameters defined in the United States Constitution. *See also* DELEGATED POWERS, 10.

Significance   Taken together, the reserved and delegated powers theoretically provide a clear line of separation between the powers of the federal government and of the states. Ideally, both the federal government and the states possess certain sovereign rights. Historically, however, this view has often been contradicted by the facts. The line of demarcation between federal and state powers is at best vague (e.g., commerce). The strength or weakness of either federal or state power is contingent on the United States Supreme Court's interpretation of the necessary and proper clause (Article I, Section 8). This clause grants Congress the authority to enact those laws that are "necessary and proper" for the implementation of the delegated powers. The (John) Marshall Court (1801–1835) interpreted this clause somewhat loosely, granting the federal government increased authority over the states. From the (Roger B.) Taney Court (1834–1864) until the 1930s, the Tenth Amendment was invoked to protect the rights of the states. From 1937, the Supreme Court has consistently ruled in favor of the federal government, demonstrating minimal concern for the reserved powers guaranteed to the states. Still the fine line between federal and state power remains blurred, as new demands and challenges force the courts to redefine the concept of reserved powers.

Separation of Powers   (25)

A cardinal principle in the U.S. political system that proclaims the three branches of government—the legislative, executive, and judicial—constitutionally equal to and independent of each other. The separation of powers prevents a dangerous concentration of power in any one branch of government. Each branch has the power not only to perform its primary responsibilities, but also to prevent others from exceeding their constitutional limits. This protection was established in the first three articles of the Constitution. Article I, Section 1 states that "All legislative Powers herein granted shall be vested in a Congress of the United States"; Article II, Section 1, that "The executive Power shall be vested in a President of the United States of America"; and Article III, Section 1, that "The judicial Power of the United States, shall be vested in one supreme Court, and in such inferior Courts as the Congress may from time to time ordain and establish." The principle of separation of powers is found in every state constitution—either enumerated or implied. *See also* CHECKS AND BALANCES, 3; CONSTITUTION, 8; STATE CONSTITUTIONS, 26.

Significance   The principle of separation of powers is deeply rooted in U.S. political thought. The concept derives from the fear that a government in which all powers are held in one hand, or in the hands of one group, branch, or organ, could become all-powerful and tyrannical. The foremost examples of these principles are found in the United States Constitution and system of government. For example, the president holds the executive power, which he exercises through his cabinet and the executive departments and agencies. The Congress holds the legislative power, which is shared by the Senate and House of Representatives. Congress makes the law, but the president enforces it, and the courts interpret and apply it. The Supreme Court used the concept of separation of powers in *Immigration and Naturalization Service v. Chadha* (103 S.Ct. 2764: 1983) to declare that a legislative veto to invalidate an act of the executive branch is unconstitutional as a violation of the separation of powers. In 1986, the Court ruled that the across-the-board spending cuts mandated by the Gramm-Rudman-Hollings Act of 1985 were unconstitutional because they encroached on presidential authority by giving executive power to the comptroller general (a congressional officer).

State Constitutions (26)
Fundamental laws governing the states. State constitutions are basically similar to the federal constitution; all declare the powers of the government and the restrictions placed on it. All state constitutions provide three separate branches of government—the legislative, executive, and judicial, and all enunciate the doctrine of separation of powers among the three branches of government. All state constitutions incorporate a "bill of rights" or a "declaration of rights." Every state has a bicameral (two-house) legislature, except Nebraska, which has a unicameral (one-house) legislature. All state constitutions include the provision of judicial review, which allows the courts to nullify actions of the executive branch that conflict with the law. The state legislatures have general rather than enumerated (explicitly provided) powers. Unlike the national government, executive authority in the states is frequently fragmented among such officials as the governor, lieutenant governor, attorney general, secretary of state, and state treasurer. Judicial powers are distributed among a variety of independently organized courts. *See also* CONSTITUTION, 8; FEDERALISM: COOPERATIVE FEDERALISM, 30.

Significance State constitutions are usually extremely long and detailed. Some state constitutions are as long as 50,000 to 70,000 words and contain as many as 2,000 to 3,000 amendments. The United States Constitution, on the other hand, is approximately 6,000 words and contains only 26 amendments. The United States Constitution provides both guarantees and limitations on the states. The United States, for example, is obliged to guarantee a republican government to the states. It also protects the states against invasion and domestic violence. The states have an obligation not to secede from the union. Although the federal government has authority in many areas, it often relies on the cooperation of state and local governments to achieve its objectives through a system known as "cooperative federalism."

Uniform State Laws (27)
Similar rules and regulations developed cooperatively by the states. Uniform state laws are encouraged by the federal government. In addition to achieving some measure of uniformity through compacts or agreements, the states may achieve some uniformity by individually passing similar types of laws and procedures. The National Conference of Commissioners on Uniform State Laws has proposed over 100 uniform laws in the states since its founding in

1892. The conference is associated with the Council of Governments (COG), which acts as a secretariat for the conference. The COG is composed of representatives from the various state governments. Participation is voluntary; any government may withdraw at any time. The COG is a research and recommending body, and it receives financial support from the state and federal governments. *See also* COUNCILS OF GOVERNMENTS (COGS), 233; FULL FAITH AND CREDIT CLAUSE, 15; INTERSTATE COMPACT, 48.

Significance   Uniform state laws are well-meaning in concept, but the process has proved extremely vexing. The diversity of laws that exist in the 50 states is a problem of immense proportions. Still, in some areas, the states have adopted uniform laws, including those dealing with negotiable instruments, stocks transfers, sales, partnerships, bills of lading, and family matters. Confusion exists in such matters as marriage, divorce, and traffic laws, to mention only a few. The courts in different states, operating under diverse laws, often interpret statutes and rules differently. The business community and citizens in general are frequently interested in adopting uniform state laws as a matter of convenience. But their efforts have fallen on the deaf ears of political leaders and legislators who are often more interested in the "sovereignty" of the states than in uniformity in matters of rules and regulations. Despite the federal government's attempt to encourage cooperation among the states, nearly 100 years have passed since the inception of the National Conference of Commissioners on Uniform State Laws. Except for a handful of agreements between the states, little of consequence has occurred.

Unitary State   (28)
A system of government in which all power is vested in a central government. Unitary states may delegate specific powers to local or subdivisional governments (e.g., states, provinces, cities, towns, prefectures, and so on), but possess the authority to revoke those powers at any time. Unitary governments exist in Great Britain, Sweden, Italy, Israel, and France, among many others. A unitary state stands in direct opposition to a federal system, in which power is constitutionally shared by the national government and the states. In France, for instance, highways, education, welfare, land, and police protection are federal functions; the constituent units merely implement policy. Typically, a unitary government is preferred in small nations, where government authorities seek to promote efficient solutions to national problems and the perpetuation of national values. Although

intergovernmental units exist, they do so as "conveniences" to the central government. Still, local autonomy plays a prominent role in some unitary states and serves to counterbalance, to the extent possible, the centralization of power at the national level. *See also* CONFEDERATION, 7; FEDERALISM, 29; SOVEREIGNTY, 50.

Significance   Unitary states are predicated on the assumption that government authority properly rests with the highest level of power (e.g., the monarch). Unitary governments are often instituted to reduce the tensions and divisions that accompany cultural and racial diversity. However, as political scientist James F. Barnes suggests, "this does not mean that deviation and diversity are never permitted. It is simply that in unitary states the psychological and political momentum is dominated by the center and the expectation of unity."[1] Despite efforts to accommodate regional differences, there exists considerable pressure in many unitary states to provide additional authority to the various constituent units. This is true in such nations as Ghana, Sudan, and the Philippines, where internal ethnic and religious pressures have forced the central government to grant increased authority to local and subdivisional units. Similar challenges have been raised in Canada, Belgium, and France, where language differences have often created public discontent. In unitary states, politics reflects the omnipresent role of the central government in the daily affairs of the people. All major institutions, be they political parties or interest groups, reflect national goals and objectives. Thus, as Barnes notes, "local politics in unitary states tend to be national politics in miniature, and local issues and personalities can be overwhelmed by the intrusion of national affairs into the local community."[2] Although unitary states frequently grant limited autonomy to their constituent units, this autonomy is contingent on implementing the policies and programs of the central government. When local officials fail to maintain the support and favor of the national authorities, they face swift sanctions and the loss of power.

2. Intergovernmental Relations

Federalism   **(29)**
A system of government in which power is constitutionally shared
between a national government and its constituent states. Federalism
represents the middle road between a unitary system of government
(where power flows from the national government) and a confederacy (where power resides in the states). Under a federal system,
neither the national government nor the states are supreme; both
enjoy their respective spheres of power and responsibility. The
United States Constitution provides for a system of shared powers.
The national government's powers are chiefly enumerated in the first
three articles of the Constitution. State powers are not specifically
enumerated, but are protected by the Tenth Amendment, under the
reserved powers clause. This clause delegates those powers to the
states that are not specifically granted to the national government,
nor prohibited by it to the states. The Supreme Court serves as an
arbiter in determining questions of state versus national power. *See
also* CONFEDERATION, 7; SOVEREIGNTY, 50; STATES' RIGHTS, 51; UNITARY
STATE, 28.

Significance   Federalism was adopted by the Constitutional Convention of 1787. At the time, the founding fathers were acutely aware
of the strengths and weaknesses of unitarism and confederalism.
Unitarism prevailed during the colonial period, when the colonies
were still under the dominion of England. Strong opposition to
unitarism, combined with the states' desire to retain their newly
acquired freedom, resulted in the formation of a confederacy. Like
unitarism, confederalism proved ineffective, as the national government lacked sufficient power to govern the nation and to raise and

spend revenue. To prevent the dissolution of the republic, the Constitutional Convention adopted a federal system, which was viewed as a compromise solution between unitarism and confederalism. Unlike the above two systems, federalism sought to define and balance the powers of the national government and the states. Throughout U.S. history, the Supreme Court, in a series of landmark decisions, has sought to interpret the Constitution as it relates to the powers of the national government and the states. Its most important single decision was that in *McCulloch v. Maryland* (4 Wheat. 316, 1819), in which it established the principle of implied powers (powers that flow from the enumerated powers and the elastic clause of the Constitution), and which provided the constitutional basis for expanded national power.

Like all systems, federalism boasts numerous strengths and weaknesses. According to political scientist William H. Riker, federalism boasts six major advantages: (1) it permits diversity and diffusion of power; (2) it permits local governments to better handle their local problems; (3) it provides more access points for political participation; (4) it protects individual rights against concentrated government power; (5) it fosters experimentation and innovation; and (6) it suits a large country with a diverse population.[1] On the other hand, Riker notes six main drawbacks of federalism: (1) it makes national unity difficult to achieve and maintain; (2) it allows local governments to block national policy; (3) it encourages economic inequality and racial discrimination; (4) it promotes uneven law enforcement and justice; (5) it places responsibility in smaller units that may lack expertise and money; and (6) it engenders local dominance by special interests.[2]

Federalism: Cooperative Federalism   (30)

A concept of intergovernmental relations that views the national government and the states as cooperative partners, rather than as antagonistic competitors in the pursuit of power. Cooperative federalism reached its apex in the 1950s, though its roots were sown two decades earlier. The impact of cooperative federalism is most evident in such areas as public finance, social programs, governmental administration, and state and local politics. According to political scientists Morton Grodzins and Daniel J. Elazar, cooperative federalism in the United States embodies seven major premises.[3] These include: (1) U.S. federalism is characterized by shared functional responsibilities at virtually all levels; (2) this sharing derives from U.S. history and politics; (3) shared functions are only made possible by the drastic reduction of the importance of state and local government; (4)

strengthening state governments will not significantly diminish the present functions of the federal government, nor will it slow the increase of new functions; (5) genuine decentralization flows from independent centers of power and functions despite the chaos inherent in the U.S. political system; (6) sharing functions and powers depends on a collegial, noncompetitive approach to government policy making; and (7) the U.S. political system is one government serving one people. Cooperative federalism is a functional and pragmatic theory, one that is mirrored in the day-to-day operations of the federal, state, and local governments. *See also* FEDERALISM, 29; GRANTS-IN-AID, 45.

Significance   Cooperative federalism represents a marked departure from earlier views of federalism, particularly dual federalism, which experienced a decline following the Great Depression of the 1930s. The United States Supreme Court eschewed cooperative federalism until 1937, following President Franklin D. Roosevelt's unsuccessful effort to restructure the Court. Soon thereafter, the Supreme Court revised its opposition to New Deal legislation and embraced Roosevelt's broad view of federal taxing power. In short order, the Court upheld the constitutionality of Social Security, unemployment compensation, and government grants as legitimate examples of federal-state cooperation. At the same time, the Supreme Court began to limit state authority in several functional areas, upholding Congress's authority in these domains. This was evident in Supreme Court rulings that overturned the states' authority to establish voting requirements, apportion legislatures, and maintain segregated schools. Cooperative federalism led to a significant increase in federal assistance to state and local governments, most notably in the form of grants-in-aid. The states followed suit and dramatically increased their assistance to local municipalities. What emerged was a new view of intergovernmental relations that resulted in increased contact and interaction and the melding of powers and responsibilities.

Federalism: Creative Federalism   (31)

An approach to intergovernmental relations, associated with President Lyndon B. Johnson, in which the president initiated a national War on Poverty and increased the use of grants-in-aid to address U.S. racial and urban ills. Creative federalism marked a departure from cooperative federalism, in which the federal government employed its power and influence to pressure and/or entice the states to implement programs and accept responsibilities that they would have preferred, in many cases, to avoid. Prior to the advent of creative federalism, federal-state relations were marked by myriad tensions, chief of which involved federal charges of inefficient administration at the state level, as well as countercharges by the states of excessive federal regulations and paperwork. Still, this period was characterized by a general consensus as to the value of the projects that were jointly administered. However, under creative federalism, that consensus was often threatened. In his book *Public Policy and Federalism: Issues in State and Local Politics,* Jeffrey R. Henig observes: "Now, in areas such as civil rights, job training, welfare, and housing for the poor, federal officials were deliberately using the carrot and the stick of grants-in-aid to redirect state and local efforts in the name of broader national goals."[4] This approach reflected the federal government's belief that the states lacked the resolve to address the problems of racial injustice and urban poverty. *See also* FEDERALISM, 29; FEDERALISM: COOPERATIVE FEDERALISM, 30.

Significance   Creative federalism represented a dramatic departure in federal-state relations. During the Johnson administration, the federal government initiated over 200 new social and economic programs, often bypassing the states in favor of direct local assistance. Indeed, between 1960 and 1970, federal aid to the states skyrocketed from $7 billion to $24 billion, while federal aid to urban areas mushroomed from 55 percent to 70 percent of the total. Creative federalism engendered fierce criticism from state and local officials. Although they frequently endorsed the policy goals underlying these programs, they bitterly resented the administrative requirements of creative federalism, which had created an unwieldy, fragmented, and inflexible system—one that threatened state and local autonomy and increased waste and inefficiency. A prime target was the federal government's insistence on matching requirements, which, according to state and local officials, forced them to alter their budget priorities to satisfy federal requirements, at the cost of programs that were more relevant and cost-efficient. Most of all, state and local officials resented the federal government's intrusion into such state and local prerogatives as education and law enforcement, which they viewed as a threat to their autonomy and independence.

Federalism: Dual Federalism   (32)

The principle that the national government and the states each possess spheres of authority, with each supreme in its sphere. Dual federalism conceived the federal-state relationship as marked by two coexistent power centers, each vying for dominance in major functional areas. In his book *Toward a Functioning Federalism,* political scientist David B. Walker divides dual federalism into two historical stages: the pre–Civil War period (1789–1860) and the period from the attack on Fort Sumter to the beginning of the Great Depression (1861–1930).[5] According to Edwin S. Corwin, the first stage was based on four postulates: (1) the national government has enumerated powers only; (2) there are few purposes it may constitutionally promote; (3) within their individual spheres, both the national government and the states are sovereign and hence supreme; and (4) the relationship between these two centers is based on tension rather than cooperation.[6] The second stage, argues Walker, demonstrated four distinct trends: (1) the theory of functional assignments remained intact; (2) the national government enhanced its position—constitutionally, judicially, fiscally, and in regulatory matters; (3) state and local governments expanded their power and authority; and (4) the states and localities grew in terms of revenue, expenditures, and personnel.[7] *See also* FEDERALISM, 29; RESERVED POWERS, 24; SOVEREIGNTY, 50.

Significance   Dual federalism arose out of the debate over the interpretation of the commerce clause of the United States Constitution. Applied to commerce, dual federalism recognized the existence of interstate commerce, which only the Congress could regulate, and intrastate commerce, which was the province of the states. The United States Supreme Court was empowered to serve as the umpire of the federal system, deciding specific cases involving commerce. Dual federalism reached its zenith immediately following the Civil War. It replaced the previously held "compact theory," which invested total sovereignty in the member states. Implicit in this new phase of dual federalism was the acceptance of a stronger national government. From 1937 on, dual federalism declined in importance, owing to the development of a closer-knit nation-state (both geographically and economically), which was brought about by two world wars and the Great Depression. With these events came the realization that such issues as social welfare, education, health care, housing, and economic growth were better addressed by the national government than by the individual states. As for dual authority, the Supreme Court has consistently upheld the doctrine of national supremacy, as enunciated by the Marshall Court (1801–1835), and the expansion of national authority, which served to reduce the influence of dual federalism as a substantive theory or principle governing federal-state relations.

Federalism: Horizontal Federalism   **(33)**

The constitutional and voluntary relationship among states and localities. Horizontal federalism contrasts with vertical federalism, which denotes the relationship between the national government and the states. The United States Constitution imposes several formal requirements on the states, among them, that: (1) each state give full faith and credit to every other state's public acts, records, and judicial proceedings; (2) each state grant to every other state's citizens the privileges and immunities of its own citizens; and (3) each state agree to render fugitives in another state back to their home state when requested to do so by that state's chief executive. In addition to these constitutional requirements, horizontal federalism also provides for several voluntary actions between states, including (1) uniform laws, (2) reciprocal agreements, (3) interstate compacts, and (4) consultation and joint action. *See also* FEDERALISM, 29; INTERSTATE COMPACT, 48; INTERSTATE/INTRASTATE RELATIONS, 49.

Significance   Horizontal federalism promotes cooperation and collaboration, as well as innovation and reform. It also fosters uniformity and consensus, education and participation. However, this should not suggest that all states are equally innovative in their approach to public policy. In one study, political scientist Jack L. Walker surveyed 88 government programs.[8] He found that the most innovative states included New York, Massachusetts, California, New Jersey, and Michigan, while the least innovative were Mississippi, Nevada, Wyoming, South Carolina, and Texas. The most innovative states tended to be larger, more urbanized, and wealthier. Furthermore, they were characterized by strong two-party systems, equitable apportionment, and comprehensive government support services. The states cooperate in numerous voluntary ways. This is most often accomplished through the dissemination of information, which occurs through publications, symposia, and research. Most important are the Governors' Conference and the Council of State Governments, which has numerous affiliates. Founded in 1933, the Council sponsors research, provides information to state officials, and publishes numerous works, including the annual *Book of the States*. It also serves as a secretariat for several other related organizations, among them the Governors' Conference, Conference of Chief Justices, National Association of Attorneys General, and the National Legislative Conference. These organizations bring together government officials in similar positions in order to discuss common problems and experiences. For example, the National Conference of Commissioners on Uniform Laws, which is a Council affiliate, has attempted, with mixed results, to address the differences in state laws in regard to business and industry, marriage and divorce, and traffic and congestion.

Federalism: Marble Cake Federalism   (34)

A model of intergovernmental relations that defines U.S. federalism in terms of shared responsibilities and joint action. Marble cake federalism was popularized by political scientist Morton Grodzins as an alternative explanation of U.S. federalism, which was based on separation of powers. According to Grodzins, "The American form of government is often, but erroneously, symbolized as a layer cake. A far more accurate image is the rainbow or marble cake, characterized by an inseparable mingling of differently-colored ingredients, the colors appearing in vertical and diagonal strands and unexpected whirls. As colors are mixed in the marble cake, so functions are mixed in the American federal system."[9] Grodzins challenged the view that the federal system was adversarial in nature, in which the states endeavored to check the expansion of federal power. Instead, he argued, the federal-state relationship is rooted in cooperation, which dates back to the nineteenth and early twentieth centuries. In his view, cooperative federalism reached its apex during Franklin D. Roosevelt's New Deal and afterward. Grodzins took exception to the notion that federal power threatened to undermine state sovereignty, arguing to the contrary that it both enhanced and strengthened it. He also insisted that a strong federal government was essential to prevent parochial and private interests from undermining the national interest. *See also* FEDERALISM, 29; FEDERALISM: COOPERATIVE FEDERALISM, 30; FEDERALISM: DUAL FEDERALISM, 32.

Significance   Marble cake federalism describes in part, but not wholly, the inherent relationship between the federal government and the states. Clearly, U.S. federalism is marked by cooperation and joint action, but it is also marked by rivalry and disagreement. Neither model—the competitive nor the cooperative—accurately explains the present relationship. On the one hand, the founding fathers sought to fashion a system in which the national government was not dependent on the states to administer its basic functions. As a result, they provided for separate powers—some powers were delegated to the national government, while others were reserved to the states. On the other hand, the framers recognized the importance of sustained interlevel interaction, in which both the federal government and the states worked jointly to promote the national interest. Despite countless examples of cooperation, federal-state relations have, from the nation's inception, been marred by conflict and tension (e.g., school desegregation, reapportionment, environmental protection). Still, marble cake federalism describes, to a large extent, the cooperative nature of the federal system and the importance of preventing special interests from threatening the general welfare.

Federalism: New Federalism   (35)

A national policy to return federal tax money to state and local governments to use as they wish. New federalism is predicated upon a broad restructuring of federal-state relations. Essentially, it seeks to return power—in the form of federal tax dollars—to state and local governments, where local options and sound administration exist. The term *new federalism* was first coined by President Richard M. Nixon, who believed that the federal government had to be "more sensitive, receptive, and responsive to the views and wishes of state and local officials."[10] Thus, Nixon proposed that federal monies be distributed to the states free from federal constraints. This could best be accomplished, argued the president, by the consolidation of categorical grants into block grants and general revenue sharing. *See also* GRANTS: BLOCK GRANT, 40; GRANTS: CATEGORICAL GRANT, 41; GRANTS: REVENUE SHARING, 44.

Significance   New federalism, as conceived by President Nixon, sought "to reverse the flow of power and resources from the states and communities to Washington and start power and resources flowing back from Washington to the states and communities and, more important, to the people all over America."[11] To a large extent, new federalism reflected the president's dissatisfaction with the growth of federal influence at the state and local levels during the (John F.) Kennedy and (Lyndon B.) Johnson administrations, and his dismay over the more than 200 categorical grants approved during the Johnson presidency. President Nixon sought to reverse this trend by endorsing two new laws: the 1968 Intergovernmental Cooperation Act, and 1972 State and Local Fiscal Assistance Act. The former mandated that the viewpoints of state and local authorities be considered during the planning stages of any federally funded program, while the latter provided for a system of general revenue sharing. Despite the president's efforts to curb federal power, the number of categorical grants continued to increase. Indeed, 90 new categorical grants were approved during the Nixon presidency, while 70 more were approved by the (Jimmy) Carter administration. The net effect was to increase local dependency on federal monies and to bypass state government in the process. Upon assuming office, President Ronald W. Reagan adopted the slogan of "New Federalism" and attempted to reverse the present trend by supporting passage of the 1981 Omnibus Budget Reconciliation Act. This act consolidated 20 percent of the existing categorical grants into nine block grants. Under the Reagan administration new federalism took on several distinctive characteristics: (1) a reduction in federal funds to state and local governments; (2) an increase in block grants, with a concurrent reduction in categorical grants; and (3) a reduction of unnecessary red tape and paperwork. President Reagan's new federalism has significantly altered federal-state relations. Although the final results are as yet unknown, forecasters predict: (1) an increase in state and local responsibility for budgetary matters previously dealt with by the federal government; (2) an increase in participation among private citizens and businesses in the areas of human services and economic development; (3) an increase in the present gap between prosperous and ailing regions; and (4) an increase in competition between cities and suburbs for scarce federal funds.

Federalism: New Partnership Federalism (36)

A theory of intergovernmental relations, implemented by President Jimmy Carter, which represented a combination of creative federalism, new federalism, and the president's own populist and technocratic beliefs. New partnership federalism emphasized four salient themes: managerialism, proceduralism, fiscal conservatism, and programmatic flexibility. Specifically, new partnership federalism, as outlined in a Carter administration report entitled "New Partnership to Conserve America's Communities," proposed: (1) improvements in local planning and management capacity and in the administration of existing federal programs; (2) fiscal assistance for the most distressed communities; (3) greater state involvement in aiding their urban communities; (4) increased participation of neighborhood and volunteer groups; (5) improvement of urban physical and cultural environments; (6) incentives for private-sector investment and development; (7) job opportunities for the long-term unemployed; (8) increased opportunities for the disadvantaged; and (9) improved and expanded health and social services.[12] President Carter embraced several of the tenets of his immediate predecessors, but he emphasized the importance of improved targeting of federal assistance to America's most distressed communities, the need to stimulate increased private investment, and the necessity of reducing unnecessary paperwork

and red tape. *See also* FEDERALISM: CREATIVE FEDERALISM, 31; FEDER-
ALISM: NEW FEDERALISM, 35; GRANTS: BLOCK GRANT, 40; GRANTS:
CATEGORICAL GRANT, 41.

Significance   New partnership federalism was instituted, note political scientists Jack Knott and Aaron Wildavsky, "to achieve a more
efficient and more simple system—structurally, administratively, and
programmatically."[13] To realize the president's programmatic and
administrative objectives, new partnership federalism advocated categorical grants, procedural reforms, the continuance of revenue
sharing and block grants, improved federal-local cooperation, increased substate regional responsibility, and a reduction in the federal
fiscal role in intergovernmental programs, but not a reduction in the
number or variety of programs nor in the federal government's
regulatory efforts in the field of grants-in-aid. Despite the prescrip-
tive thrust of new partnership federalism, the Carter administration's
initiatives were beset by numerous ideological ambiguities; these
stemmed, on the one hand, from the president's commitment to
urban areas and, on the other, from his innate fiscal conservatism.
Although the Carter approach underscored the necessity of administrative reform and fiscal restraint, it did little to reorganize the
federal grant system, which encouraged many of the president's
critics—including his successor, President Ronald W. Reagan—to
question the efficacy of new partnership federalism and to propose a
dramatic alternative, new federalism.

Federalism: Picket-fence Federalism   (37)

A view of intergovernmental relations that emphasizes the interrela-
tionships between various levels of government and the functions
they perform. Picket-fence federalism was coined by former North
Carolina governor Terry Sanford, who sought to describe the political
implications of the federal grants system. According to Sanford, "The
lines of authority, concerns and interests, the flow of money and the
direction of programs run straight down like a number of pickets
stuck into the ground. There is, as in a picket fence, a connecting
cross slat, but that does little to support anything. In this metaphor it
stands for the governments. It holds the pickets in line; it does
nothing to bring them together."[14] Picket-fence federalism is based
on two major assumptions: first, initiative and control flow from
federal administrators to their counterparts at the state and local
levels and, second, widespread bureaucratic alliances and linkages
across   levels   of   government—primarily   through   grant-in-aid

programs—that serve to reduce the influence of elected officials. *See also* FEDERALISM, 29; GRANTS, 39; GRANTS-IN-AID, 45.

Significance   Picket-fence federalism argues that the categorical grant system has produced anxiety, turmoil, and competition between the federal government and the state and local units. In addition, it has intensified conflicts between program specialists (bureaucrats) and policy generalists (elected and appointed officials), as the latter have lost meaningful control of government programs. At the same time, special interests have proven increasingly successful in influencing both program specialists and policy generalists, and this has politicized the policy process. In addition, the grants system has exacerbated existing rivalries between program areas (e.g., health, welfare), with the result that program specialists at all levels have been forced to forge political alliances with federal officials, often at the expense of governors and mayors, to secure federal grants. As an explanatory model, picket-fence federalism has become the target of mounting criticism. In their book *The Politics of Federal Grants*, George E. Hale and Marian Lief Palley argue: "The picket-fence assumptions overstate the role of federal officials by ignoring the two-way nature of bargaining and compromise between national and subnational officials. Second, these assumptions underestimate both federal administrative fragmentation and the political clout of state and local officials. Furthermore, like other models, the picket-fence analogy concentrates on the issue of 'Who governs?' largely at the expense of the day-to-day operations of the grant system."[15] Clearly, federal administrators play a prominent role in the intergovernmental process, and this role has increased due to the growing importance of federal assistance. However, less clear is how significant is their actual role, which depends, to a large extent, on how one evaluates their position, influence, and power, as well as on the formal and informal limitations inherent in the system. Picket-fence federalism tends to magnify the role of federal actors, at the expense of state and local officials, who may, in fact, enjoy greater influence than the picket-fence theorists understand or will admit.

Federalism: Regulatory Federalism   (38)

Describes the development of federal programs that were aimed at, or implemented by, state and local governments. Regulatory federalism emerged in the 1960s, the result of numerous federal laws that imposed various requirements on the states. For example, in 1974 Congress enacted legislation that barred federal highway funds to any state that failed to adopt the 55-miles-per-hour speed limit. In 1970, the Clean Air Act Amendments established national air quality standards for the entire country, which required the states to develop plans to implement those requirements. In 1983, Congress approved the Clean Water Act, which compelled the cities to spend approximately $120 billion to construct wastewater treatment plants. Congress passed myriad other laws, all of which imposed various requirements on the states. These included the 1964 Civil Rights Act, the 1965 Highway Beautification Act, and the 1970 Occupational and Safety Act. These measures encompassed numerous areas, among them education, environmental protection, employment, age discrimination, endangered species, and handicapped persons. *See also* FEDERALISM, 29; SOVEREIGNTY, 50; STATES' RIGHTS, 51.

Significance   Regulatory federalism reflected the federal government's commitment to provide for the general welfare—to develop national standards that reflected national priorities. Many of the measures adopted were aimed directly at state and local governments. For example, the 1972 Equal Employment Opportunity Act prevents discrimination by states or municipalities on grounds of race, religion, sex, and national origin. Other laws apply to all federal programs. For instance, the 1964 Civil Rights Act prohibits discrimination in any program that involves federal funds. Still other laws "cross over" and establish rules in one policy area in order to influence another one (e.g., a 1984 law that withholds up to 10 percent of federal highway funds from states that fail to raise the drinking age to 21). Finally, some measures (e.g., the 1970 Clean Air Act Amendments) set overall standards but obligate the states to implement them. Many of these laws enjoyed widespread public support. Even so, they frequently created massive red tape and paperwork, which served to spark strong opposition from state and local officials. Numerous other objections were also raised, including the charge that such legislation threatened to undermine state and local priorities, requiring officials to relinquish their own authority or to adopt standards that may or may not reflect their own goals and objectives. Moreover, it is one thing to pass a law; it is another to enforce it. To do so, the federal government is dependent on state compliance and cooperation. This, too, may pose problems, as is the case with the 55-miles-per-hour speed limit, where some states, such as Nevada, actively oppose the law. Clearly, federal enforcement is limited. This is compounded by the fact that enforcement frequently rests with several agencies, each of which must work in concert to ensure compliance. In addition, these measures grant broad power to the enforcement agencies, which are frequently subject to political pressures and may, if they are not themselves monitored, either refuse to enforce the law, enforce it unevenly, or enforce it in ways that overreach their authority. Finally, these agencies, owing to legislative and administrative authority, may become captured or controlled by the very interests they are charged with regulating.

Grants (39)

Financial assistance from a higher governmental body to a lower one. Grants may take several forms, ranging from early land grants to state governments to a variety of monetary grants for general and specific purposes. One of the earliest federal grants was the Land Ordinance of 1785, which authorized states to use federal lands for public schools. Prior to the Civil War, there were few federal grants, owing, in large part, to the strong emphasis on the Tenth Amendment and states' rights. Advocates of states' rights viewed federal grants as an unwise incursion into state affairs. This was evident in President Franklin Pierce's veto of an 1854 bill that provided federal land to states for mental health facilities. A marked shift in attitude occurred with the passage of the Morrill Act of 1862, which offered public lands to states for financing land grant colleges. Later, the Hatch Act of 1887 offered the first cash grant to states for the development of agricultural experiment stations. However, the major stimulus for federal grants was the ratification of the Sixteenth Amendment in 1913, which authorized Congress to levy taxes on incomes. This amendment guaranteed an automatic growth in federal revenues and a substantial grant base. *See also* GRANTS: BLOCK GRANT, 40; GRANTS: CATEGORICAL GRANT, 41; GRANTS: FORMULA GRANT, 42; GRANTS-IN-AID, 45; GRANTSMANSHIP, 46.

Significance   Grants have been the subject of considerable criticism since their inception and have been viewed as a source of unwarranted interference in the internal affairs of the states. This criticism was reflected in President Pierce's 1854 veto and in the (Roger B.) Taney Court's (1836–1863) emphasis on safeguarding states' rights. The ratification of the Sixteenth Amendment, combined with the Great Depression two decades later, led to the adoption of a new theory of cooperative federalism, in which federal, state, and local governments work cooperatively with one another to address mutual needs and concerns. This new accord garnered increased support with the United States Supreme Court's 1937 decision in *Steward Machine Co. v. Davis* (301 U.S. 548), which derived from the passage of the Social Security Act of 1935. The Supreme Court held the act to be a cooperative attempt to find a method by which all these public agencies could work together toward a common end.

Federal grants continued to proliferate due to a marked increase in categorical grants. With the onslaught of the 1960s and the (Lyndon B.) Johnson administration's emphasis on social service programs, the number of categorical grants increased significantly. This provoked a renewed interest in states' rights and the appropriate role of the federal government in state affairs. The (Richard M.) Nixon, (Gerald R.) Ford, and (Jimmy) Carter administrations endeavored to reverse this trend through the use of block grants and revenue sharing. Even so, their efforts had little impact on the growth of categorical grants. The (Ronald W.) Reagan administration launched an ambitious program to reduce the federal budget by instituting major budget cuts and employing block grants and revenue sharing to a greater degree than had previous administrations. Still, the fear remains that state and local governments may become too reliant on federal grants, to the point that it may be difficult, if not impossible, to reverse the present trend with politically acceptable methods.

Grants: Block Grant   (40)

A type of federal grant-in-aid to state and local governments for broadly defined purposes. Block grants are awarded for a variety of purposes, ranging from crime prevention (e.g., the 1968 Omnibus Crime Control and Safe Streets Act) to community development (e.g., the 1974 Housing and Community Development Act). The dollar amounts of such grants are determined by a formula based on the economic and demographic features of a state or locality. State and local matching funds are rarely required, and federal supervision is minimal. This enables block grants to serve as an important fiscal policy tool by decentralizing the federal government's role in state affairs. Block grants afford state and local administrators greater latitude in the precise use of funds than do categorical grants. The creation and funding of block grants frequently derive from the consolidation of existing categorical grants. For example, categorical grants earmarked for a housing project, a community park, or building renovation are frequently consolidated into one grant under the broader rubric of community development. City and state administrators determine how much of each grant is designated to each area. *See also* GRANTS, 39; GRANTS: CATEGORICAL GRANT, 41; GRANTS: FORMULA GRANT, 42; GRANTS-IN-AID, 45.

Significance   Block grants were instituted in 1966 with the passage of the Partnership for Health Act, and are viewed as an alternative to categorical grants. Block grants were originally conceived to serve three main objectives: (1) to achieve greater economy and efficiency by consolidating existing categorical grants under a broader heading; (2) to enhance program visibility and public support; and (3) to decrease federal involvement in local affairs by delegating autonomy and power to local officials in deciding how monies should be spent. Block grants have served to promote increased economy and efficiency by reducing the level of paperwork and red tape. Despite this fact, there has been relatively little expansion of the block grant program in the last ten years. In fact, block grants comprise less than 14 percent of the federal grant-in-aid program, as strong congressional support of categorical grants has precluded expected program growth. Block grants have also allowed state and local officials increased freedom in the use of grant monies, although federal regulations have served to reduce the freedom and flexibility of such grants. President Ronald W. Reagan has made widespread use of the block grant program, as well as encouraged Congress to give greater consideration to the expanded use of block grants.

Grants: Categorical Grant (41)

A federal grant-in-aid program in which funds are earmarked to state and local governments for specific purposes only. Categorical grants are the oldest form of federal assistance to state and local governments. There are several types of categorical grants: project grants, formula grants, and project-formula grants. Project grants are submitted through specific federal agencies and awarded on the basis of the competitiveness of the project (e.g., low-income housing). Formula grants are disseminated through the legislative process and awarded on the basis of eligibility requirements (e.g., Medicaid). Project-formula grants are distributed by formula to states, to whom communities make application for project funds (e.g., industrial development). Frequently, categorical grants impose a matching requirement, under which state and local governments are required to contribute a stated percentage of the federal grant. This requirement seeks to eliminate waste, fraud, and mismangement. *See also* GRANTS, 39; GRANTS: BLOCK GRANT, 40; GRANTS: FORMULA GRANT, 42; GRANTS-IN-AID, 45.

Significance Categorical grants are the most popular form of federal assistance. Of the various grants, they allow federal officials the widest latitude in ascertaining local need and structuring program objectives and delivery. Since their inception, they have served to redistribute funds from the most prosperous states to the least prosperous ones. They originated from the need to combat the economic woes of the Great Depression of the 1930s. Since that time, they have continued to increase at a steady rate, despite attempts—both past and present—to curtail their use. Major objections to categorical grants include: (1) they create unnecessary red tape and paperwork; (2) they produce funding uncertainty; (3) they impose burdensome regulatory requirements; and (4) they redistribute power within state and local governments. President Ronald W. Reagan has sought to consolidate the categorical grant program into block grants and general revenue sharing. Clearly, recent history demonstrates that federal assistance appears to be crucial if the nation is to solve its present urban crisis. With the steady increase in federal assistance—frequently in the form of categorical grants—many state and local governments have become overly dependent on federal funds. At the same time, federal officials have been forced to reduce the number of categorical grants, to the point where many states and local governments are incapable of offsetting the loss of federal revenue. Future trends suggest that state and local governments will have to explore alternative sources of funding or seriously face major cutbacks in public services. Unfortunately, many cities lack the resources required to adequately fund vital public services. For those cities, the reduction in categorical grants could pose severe economic and political consequences. If U.S. cities are to survive, they will have to make difficult choices that could spell either opportunity or disaster.

Grants: Formula Grant   (42)

Federal or state monies distributed to all eligible recipients based on criteria established by Congress. Formula grants are, in essence, entitlement grants to which state and local governments can lay claim. For example, in the case of the visually impaired, all needy blind persons in every state can receive federal assistance as a matter of "right." Block grants and general revenue sharing are essentially formula grants, while categorical grants can either be project, formula, or a combination of the two. Categorical grants based on formulas can either be open-ended reimbursements of incurred costs (e.g., Medicaid), or close-ended grants, which specify amounts that can be expanded (e.g., Public Library Service). Formula grants constitute approximately one-third of all categorical grants. However, they represent three-fourths of all federal transfer payments to state and local governments. Grant formulas are typically based on the economic and demographic characteristics of a state or locality, except those which pertain to the express eligibility of recipients (e.g, Aid to Families with Dependent Children). *See also* GRANTS, 39; GRANTS: BLOCK GRANT, 40; GRANTS: CATEGORICAL GRANT, 41; GRANTS-IN-AID, 45.

Significance   Formula grants are the most popular method of distributing federal funds to state and local governments. This stems from their reliance on a fixed legal formula that determines allocations to eligible recipients, and not on the discretion of federal administrators, as is true of project grants. Formula grants ensure a broad perspective and approach to the specific problem and guarantee each region its fair share of federal funds, thereby avoiding favoritism. Formulas also insulate federal agencies from political pressure to award grants, using three related processes: (1) a decentralized selection process, which permits regional or area office evaluation; (2) specific guidelines, which are written into administrative allocation formulas to divide funds among many jurisdictions; and (3) an ambiguous assessment process, which permits civil servants to ensure that states or areas are not denied a project. Federal agencies rely on stated minimums, maximums, and quotas in allocating funds rather than on the merits of the project. One such example is the Economic Development Administration's (EDA) criteria for public works grants: (1) appropriations allocated to EDA regional offices are based on area size and population; (2) legislative formulas limit each state to a maximum of 15 percent of the national total; (3) every state is guaranteed a minimum of one area that can receive EDA public works grants; (4) projects in excess of $1 million are discouraged; and (5) there is a limit on the number of projects in any urban area.[16] Since formulas are based on economic and demographic criteria, they tend to represent a stable and consistent approach to federal grants over time. Their redistributional qualities are favored by congressional interests, thus making the formulas difficult to change once established by law.

Grant: Matching Funds   (43)

A financial requirement explicit in many grant programs wherein one level of government agrees to contribute a specific share of the money if the other will provide a specific amount for the same program. Matching funds are required in many federal-state, federal-local, and state-local grant programs (e.g., categorical grants). For instance, if a proposed mental health facility will cost $20 million, the federal government may encourage the city to build it by agreeing to pay $18 million of the cost if the city will assume the remaining $2 million. Many categorical grant programs require a 10 percent match, while others require an equal contribution. In recent years, state and local governments have contributed about $1 for every $2.39 they received from the federal government. There are several types of matching, one of which is in-kind matching. Under this type, the state or local government agrees to contribute its share in the form of personnel, equipment, or facilities equal to the stipulated amount. Typically, state and local governments must raise their match through taxation, as general revenue-sharing funds may not be used for matching purposes in any agreements between the federal government and state and local units. *See also* GRANTS: CATEGORICAL GRANT, 41; GRANTS: REVENUE SHARING, 44.

Significance   Matching funds were commonplace in the 1960s and early 1970s. However, recent trends point to a decrease in the dollar match and an increase in the number of statutory nonsupplant or maintenance-of-effort requirements. For example, the percentage of grant programs requiring low or 50-50 federal matching declined from 32.6 percent of the 1960s total to 13.7 percent of its 1976 counterpart. At the same time, the percentage of grants requiring a high or total federal participation increased from 63 percent to over 80 percent of the 442 programs that were funded in 1976. Generally, the federal government has eschewed matching funds in favor of increased involvement. With the concomitant increase in the number of 100 percent federally funded programs, the number of federal requirements has multiplied. As of 1976, nearly 20 percent of all categorical grants included statutory nonsupplant or maintenance-of-effort requirements. As regards formula grants, the amount rose to over 40 percent. However, as political scientist David B. Walker observes, "in practice, it frequently is difficult to monitor and enforce such 'strings,' which suggests that the increase in low and no-match requirements is more significant than the parallel trend of more nonsupplant and maintenance-of-effort conditions."[17] This trend demonstrates, as many experts have argued, that matching requirements failed to ensure the kind of state and local fiscal accountability and responsibility expected. Apparently, the federal government believes that this goal is best accomplished through increased federal involvement and stricter guidelines.

Grant: Revenue Sharing   (44)

A grant program providing federal aid to state and local governments not earmarked for specific purposes. Revenue sharing enables state and local governments to define their own needs and to use federal funds to address them. Generally, these monies have been targeted for public safety, environmental protection, public transportation, recreation, health care, libraries, and financial administration. Initially, revenue sharing was conceived to reduce fiscal disparities within the federal system and to increase state and local control over expenditures. It reflected the belief that local government has a problem requiring a solution, that the state has the authority to solve the problem, and that the federal government has the resources to correct the problem. *See also* FEDERALISM, 29; FEDERALISM: NEW FEDERALISM, 35; GRANTS, 39; SOVEREIGNTY, 50.

Significance   Revenue sharing exists worldwide. It serves as a means by which central governments seek to disburse funds to their states and localities. In the United States, revenue sharing was first proposed by Representative Melvin R. Laird (R-Wisc.). Controversial in nature, the idea gained momentum in 1964 when Walter W. Heller, chairman of the Council of Economic Advisors, suggested that 1 percent of federal income tax revenue be distributed unconditionally to states, with specific amounts contingent on demographic and economic considerations. The quest by the (Richard M.) Nixon administration to incorporate revenue sharing into its new federalism program proved successful with the 1972 congressional enactment of the State and Local Fiscal Assistance Act. This measure allocated government monies to state and local governments in the proportions of one-third and two-thirds, respectively. In 1976, Congress extended the program for an additional five years. However, the (Ronald W.) Reagan administration discontinued the funds allocated to the state level, thereby reducing the total amount budgeted for revenue sharing. This action marked a significant turnaround from Heller's original proposal, which called for funds to be distributed to states and not to localities. In true federalism, local municipalities are considered "creatures of the state," and are viewed as the responsibility of the state, not the federal government. Despite its advantages, revenue sharing has been the target of several criticisms, including: that it is merely a substitute for other grants, which represents little or no net gain in total revenue for state and local governments; that it encourages governmental fragmentation; that local governments have often misused these funds; and that the distribution formulas frequently discriminate against poorer rural and urban communities.

Grants-in-aid   (45)
Funds made available from the national or state government to a state or local government for a specific purpose, in accordance with

the guidelines imposed by the granting authority. *Grants-in-aid* is a broad term used to describe several types of monetary transfers. These include categorical grants (project, formula, and project-formula) and block grants (formula). Overall, the grants-in-aid program seeks to promote federal policy priorities, while encouraging state and local policy innovation that would prove difficult, if not impossible, without federal support. Specifically, grants-in-aid were instituted to (1) establish minimum national program standards; (2) equalize state resources; (3) improve state programs; (4) encourage program experimentation and evaluation; (5) streamline governmental administration; (6) promote specific policy goals; and (7) increase state authority and responsibility. *See also* GRANTS, 39; GRANTS: BLOCK GRANT, 40; GRANTS: CATEGORICAL GRANT, 41; GRANTS: FORMULA GRANT, 42.

Significance   Grants-in-aid owe their existence, in large measure, to the ratification of the Sixteenth Amendment, which authorized Congress to levy income taxes. This amendment provided Congress with an ever-expanding revenue base with which to implement federal fiscal policy objectives. Prior to the 1960s, federal funds were targeted to assist state and local governments to achieve their individual objectives. Between 1960 and 1972, this emphasis shifted markedly, with grants aimed at realizing federal program goals. One such example is urban renewal, where federal funds were used to finance three-fourths of the program, with only one-fourth contributed by the states. This program underscored the federal commitment to urban renewal, but it did not necessarily reflect state and local priorities. Another example is the federal highway program, where over 90 percent of the funds were provided by the federal government and only 10 percent by the states. In recent years, state and local governments have become increasingly dependent on grants-in-aid. Their interest is, for the most part, economic. Poorer states and localities desperately require such assistance, while wealthier states and localities believe that they must compete for their fair share of tax dollars to avoid raising new taxes. Despite their advantages—and they are many—grants-in-aid have provoked widespread criticism, owing, largely, to the lack of state and local discretion. This has resulted in a renewed interest in revenue sharing and block grants, which provide wider latitude. Public criticism of the grant-in-aid program culminated in a major reorganization, in which ten federal regions were established in 1969 to promote greater decentralization and to streamline grant administration. Still, grants-in-aid are the subject of state and local concern stemming, in part, from program overlap, extensive paperwork, and cumbersome rules and regulations. Criticism runs high, and corrective remedies remain elusive.

Grantsmanship (46)

The study, analysis, and acquisition of grant money from public and/or private sources. Grantsmanship has become a prized political skill, owing to marked changes in the character of the grants process. During the past three decades, the scope of federally supported activities has changed, as have the methods by which grants are secured. The earlier expansion of government grants was a direct by-product of shifting political attitudes and economic conditions. The growth of the grants system was precipitated by several factors, including political party decline, decentralized congressional policy making, influential interest groups, administrative flexibility, and weak state governments. In recent years, there has been a significant decline in federal assistance to state and local governments. This has created the need for grants specialists—individuals adept at program planning and proposal writing. As federal assistance becomes tighter, grants professionals become increasingly important at all levels of government. Indeed, state and local governments can ill afford the luxury of inaction and inexperience. As George E. Hale and Marian L. Palley suggest, "The number of grants programs and the complexity of their rules and regulations reinforces the role of administrators at all levels of government."[18] *See also* GRANTS, 39; GRANTS: MATCHING FUNDS, 43; GRANTS: REVENUE SHARING, 44.

Significance Grantsmanship has magnified the influence of trained specialists—individuals who possess the skills required to write fundable grants. These skills can be acquired in many ways, among them, on-the-job training, specialized courses, seminars and workshops, and tutorial assistance. Regardless of the method, a fundable grant must reflect careful planning, clear reasoning, skillful organization, meticulous research, persuasive writing, and aggressive follow-up. Grants professionals who possess these talents—and are able to secure public and/or private funding—are in short supply and high demand. Recent national developments have altered the nature of grantsmanship. The present system is fraught with uncertainty, as the federal government and the private sector have reduced the level of grant assistance. Thus, the competition for scarce grant dollars has increased. Inflationary pressures, increased defense spending, massive entitlement programs, and other national and international

problems are certain to squeeze the already shrinking grants program. For example, reduction in revenue-sharing funds during the
1980s portends increasingly difficult times for grant applicants.
These developments suggest that aggressive lobbying activities will
become increasingly important. Clearly, stiffer competition is inevitable, as state and local jurisdictions compete against one another for
the dwindling federal grant pie.

Home Rule   **(47)**
Power granted to local governments to draft charters and to manage
their own affairs. Home rule limits state intervention in local matters
by permitting local governments to determine their own governmental structures, raise revenues, promote the general welfare, and
regulate local activities. Home rule may be mandated or permitted by
state constitution or be approved by legislative enactment without
specific constitutional authorization. In addition, state legislatures
may grant home rule charters under special acts, general laws, or
optional plans. Home rule, observes political scientist Rodney L. Mott,
serves three objectives: (1) it grants local governments the power and
flexibility to satisfy increasing demands for local services; (2) it
permits local governments to determine the kind of government best
suited to their needs; and (3) it usually protects local governments
from state intervention, while protecting the state from the constant
pressures of local governments for additional power to respond to
new challenges.[19] In recent years, government reformers have cham-
pioned the cause of home rule. Today, over three-fourths of the
nation's largest cities have been granted home rule. *See also* FEDERAL-
ISM, 29; REPRESENTATIVE GOVERNMENT, 23; SOVEREIGNTY, 50.

Significance   Home rule promotes, according to its proponents,
democracy, self-government, and citizen interest. Although home
rule has served to strengthen local government and to increase local
control, it has several important limitations. In many cases, local
officials must still secure legislative approval of governmental initiatives. Furthermore, home rule cities may not approve ordinances that
conflict with either the state constitution or relevant state laws. They
also may not pass ordinances that affect a "state interest" (one that
transcends local matters, e.g., consumer protection, traffic regulations, waste disposal). These areas typically affect not only local
residents, but those who reside outside the city. Generally, state courts
have held, reports the Chicago Home Rule Commission, that such
limitations also apply to closing hours for taverns, speed limits within

municipal boundaries, and regulation of public school teachers. While home rule does not supplant state supremacy, it does encourage increased discretion and flexibility at the local level. Still, as its critics argue, home rule is not without its drawbacks. For example, it may produce a lack of coordination, political infighting, parochialism, capriciousness, and unpredictability. Whatever its theoretical benefits, home rule must be evaluated in terms of the basic goals and objectives of government: efficiency, effectiveness, innovativeness, and equity.

Interstate Compact   (48)

A formal agreement between two or more states, which requires congressional ratification. This process of approval of interstate compacts ensures federal oversight of agreements between states that seek to settle disputes or problems, and guards against attempts by states to increase their power at the expense of the Union. As stated in Article I, Section 10 of the Constitution, "No State shall, without the Consent of Congress . . . enter into any Agreement or Compact with another State, or with a foreign Power." Once a compact is ratified by Congress, it becomes legally binding on all signatory states. Interstate compacts are primarily employed to address particular rather than technical problems. However, not all compacts require congressional ratification. Formal approval is typically required if a compact tends "to increase the political power of the states, which may encroach upon or interfere with the just supremacy of the United States" (*Virginia v. Tennessee*, 148 U.S. 503: 1893). *See also* FEDERALISM: HORIZONTAL FEDERALISM, 33; INTERSTATE/INTRASTATE RELATIONS, 49.

Significance   Interstate compacts originated in the American colonial era, as a means of resolving boundary disputes. Until 1920, such dispute settlements constituted the majority of the 36 compacts that had been signed. Congressional ratification was instituted to restrict the states from entering into military or economic agreements with other states or foreign countries that might jeopardize the safety and welfare of the nation. Since 1920, the number and diversity of interstate compacts have increased. One of the best-known compacts was concluded between New York and New Jersey in 1921, to establish the New York Port Authority. This agreement sought to regulate transportation problems in and around New York harbor. In the 1930s, interstate compacts extended to regional problems associated with such issues as pollution abatement and to the national level in the creation of such compacts as the Interstate Compact for

Supervision of Parolees and Probationers. The history of interstate compacts reveals several major trends, including: (1) regional rather than bilateral compacts; (2) the acceptance of compacts as a viable method of interstate cooperation; (3) the promulgation of compacts as a means of securing intergovernmental cooperation in such functional areas as education, health, and welfare; (4) the creation of facilitative compacts to provide legal avenues for interstate governmental action; and (5) the emergence of interstate-federal compacts to merge constitutional powers at the federal and state levels. The 1970s and 1980s have been marked by adjoinders to existing compacts rather than an increase in the number of new ones.

Interstate/Intrastate Relations (49)

Pertaining to the internal affairs of a state and its relationships with other states. Intrastate relations define those relationships existing within the boundaries of a state. Each state possesses jurisdiction over its respective counties and cities. The United States Constitution does not refer to local governments. They are considered "creatures of the state," and a state is empowered with total discretion in assigning or denying specific governmental powers to its localities. Interstate relations define the relationships between states. The Constitution sets forth several specific guarantees in this area, including: (1) the full faith and credit clause (Article IV, Section 1); (2) the provisions and immunities clause (Article IV, Section 2); (3) the interstate extradition clause (Article IV, Section 2); (4) the interstate lawsuits clause (Article III, Section 2); and (5) the compact clause (Article I, Section 10). These clauses are designed to improve and enhance interstate relations. *See also* DILLON'S RULE, 234; FEDERALISM: COOPERATIVE FEDERALISM, 30; INTERSTATE COMPACT, 48.

Significance   Interstate/intrastate relations are important factors in U.S. federalism. Intrastate relations were first enunciated by Judge John F. Dillon, an authority on municipal corporations in his 1872 treatise, *Commentaries on the Law of Municipal Corporations*. Since local governments are the creations of state governments—and derive their powers from these governments—disputes arising among states and localities are typically settled by state courts. In 1923, the United States Supreme Court affirmed Judge Dillon's argument in *Trenton v. New Jersey* (262 U.S. 182), ruling, "The City is a political subdivision of the State, created as a convenient agency for the exercise of such governmental powers of the State as may be entrusted to it." While intrastate matters are theoretically the province of state governments, provisions for interstate relations are specifically stated in the United States Constitution. These provisions proved both desirable and necessary. Under the Articles of Confederation, no such provisions were included. As a result, the central government lacked legal authority to arbitrate or settle disputes between states. The Constitution addresses this question in Article IV, Sections 1 and 2. The full faith and credit clause guarantees that no citizen can avoid fine or imprisonment in one state by fleeing to another state. The privileges and immunities clause requires that out-of-state citizens be accorded fair treatment. A citizen cannot be additionally penalized or discriminated against should that citizen commit a crime in another state. The interstate extradition clause provides for the return, upon gubernatorial demand, of any criminal who flees from one state to another. In 1861, in *Kentucky v. Dennison* (65 U.S. 66), the Supreme Court held that it did not possess the constitutional authority to force gubernatorial compliance. Compliance, argued the Court, derives from the spirit of the Constitution. Where lawsuits arise between states, the United States Supreme Court is delegated the role of arbiter. Typically, the Supreme Court will encourage states to settle disputes through interstate compacts.

Sovereignty (50)

The concept that a state or nation is defined by its ability to enact and enforce laws and policies within its domain. Sovereignty implies freedom from the control or interference of another state or nation. In the United States, sovereignty has a twofold definition: externally, it can be defined in terms of the federal government's relationship to other nations, while internally, it can be defined in terms of its relationship to its citizenry and their state governments. In the area of international relations, the federal government exercises supreme authority in the realm of foreign policy. Internally, each state is sovereign and legally equal to all other states. In addition, internal sovereignty defines each state's power and authority over its citizens. The term *popular sovereignty* refers to the right of the people to alter or abolish a government when it abrogates its constitutional mandate. *See also* CONFEDERATION, 7; FEDERALISM, 29; POPULAR SOVEREIGNTY, 19; STATES' RIGHTS, 51; UNITARY STATE, 28.

Significance Sovereignty was a salient concern of the states at the time of the nation's founding. Between 1777 and 1789, the United States existed as a confederacy of sovereign states under the Articles of Confederation. At that time, sovereignty resided in the states. Each state possessed a veto power over major policy initiatives proposed by the national government. The impotency of the national government resulted in the creation of a Constitutional Congress to formulate a new national government. Of primary concern was the degree to which the national government should be sovereign. With the ratification of the United States Constitution in 1789, the existing system was transformed from a confederacy to a federacy. The founding fathers believed that a federal form of government would ensure a far stronger national government than a confederation. This resulted in the diminution of the powers of the individual states—hence, the concept of limited sovereignty. The attempt to address this question of sovereignty was evident in the establishment of Congress. To preserve the notion that all states would be sovereign equals, the founding fathers provided that the Senate would be equally represented by two senators from each state, regardless of population. This appeased the smaller states, which feared the potential power of the larger states. The principle of popular sovereignty was provided for in the House of Representatives, where representation would be based on population, with each state guaranteed at least one representative. The present-day conflict over sovereignty, however, lies not in representation or the sovereignty of one state versus another, but between the states and the federal government. Unfortunately, the adoption of the Tenth Amendment, which sought to guarantee states' rights, did little to clarify the relationship of the two sovereigns. Thus, the dividing line between state and federal sovereignty is vague and marked by concession. The question is not whether the states will surrender sovereignty to the national government, but how much and in what areas.

States' Rights   (51)

The doctrine that a state enjoys supreme sovereignty over its internal affairs. States' rights is based both on Article II of the Articles of Confederation, which grants sovereignty, freedom, and independence to the states, and the Tenth Amendment to the United States Constitution, which guarantees that those powers not granted to the federal government, nor prohibited to the states, are reserved to the states, or to the people. States' rights proponents view federalism as state-centered, as opposed to nationally centered. Governmental power is seen as finite in scope. An increase in federal power invariably spells a decrease in state power. To combat the federal government's incursion into state affairs, states' rights advocates contend that the states possess the rights of secession (voluntary withdrawal from the Union), nullification (the right of a sovereign state to declare a national law null and void), and interposition (the authority of a state to protect its citizens against any national action it perceives as unjust). *See also* CONFEDERATION, 7; FEDERALISM, 29; SOVEREIGNTY, 50; UNITARY STATE, 28.

Significance   States' rights has long been the battlecry of the states in their efforts to combat the excessive growth of federal power. With their newly won independence from Great Britain, the states were reluctant to relinquish their freedom to a new, strong central government. The states' commitment to independence and sovereignty was embodied in the Articles of Confederation, which provided for a weak central government—one that often proved incapable of solving interstate disputes. With the ratification of the United States Constitution in 1789, a federal system replaced the original confederacy. This led to the development of strong central government. It also left unresolved the question of states' rights. States' rights proponents argued that both the Union and the Constitution were predicated on the absolute and independent sovereignty of the member states. The states' rights controversy was further heightened by the battle over slavery, which raised the question of whether the federal government possessed the authority to contain and/or abolish slavery. If so, could the states exercise their sovereign rights by maintaining slavery and by legally seceding from the Union? This question was ultimately settled by the Civil War and later affirmed by the 1869 Supreme Court ruling in *Texas v. White* (7 Wall. 700), in which the Court ruled against the right of secession. The states' rights controversy has reemerged in recent years, particularly as it relates to the proper relationship between the federal government and the states. Many states have voiced strong concern over federal legislation that has either preempted or supplanted state legislation in areas historically considered the province of the states. Recent examples include noise control, water quality, highway beautification, and civil rights. In recent years, President Ronald W. Reagan has revived the issue of states' rights by arguing, as he did in his 1981 Inaugural Address, that "The states created the federal government through the Constitution."[20] Under Reagan's new federalism, the states' rights argument has received new expression. In practice, it reflects the president's commitment to the decentralization of federal power, while granting states and localities increased responsibilities over internal affairs.

3. Parties and Elections

At-large Election (52)

The election of members of a legislative body who do not run in precincts, wards, or districts but are selected by the voters as a whole. At-large elections differ markedly from district contests, in which candidates run from geographical areas. The type of election—at-large or district—will, in many cases, dictate the outcome of the contest. In at-large elections, candidates must appeal to the entire community to secure a plurality (the largest number, as opposed to a majority) of the vote. Typically, the victorious candidate must reflect the dominant values of the community, instead of championing local neighborhood interests. In theory, at-large elections promote community-wide solutions to municipal problems. Today, 66.5 percent of U.S. cities elect their council members at-large; 14.5 percent by district; and 19 percent by a combination of the two. *See also* GENERAL ELECTION, 57; NONPARTISAN ELECTION, 63; PRIMARY ELECTION, 76.

Significance At-large elections were instituted to promote the "general good" and to reduce the impact of interest group pressure. Opponents of at-large elections contend that they penalize minority candidates, who, in many cases, are incapable of winning such contests. For example, Hispanics may represent 65 percent of the population in a particular section(s) of the city, but constitute only 10 percent of the total population. In an at-large election, they may find it difficult, if not impossible, to garner a plurality of the vote. However, in a district election, they may boast sufficient voting strength in one or two districts to be elected. Critics also maintain that at-large elections force candidates to mirror the "prejudices" of the majority and, at times, support public opinion even when it is wrong.

On the other hand, proponents of at-large elections argue that such contests reduce log rolling (the exchange of political favors for mutual benefit), interest group control, and political demagoguery. Moreover, they suggest that at-large elections encourage talented individuals from the same area to run for public office, as such contests may permit simultaneous election. However, as political scientist Thomas R. Dye notes (as regards city council elections), "There are no significant differences in the social status, occupations, or experience of council members elected at-large and by wards."[1] In the end, at-large elections represent a mixed bag—that is, they encourage community-wide solutions, while minimizing the opportunities for minority group representation.

Australian Ballot (53)

A secret ballot compiled, disseminated, and validated by election officials at public expense. The Australian ballot, which originated in 1890, was a direct response to earlier methods of voting, in which citizens cast their ballots orally or on differently colored sheets, prepared by the parties. This system produced coercion and intimidation, particularly where voters were required to cast their ballots publicly. The type and format of ballots have a major impact both on the results of elections and on the level of participation. The *long ballot* (or *bedsheet ballot* or *'jungle ballot'*) is the most common state and local ballot. This ballot features a long list of offices, candidates, and issues to be decided. It stands in contrast to the *short ballot*, which contains relatively few offices (e.g., the national election ballot). The long ballot was established during the Jacksonian period (1830s) and reflected the popular belief that democracy was best served by an increase in the number of elected officials. This assumption is challenged today by many observers, who contend that the shorter the ballot, the more likely it is that the voter will know the candidates, their qualifications, and the issues. Moreover, the long ballot enables many elected officials to retain their positions as a result of voter apathy and indifference. The short ballot, which was initiated in the early twentieth century, has succeeded in simplifying the voting process, but has failed to resolve many of the more substantive questions. *See also* POLITICAL ACCESS, 68; VOTER QUALIFICATIONS, 81.

Significance   The Australian ballot ensured secrecy, but it did not eliminate the complexities inherent in voting. In addition to the controversy surrounding the long versus the short ballot, a similar controversy surrounds the format of the ballot. In this regard, there are two main forms: the *office-block ballot* or *Massachusetts ballot*, and the *party-column ballot* or *Indiana ballot*. The office-block ballot groups candidates together under the offices they seek, while the party-column ballot arranges candidate names in one column based on party affiliation. The office-block ballot, employed in 20 states, is disdained by party leaders, who believe it places undue emphasis on the office, as opposed to the party, and tends to discourage *straight-ticket voting* (voting for all candidates of one party for all offices). The party-column ballot, adopted in 30 states, simplifies the voting process and allows straight-ticket voting (voters may mark a single "X" or pull a single lever). On the other hand, the party-column ballot encourages citizens to vote based on party affiliation, as opposed to candidates and issues.

County Chairperson   (54)

An official who administers the party's affairs at the county level and implements its programs and policies. County chairpersons are usually elected by precinct captains (individuals who head the basic unit of the election process at the lowest organizational level). Ideally, county chairpersons organize the local election machinery and provide an important communications link with the state central committee (the main governing body of a political party within a state). In this regard, county chairpersons play a salient role in melding the party together. If the party's organizational structure is to function, then the county chairpersons must communicate effectively with party officials both above and below them in the organizational hierarchy. This is no mean feat, as there is little communication between precinct captains, county officials, and state party leaders. *See also* COUNTY COMMITTEE, 55; STATE PARTY CHAIRPERSONS, 79.

Significance   County chairpersons are, in the view of most experts, the kingpins of the party's organizational structure. For myriad reasons, they exercise considerable political influence, which is why, for example, most governors and even presidents go to enormous lengths to court the nation's county chairpersons. County chairpersons perform numerous tasks, among them, campaign planning, candidate recruitment, political fundraising, patronage appointments, and organizational development. In many cases, county chairpersons' power is magnified by the fact that they recruit precinct captains who, in turn, are responsible for developing support for their election. Moreover, county chairpersons are deeply involved in presidential politics, particularly in terms of identifying potential candidates. Although they do not select their party's presidential nominees, they do provide important feedback—namely, how the various candidates are viewed by the professionals. Despite their importance and heavy workload, most county chairpersons do not receive a salary, have little staff assistance, and operate with a minimal budget. Still, their contributions are far greater than one might expect, given their meager resources. Today, there are over 3,000 Republican and 3,000 Democratic county chairpersons. For the most part, they operate autonomously. Since they are elected by their constituents, they cannot be removed by the state or national party committees.

County Committee (55)

The governing body of the party at the county level and the major organ of the state party apparatus. The county committee consists of individuals selected at one of two organizational levels: the precinct and the city or ward. The most common method is selection at the precinct (the basic unit of the election process at the lowest organizational level). There are over 178,000 precincts (Democratic and Republican) in the United States. These precincts report to approximately 6,200 county organizations. The precinct chairperson or captain (the individual who heads the precinct) is elected in the party primary or at the precinct convention. The precinct chairperson is a member of the county committee, which, in turn, elects the county chairperson. At the other level (the city or ward), precinct chairpersons are appointed by the ward (the division of a city for purposes of electing individuals to the city council) or citywide. This system presently exists in Chicago, Illinois. *See also* COUNTY CHAIRPERSON, 54; STATE CENTRAL COMMITTEE, 78; STATE PARTY CHAIRPERSONS, 79.

Significance   County committees are extremely active in state politics. However, like other party organs, they lack both discipline and cohesion. Generally, the county committee is composed of a county chairperson (the official who administers the party's affairs and implements its programs and policies), an executive committee, and a core of activists. These individuals make decisions, recruit candidates, raise funds, and speak for the party. The county committee is elected locally and enjoys considerable autonomony. For many reasons, county committees are extremely important. First, the county is a major source of *patronage* (the power to make partisan appointments to office or to confer other favors), which is dispensed for party service. Second, county lines are widely accepted as a legitimate means of creating other political jurisdictions (e.g., congressional districts). Third, the county is a prominent administrative unit of the state and a hub of commercial enterprise. Fourth, as increasing numbers of municipalities have dispensed with the nonpartisan ballot (where candidates run for office without benefit of party affiliation), the county has become a major focus of party activity. Fifth, the county elects myriad public officials, who possess considerable influence in the policy-making process. Sixth, state statutes enhance the stature of county committees, as their members often serve on parallel committees and on the state central committee (the main governing body of a political party within a state).

Extralegal Political Organizations (56)

Parties or clubs that are auxiliary and/or alternative to the official party organization. Extralegal political organizations serve as embellishments to the formal party apparatus. These organizations take two forms: auxiliaries to party organizations and alternatives to them. These extralegal parties or clubs occupy an important place in the party machinery. In many cases, they were established by party members to accomplish a specific purpose. For example, women's groups have been created to promote women's rights and other feminist issues. These unofficial organizations vary in size, shape, and purpose. Some were conceived to challenge the regular party organization (e.g., Mississippi Freedom Democratic party), while others were designed to stimulate heightened interest in political issues (e.g., California Democratic Council). Major extralegal political organizations include the California Republican Assembly, Republican and Democratic voluntary associations in Wisconsin, and the New Democratic Coalition in New York City. Similar groups have been spawned in Pennsylvania, Ohio, and Illinois (including the influential Independent Voters of Illinois). *See also* PARTY ACTIVISTS, 64; POLITICAL PARTY, 71.

Significance   Extralegal political organizations have, at times, achieved remarkable results, often overshadowing the performance of the official party apparatus. Indeed, at times, the national committees have cooperated more closely with these organizations than they have with the official party machinery. Generally, members of these groups are dues-paying, well educated, and middle-class. Despite their effectiveness, they differ markedly from the usual political organizations of the past, in that they eschew political patronage (the power to make partisan appointments to office or to confer other favors), demonstrate a keen interest in issues and ideology, and possess solid professional credentials. In addition to these groups—which both cooperate with and, at times, compete with the official party machinery—both parties boast numerous auxiliary organizations, which usually surface at election time. These include such groups as Volunteers for Carter, Businessmen for Reagan, Citizens for Mondale, and Independents for Bush, among others. In some cases, these groups are closely tied to the official party organization, while in others they function quite independently. Typically, they raise funds, plot strategy, organize events, and solicit voter support. They permit many individuals to become involved in party politics who would prefer not to be formally affiliated with the official party apparatus. There are myriad extralegal political organizations, including youth groups (e.g., the Young Democrats and Young Republicans) who recruit and train young candidates and raise funds for party campaigns. Like other extralegal political organizations, their effectiveness varies. Some are ostensibly social in nature and perform little grassroots work, while others provide the talent and personnel of which campaigns are made. Extralegal political organizations have, in several instances, dramatically changed the face of state parties and have, on occasion, emerged as a viable alternative to the regular party organization.

General Election   (57)

An electoral contest, usually held following a primary election, to fill various local, state, and national offices. A general election pits the nominees of each party against one another. Candidates work assiduously to reach the voters, often spending vast sums of money to garner the necessary votes. Regardless of how well candidates fare in the party primary, if they win that election their battle is only half won; they must then win the general election. In the primary, their goal is to secure enough votes from party members to win the nomination. In the general election, their task is greater. First, they must try to heal the wounds created by the primary, bring the various factions together, and forge a united effort. Second, they must make a major attempt to reach the large bloc of undecided voters and persuade them to support their candidacy. Third, they must make some effort, depending on the district, constituency, issues, and circumstances, to attract as many votes as possible from the opposing party. The task before them requires a major effort: a campaign that is well organized and conducted effectively from start to finish, and one that addresses the diverse interests of as large a cross section of the electorate as possible. *See also* AT-LARGE ELECTION, 52; NONPARTISAN ELECTION, 63; PRIMARY ELECTION, 76.

Significance   General elections are replete with contradictions. The textbook profile of the typical U.S. voter bears little resemblance to today's actual voter. Classical democratic theory posits a voter who is well informed, involved, and interested in government affairs; a voter who is willing to invest the required time and effort to study the candidates and issues; and who then, in the solitude of the voting booth, selects those individuals who are most qualified to lead. The facts, however, bespeak another type of voter. Many of today's voters are uninformed on political issues. They have only a vague sense of what is at stake, and rarely do they understand the nuances and complexities that are involved. Instead, they vote on instinct or whim for the candidates who come closest to espousing their own views on two or three issues of select concern at the time. More often, they vote based on party affiliation, routinely supporting those candidates who carry their party's banner. On occasion, they will vote on the basis of the candidate's style, charm, appearance, or charisma, associating those qualities with the ability to govern. The implications of such voting are great. They suggest, more and more, that "the medium is the message"—that public relations packaging and mass media advertising are indispensable tools in winning elective office. Successful candidates must build a broad-based coalition of voters. This, in turn, forces them to avoid issues and eschew controversy. Candidates can ill afford to antagonize those voters who determine victory or defeat. All too often, the wrong candidate is elected—the pied piper who promises the sky and then fails to deliver—making the problem of accountability extremely difficult. Since the voters know little of the issues, or the candidates, they are incapable of holding elected officials accountable for their promises.

Gerrymandering   (58)
The manipulation of electoral district boundaries, usually by the majority political party in a state legislature, for the political advantage of an incumbent, party, or group. Gerrymandering often produces oddly shaped districts, violative of history and common sense, to accomplish its desired effect. The term originated in 1812, when a district in Essex County, Massachusetts, was described as resembling a salamander. In deference to Governor Elbridge Gerry of Massachusetts, the misshapen district was described as a *gerrymander*. Gerrymandering may take one of several forms, including *packing* and *cracking*. A district is packed when its lines are drawn to concentrate party voters into a safe district. If the majority party wishes to minimize the partisan concentration of the opposition, it

may crack a district into more than one district, so as to spread that party's vote. Gerrymandering is reinforced by the consistent voting patterns of the electorate. *See also* INCUMBENT'S ADVANTAGE, 60; POLITICAL ACCESS, 68; RACIAL DISTRICTING, 77.

Significance   Gerrymandering, unlike *malapportionment* (the drawing of legislative district boundaries which are both unfair and unequal), does not violate the United States Constitution or federal law. Lines may be drawn in many configurations to allow equally sized districts. Gerrymandering is regarded as one of the fine arts of the political process. When state legislatures draw district lines, the majority party seeks to maximize the number of congressional and state legislative seats they are likely to win. Thus, by packing and cracking, the legislature can distribute voters into districts of relative partisan strength. Opposition voters may be gerrymandered into a district where their party can win by a large margin, while limiting the number of districts they can win. Or the opposition party's voting strength can be dissipated by spreading it over a number of districts. In cases where each of the two parties controls one of the houses of the state legislature, district lines are likely to be drawn to favor incumbents rather than to alter partisan balance. Gerrymandering not only redistributes partisan advantage, but also concentrates or disperses voters by such characteristics as income, race, occupation, and education. In most cases, gerrymandering produces a large number of safe districts, which increase the advantages of incumbents and make it difficult, if not impossible, for opponents to mount a serious challenge. It may, in some cases, result in the party receiving fewer votes statewide than the opposing party yet winning a majority of seats in the legislature.

Grandfather Clause   (59)
A means by which an individual could register to vote without taking a literacy test if he or she were a "lineal descendant" of a person who had voted prior to 1860 or 1870, thereby disfranchising blacks whose ancestors were slaves and could not vote. The grandfather clause was an ingenious device to permit illiterate whites to vote, while the literacy test continued to exclude similarly or better-educated blacks. These provisions differed markedly in form and content, but their intent was identical: to prevent blacks from registering while providing ample opportunities for whites to do so. For example, one such measure provided that any man, or his descendant, who had served in

one of a number of specified wars (or in some states, who had voted before 1867) was eligible to register and vote. This grandfather clause disqualified blacks and admitted even the most backward whites. Obviously, it was not difficult for a southern white to produce evidence of a soldier or an ancestor. In the case of blacks, however, it was impossible, as most were barred from military service. *See also* LITERACY TEST, 62; POLITICAL ACCESS, 68; POLL TAX, 74; WHITE PRIMARY, 83.

Significance   The grandfather clause was eventually struck down in 1915, when the United States Supreme Court ruled, in *Guinn v. United States* (238 U.S. 347), that Oklahoma's grandfather clause violated the Fifteenth Amendment. The Court stated that although the grandfather clause did not mention race or color, it was clearly discriminatory because the only reason for setting a date of 1867 or earlier was to deny blacks the right to vote. While in existence, the grandfather clause severely limited black registration. For example, in Louisiana, for the 1896 national election (the last before the disfranchising measure), 130,344 blacks were registered in the state, and black registrants were in the majority in 26 parishes (counties). For the 1900 national election, two years after the adoption of the new constitution, only 5,320 blacks were registered, and no parishes showed a majority of black registrants. While black registration fell by 125,000 (96 percent), white registration decreased by only 30,000.

Incumbent's Advantage   (60)

An advantage over a challenger enjoyed by an official seeking reelection. The incumbent's advantage in state and local races is extremely strong: eight out of ten state senate incumbents are reelected; six to nine out of ten state house members; and six out of ten state governors. In addition to incumbency, party competition, state and local issues, candidate styles and personalities, and campaign methods and techniques affect election outcomes. The advantages of incumbency include name recognition, campaign funds, political contacts, media exposure, a record in office, leverage in redistricting, and control over a vast network of resources available to an incumbent official. *See also* GERRYMANDERING, 58; POLITICAL CAMPAIGNING, 69; POLITICAL MACHINE, 70.

Significance   The incumbent's advantage is not a guarantee of electoral success, but it has proved a formidable hurdle for nonincumbent opponents to overcome. In state legislative races, incumbency is an important factor, as many districts reflect a solid one-party constituency. This partisan balance usually translates to the advantage of the candidate of the majority party. Redistricting plans by state legislatures are often shaped to favor incumbents, resulting in *safe districts*, districts virtually impossible for a challenger to penetrate. Moreover, the voters know their legislators—their names, backgrounds, and records. To stimulate increased awareness, an incumbent enjoys the privileges of a paid staff, postage, a WATS telephone line, speechwriters, caseworkers, and the publicity an incumbent official can generate. While the challenger's campaign funds are consumed by these expenses, incumbents may use their resources to fortify communications with the voters, relying extensively on television, radio, and newspaper advertisements. They can disseminate their message concerning what they have done for the district or state—tangible accomplishments versus the promises of the challenger. Moreover, many political action committees (PACs) provide campaign funds mainly for incumbents of both political parties on the assumption that these are people of power who very likely will continue to hold the office. To overcome these disadvantages, a challenger must often run several times for the same office, thereby increasing name recognition, expanding the support base, improving the campaign organization, and avoiding the pitfalls of earlier campaigns. Incumbents also possess the ability to exploit the major media, while challengers are limited to uninfluential organs. Despite these advantages, incumbency is not always an asset, particularly when the official or party in power has alienated the voters (either because of what they did or did not do). After several years in office, incumbents make enemies—often powerful enemies—who relish the opportunity to unseat them. Moreover, campaigning on one's record is not always advantageous, as Governor Christopher S. (Kit) Bond of Missouri discovered in 1976, when he was forced to explain why he had allowed utility rate increases and had not imposed steeper taxes on corporations, or as Massachusetts Governor Michael S. Dukakis discovered in 1978, when he had to explain his decision to raise state taxes and support stricter gun control legislation. In the end, incumbents possess myriad advantages. However, they must still work extremely hard to maintain their positions. There are too many variables, too much unpredictability, to assume certain victory. Indeed, incumbents often simply campaign far better than their opponents and boast records that ensure their reelection.

Language Disfranchisement (61)

The inability to vote or participate in the political process owing to a failure to understand or read the majority language of English. Language disfranchisement has sparked heated debate in recent years, especially among Hispanics, and has led to bitter charges of discrimination. Moreover, it has led some elements of the English-speaking community to demand an end to bilingualism, as it relates to voting and electoral participation, as well as school programs. This land is a nation of immigrants. Many U.S. citizens came to this country from abroad, fluent in their native tongues but unable to speak English. Others were born in this country but were, for one reason or another, reared in families where English was spoken only as a second language. Over the years, these people have been at an extreme disadvantage in registering and/or voting, as the law required them to read and write English. Where they could meet the minimum qualifications to register and vote, they often were unable to read fully the ballot and the various issues presented. Many believe that individuals should not be deprived of the right to vote or participate in the election process simply because they cannot read, write, or speak English. Others maintain that all citizens, regardless of their ethnic background, should be required to demonstrate proficiency in English and that no special allowances should be made when it comes to voting or electoral participation. *See also* LITERACY TEST, 62; POLITICAL ACCESS, 68.

Significance Language disfranchisement, as a violation of voting rights, gained legal recognition when, in 1965, after a long and arduous fight, Congress passed the Voting Rights Act. Ten years later, the act was amended to include, among other features, minority language provisions that required the states to conduct elections in one or more languages, in addition to English, where circumstances necessitated such action. For most states, this meant the addition of one language, usually Spanish, and in a few cases, two or more languages. The language of the Voting Rights Act is quite general. The new language requirements affect localities as small as Loving County, Texas, with its population of fewer than two hundred, and as large as Los Angeles County, with its population of more than seven million. Because different areas have different election procedures, the steps required to implement the law vary with local circumstances. For example, where the required minority language is currently or traditionally unwritten, such as most American Indian languages, the state or locale need provide in that language only oral publicity and oral assistance at registration and polling places. Similarly, a small jurisdiction employing paper ballots may be more able to convert to a totally bilingual election than a large jurisdiction using voting machines that limit the size of the ballot. In passing the act, Congress was concerned that information directly related to registration and voting be as available to language minority citizens as to others. At a minimum, Congress felt that citizens in covered states and locales had a right to expect that their local election officials would provide oral and, where appropriate, written assistance and information in the appropriate language(s). It also felt that publicity about elections and registration qualifications and times should be provided in the appropriate minority language(s).

Literacy Test   (62)

A suffrage requirement used to determine fitness for voting by means of a reading, writing, or "understanding" examination. Literacy tests varied widely in terms of format, content, and evaluation. In some states, the examination merely required the prospective voter to scratch a signature. In other states, literacy was demonstrated by the ability to complete a registration application. In still others, the test was more substantive (e.g., New York), requiring applicants to demonstrate understanding of several brief expository paragraphs. In addition to these tests, some states employed interpretive examinations. Originally, these tests were viewed as alternatives to literacy tests. For example, if individuals could not read or write, they might qualify to vote by describing a feature of the governmental system or state constitution. In other states (e.g., Louisiana and Georgia), the local registrar could allow illiterates to register if they could prove "good character." Still other states, such as Mississippi, required all three tests: interpretation, literacy, and good character. In Mississippi, for example, local registrars were free to select 1 of 286 sections of the state constitution for the applicant to read and interpret, with the registrar serving as sole judge of the results. *See also* GRANDFATHER CLAUSE, 59; POLITICAL ACCESS, 68; POLL TAX, 74; WHITE PRIMARY, 83.

Significance   Literacy tests were discontinued in 1970, with the enactment of the Voting Rights Act. Under this act, Congress barred the use of literacy, understanding, and good character tests as a prerequisite for registration. It concluded that literacy tests were, both in theory and practice, discriminatory—that is, they granted unwarranted discretion to local examiners, who used their authority, particularly in the South, to prevent blacks from voting. In some southern states, for example, black applicants were disqualified because they failed to interpret various constitutional passages to the satisfaction of the white board of examiners. Ultimately, the discriminatory nature of these tests in six southern states resulted in the passage of the Voting Rights Act of 1965. This act, which was further expanded in 1970 and 1975, precluded the use of such tests and authorized federal voting examiners to register blacks in those states and voting districts in which less than 50 percent of eligible voters were registered. The Voting Rights Act of 1970, which suspended all literacy tests, was upheld by the United States Supreme Court in *Oregon v. Mitchell* (400 U.S. 112) in 1970.

Nonpartisan Election (63)

A contest in which candidates' names appear on the ballot without party designations and political parties are prohibited from recruiting candidates for elective office. Nonpartisan elections are especially prevalent in smaller cities, where they are used to select councilpersons, school board officers, judges, and other municipal officials. Currently, Nebraska is the only state in which legislators are elected in nonpartisan contests. Although typically the candidate who receives a plurality of the votes wins a nonpartisan election, in some races a nonpartisan primary is held to reduce the number of candidates to two. Nonpartisanship, which emerged from the reform movement of the early twentieth century, sought to eliminate the evils of machine politics and the impact of boss rule. It reflected the popular view that the best way to reduce the tight-fisted control of political parties was to prevent them from dominating the elections process. As a result, reformers believed that nonpartisan elections would encourage voters to focus increased attention on candidates and issues, as opposed to party affiliation and boss influence. *See also* AT-LARGE ELECTION, 52; GENERAL ELECTION, 57; PRIMARY ELECTION, 76.

Significance   Nonpartisan elections have failed, despite their goal, to eliminate party control and have given rise to a host of new problems. Studies reveal that, while candidates' affiliations may not appear on the ballot, nonpartisan elections have served to increase the influence of special interest groups, which both endorse candidates and fund campaigns. Like political parties, these groups support candidates who embrace their views and raise large sums of money to advance their interests. Nonpartisan elections also encourage the electorate to vote on the basis of candidate familiarity, which increases the advantage of incumbency. Moreover, nonpartisan elections encourage voters to simplify their choices by voting on the basis of name recognition or ethnic affiliation. Furthermore, they engender low voter turnout in many races, as protest voting is made more difficult in the absence of party designations. This works to the advantage of Republican interests, as Republicans tend to vote in larger numbers and are less dependent on interest group activity to stimulate voter turnout. Finally, nonpartisan elections lessen the chances of candidates with minimal resources and connections, as well as reduce the electoral fortunes of racial and ethnic minorities and blue-collar workers, who usually fare less well in nonpartisan races. Thus, nonpartisan elections, in and of themselves, do not necessarily produce "better" candidates or promote "democratic" politics.

Party Activists (64)

Individuals who staff a party organization or a political campaign. Party activists are essential if a party hopes to elect its members to office and win control of government. To recruit activists, the party must provide a variety of incentives: material rewards (e.g., money, jobs, contracts), psychological satisfactions (e.g., excitement, prestige, camaraderie), and purposive inducements (e.g., principles, issues, social change). Obviously, these incentives are not mutually exclusive, and party activists may be motivated by a combination of them. According to political scientists Nelson W. Polsby and Aaron Wildavsky, activists fall into two main categories, "professionals" and "purists".[2] The professional is motivated by patronage, favors, and winning elections. This individual has a pragmatic style; is a party follower; believes in organizational loyalty; views politics as a full-time occupation; and comes from a lower-middle or middle-class background. The purist is motivated by the passage of favored legislation; possesses an ideological style; advocates equality in party decision making; is loyal to officeholders, clubs, individuals, or a cause; views politics as a part-time avocation; and comes from a middle-class or upper-middle-class background. *See also* EXTRALEGAL POLITICAL ORGANIZATIONS, 56; POLITICAL PARTY, 71.

Significance   Party activists are vital to the lifeblood of a political party. Clearly, a party cannot survive unless it can attract interested and dedicated supporters. Since most party activists are unpaid, this poses a special problem to the organization, namely, how to recruit, motivate, and keep party workers. At the state and local level, material rewards play an important role. For example, party activists may be selected to run for office; given contracts for equipment, construction, insurance, and other government business; and appointed by probate courts as appraisers and trustees of estates. Research suggests that material rewards have declined in importance over the years, owing, perhaps, to the fact that state and local employees are more secure today as a result of civil service reforms and unionization. For example, at one time, the governor of Pennsylvania could fill as many as 63,000 jobs; today, that number has been reduced to under 1,000. Increasingly, state and local activists have expressed greater interest in the psychological satisfactions associated with party service; many relish the contacts, status, and conviviality. Additionally, many state and local activists experience fulfillment by working for a desired goal or objective. These individuals view party service as a way to influence public policy, as well as to effect social change. This incentive has become particularly pronounced, as party activists have discovered that social satisfactions can easily be realized in sundry nonpolitical groups and organizations.

Party Competition (65)

The ability of parties to contest elections, organize the government, and ensure party responsibility. Party competition is said to exist when the majority party's margin is sufficiently uncertain that the prospects of electoral defeat are strong enough to influence the conduct of incumbents. If the balance is close, the minority party is likely to be sufficiently motivated to exploit popular discontent and propose a rival program that promises potential electoral success. In a democracy, competition is essential to promote government accountability. This, of course, is the ideal. In reality, most state parties are plagued by factionalism; cohesiveness is the exception. Overall, argues political scientist John F. Bibby, about half the state Republican organizations could be characterized as "moderately strong" and half the Democratic organizations as "moderately weak."[3] *See also* GERRYMANDERING, 58; PARTY REALIGNMENT, 66; THIRD PARTY, 80.

Significance Party competition is extremely difficult to measure. The results depend, in large part, on the methods employed. In one study, political scientist J. Austin Ranney sought to measure interparty competition by combining the party's percentage of votes in gubernatorial elections and of legislative seats along with the duration of legislative control.[4] Applying this test for the 1974–1980 period, Ranney concluded that there were 8 "one-party" Democratic states (Alabama, Arkansas, Georgia, Louisiana, Maryland, Mississippi,

North Carolina, and Rhode Island); 1 "modified one-party" Republican state (North Dakota); and 41 states divided between modified one-party Democratic and two-party rule. In another study, political scientists Malcolm E. Jewell and David M. Olson, employing the criteria of control of the governorship and the legislature from 1961 to 1982, found that there were 7 "dominant" Democratic states (Alabama, Arkansas, Georgia, Louisiana, Mississippi, South Carolina, and Texas), and 5 "majority" Republican states (Colorado, New Hampshire, South Dakota, Vermont, and Wyoming).[5] Overall, many two-party states and modified one-party Democratic states possess higher increased urbanization, greater union memberships, fewer farmers, and larger black populations. Partisanship, in large measure, is the product of socioeconomic status; since the Democratic and Republican parties appeal to different socioeconomic groups, this may explain why many of the states vote as they do. As economic circumstances change, it is reasonable to expect shifts in party loyalty. According to many experts, current trends portend several major changes in party competition. As political scientist Michael J. Ross notes, "Many of the one-party Democratic or modified one-party Democratic states are Sunbelt (southern or border) states that have received extensive migration. This population movement, and the emergence of the Republican party in the South, may lessen allegiance to the Democratic Party and increase competition between the parties."[6]

Party Realignment   (66)

A situation that occurs when a substantial number of existing voters alter their partisan allegiance or new voters identify disproportionately with one side. Party realignment suggests a long-term fundamental shift in partisan loyalties, deriving, in part, from political unheavals that threaten present party alignments. Generally, *cross-cutting* issues (e.g., disarmament, school busing, tax reform) affect both political parties. However, if one party succeeds in identifying itself with the popular side of the issue, a political realignment may occur. Clearly, the party out of power must exploit the issue if it hopes to win political power, while the party in power must squelch the issue if it wishes to maintain its majority status. During the post–World War II era, several potential cross-cutting issues have arisen, including Communism, Vietnam, racial strife, and law and order. Still, party realignment did not occur, as neither party adopted a clear-cut stand that captured the support of the nation. *See also* PARTY COMPETITION, 65; PARTY REFORM, 67; VOTING BEHAVIOR, 82.

Significance   Party realignment is a subject of considerable interest among politicians, professors, and pundits. During the 1980s much was written about the so-called Reagan revolution and whether it signaled a new party realignment. During this period, the Republicans have succeeded in winning increasingly larger percentages of such traditional Democratic constituencies as blue-collar workers, Roman Catholics, and white southerners. Clearly, President Ronald W. Reagan's unprecedented success in these Democratic strongholds contributed much to his 1984 presidential landslide. However, in spite of the president's enormous personal popularity, he failed to prevent the Democrats from winning control of the Senate in 1986. Moreover, other factors caused President Reagan's popularity to wane, particularly the 1986 Iran-Contra scandal. The key question remains whether a party will be able to maintain its new constituencies once its leader leaves office. In addition, many scholars argue that the likelihood of a party realignment is lessened by the current decline of parties and the increase in the number of independent voters. Indeed, in spite of earlier predictions of an "emerging Republican majority," conservative author Kevin P. Phillips contends that "our current volatility suggests a process of 'dealignment.'"[7] In this same vein, political scientist Walter Dean Burnham has predicted "the onward march of party dealignment."[8] Despite Republican optimism, most observers share the views expressed by Phillips and Burnham. In reality, there is scant evidence of a party realignment. Unlike previous realignments (e.g., Thomas Jefferson, 1800; Andrew Jackson, 1828; Abraham Lincoln, 1860; William McKinley, 1896; and Franklin D. Roosevelt, 1932), the Reagan revolution was not the result of a momentous public tide. Indeed, the Republicans during the Reagan years failed to win control of the United States Congress, most state legislatures and city halls, and the partisan loyalty of a majority of the U.S. public.

Party Reform   (67)

Institutional, organizational, and political changes aimed at preventing the disintegration of the party system in the United States. Party reform is essential if the two-party system is to survive. Political experts are divided as to the future of U.S. parties. On the one hand, Stephen Hess, a senior fellow at the Brookings Institution and author of several works on political parties, has written, "The obituary has been set in type, waiting. The epitaph is written. Here lie America's political parties—born of necessity, died of irrelevancy. Rest in peace."[9] On the other hand, Professor James MacGregor Burns, a distinguished political scientist and chairperson of a special commission on the future of political parties, contends that parties are essential to the realization of democracy, arguing, "What would take the place of parties? A politics of celebrities, of excessive media influence, of political fad-of-the-month clubs, and massive private financing by various 'fat cats' of state and congressional campaigns, of gun-for-hire campaign managers, of heightened interest in 'personalities' and lowered concern for policy."[10] Without parties, maintains Burns, politics would lack both organization and coherence. *See also* PARTY COMPETITION, 65; PARTY REALIGNMENT, 66; VOTING BEHAVIOR, 82.

Significance   Party reform boils down to the idea that parties should offer clear alternative courses of action to the voters and, if elected, function in a responsible, accountable manner by redeeming the pledges made in the party platform during the campaign. Most experts contend that parties must strive to become more democratic, responsible, and effective. In this regard, parties must become more issue-oriented and, to the extent possible, develop increased discipline and cohesion. For a two-party system to function, the opposition party must improve its mechanisms for defining, developing, and presenting policy alternatives. Moreover, reformists argue that parties must increase their resistance to interest group pressure, particularly where it is incompatible with their time-honored goals and objectives. Critics contend that the key to survival is accountability—that is, parties must become more accountable to the public and their members. They must say what they mean and mean what they say. They must only promise that which they can deliver and then, if granted power by an election, deliver it.

In recent years, political reformers have succeeded in democratizing U.S. parties. However, the public's faith in the party system has steadily declined. Moreover, elected officeholders and party officials continue to bemoan the deteriorating state of political parties in the United States. In the future, critics are likely to turn their attention to two major concerns: the presidential selection process and the national party's role in party building and campaign-related assistance. In the end, the fate of the party system rests in the hands of the parties themselves. It is highly unlikely that the public will rise up and demand stronger parties; leadership must come from party officials and elected officeholders. No single reform or group of reforms will cure what ails the party system. However, it is clear that meaningful, systemic reform could help to reverse the decline of the parties. Despite these problems, there is reason for optimism. State party organizations, for example, have experienced what many have described as a "resurgence." Although strengthening these organizations will not, by itself, produce programmatic or cohesive parties, it could contribute to increased party competitiveness or even reverse the trend toward personalized politics. Ultimately, the future of the party system depends upon the ability of the two major parties to develop distinct, if highly general, viewpoints on important policy issues and to ensure greater accountability on the part of elected officeholders and party officials.

Political Access   (68)

The ability to participate actively in decisions concerning the governing of society. Political access is basic to the right of a free people to govern themselves and to shape their society and its policies. It includes the right to vote, the right to participate in the decision-making process, and the right to influence the development of public policy. In a democracy, it is particularly important that all major segments of the population feel represented in the political process. Otherwise, confidence in the system will erode. Political access serves several objectives: (1) it stimulates civic participation; (2) it fosters social harmony; and (3) it is a vehicle to achieve power. Political access is an important stimulus to political participation. Obviously, if large groups of people cannot vote, they are not likely to become involved in politics. Political access also promotes positive group relations. Any society will invite violent protest if it refuses to share power with those who feel excluded. Finally, political access can advance or retard an individual's or group's position in society. Clearly, the disfranchisement of blacks and other ethnic groups has caused many negative effects. It has not only served to dilute their power and influence but has worked against their chances for economic mobility and success. This denial of political power is partly responsible for the high unemployment, poor housing, inadequate public services, unequal education, and numerous other problems that make life difficult for these groups. *See also* AUSTRALIAN BALLOT, 53; GERRYMANDERING, 58; VOTER QUALIFICATIONS, 81; VOTING BEHAVIOR, 82.

Significance   Political access involves two major dimensions: formal and informal. Formal access includes the right and/or privilege to vote, to run for office, to take part in political activities, to communicate directly with government officials, and to serve on juries. It also includes those rights specified in the Bill of Rights (e.g., freedom of speech, association, and assembly). Having the legal right to participate is, however, no guarantee of power or influence. One must also have *informal access*, that is, access to government officials, family and job connections, school and friendship ties, and certain capacities such as the ability to speak the majority language. It is necessary not only to have the right to participate but also the means to do so. This often requires time, effort, money, connections, and know-how. Group influence and/or power are also important. People identify with and act in groups, and government makes policies that affect groups. Groups wield enormous power. Individuals, acting alone, are limited when it comes to influencing government policy. Group action, therefore, is extremely important. But not all groups are equally effective. Skills, resources, numbers, and geographic location all affect voting outcomes. Groups that have these advantages are the most likely to be effective in politics.

Political Campaigning   (69)

The process by which candidates seek to win voter support in their bid for elective office. Political campaigning requires the development of a coherent strategy to reach the electorate—supporters, potential supporters, and the undecided—as well as to woo the opponent's backers. A political campaign has one main objective: to muster sufficient votes to win. Campaign resources figure prominently in the process; the cost of reaching voters via television or direct mail is extremely high. The amount of funds that candidates have at their disposal will largely determine the type of campaigns they will wage. However, money is not the sole determinant of a successful campaign; candidates can spend more than their opponents and still lose. Still, money is a vital resource, one for which there is no real substitute because most other campaign activities are dependent on money. *See also* EXTRALEGAL POLITICAL ORGANIZATIONS, 56; GENERAL ELECTION, 57; INCUMBENT'S ADVANTAGE, 60; PRIMARY ELECTION, 76.

Significance   Political campaigning begins with a candidate's decision to run. At that point, the candidate must appoint a campaign manager, establish a fund-raising apparatus, hire a campaign counsel, employ media and campaign consultants, enlist a staff, decide logistics; recruit a research and policy team, select a pollster, choose a press secretary, and organize various other activities. These are but the preliminaries. The challenger is faced with numerous obstacles in attempting to unseat an incumbent who enjoys such advantages as money, power, influence, staff, and media access. This poses a difficult but not impossible task. Incumbents seeking reelection must reactivate their support base, emphasizing their qualifications, experience, and record. Campaign techniques vary from race to race, depending on myriad factors. Still, candidates must try to reach the voters by whatever strategy they employ. To do so, they must emphasize such qualities as leadership, competence, strength, integrity, and compassion. The old-fashioned methods of door-to-door canvassing, meeting the voters, shaking hands, and kissing babies have been supplanted by newer, more sophisticated methods. Candidates now depend heavily on media advertising (television, radio, newspaper) to reach the voters. Public opinion polls are commissioned, and many candidates hire campaign management firms to coordinate the effort. Increasingly, campaigns have been conducted independently of the party organization, with candidates making the crucial decisions as opposed to party leaders. In addition, candidates seek most of their funding outside the party, soliciting personal, organizational, and corporate contributions to finance their campaigns. State and local campaigns can, depending on the race, run into hundreds of thousands or millions of dollars, and the parties, as well as the candidate, can only provide a fraction of the required funds. What money is raised must be spent wisely, in both the primary and general elections, with the ultimate objective of winning the necessary votes on election day. All is not lost, though, on an unsuccessful campaign—particularly if the candidate harbors future political aspirations. There is always the next election; a candidate may learn from past mistakes and prove more successful in the next round.

Political Machine   (70)

A tightly organized political entity, headed by a boss or small group of autocratic leaders, that controls the election process, administers the government, and formulates public policy. Political machines were, until recent times, common in many large cities and counties and, on occasion, in states. The term *political machine* refers to a state or local party that exerts inordinate influence on government institutions. It differs from a regular political party organization in that: (1) it is led by a single boss or a unified group; (2) it controls the nomination process; (3) its leaders possess working-class or lower-class backgrounds; (4) it maintains the loyalty of its supporters through tangible rewards (e.g., patronage jobs) and psychic rewards (e.g., ethnic acceptance); (5) its leaders do not usually hold elective office; and (6) it controls vast patronage (the power to make partisan appointments to office or to confer other favors). *See also* PARTY REFORM, 67; POLITICAL CAMPAIGNING, 69.

Significance   Political machines flourished for several reasons, most important of which was often the bosses' power to control the immigrant vote. In the late nineteenth century, many immigrants arrived in the United States without jobs, money, prospects, or knowlege of English. The political machines adopted these newcomers, serving as their protectors and benefactors. They provided food, shelter, leisure, and jobs in exchange for political support. The machine also provided numerous welfare benefits, financed, in part, by political graft, kickbacks on municipal contracts, and assessments on the salaries of government workers. The political machine was motivated by power, not philanthropy, and saw City Hall as the vehicle to power and profit. Political bosses not only dominated the election process at the local level, but were able to exercise enormous influence on state and national elections. Candidates were hand-picked, based on their loyalty to the political machine and in return for supporting boss rule and delivering the vote on election day. Central to the success of the machine was the vote, which, in many cases, was manufactured to serve the purposes of the bosses. Indeed, votes were manufactured for the deceased, cats and dogs, children, and fictitious people. To win elections, the machine played the game of ethnic politics, running slates of candidates who embodied the ethnic makeup of the city. They also exerted strong pressure on the business community, which profited under machine rule, and enlisted their active support. Political machines were made possible, in large measure, by the unholy alliance between the bosses and the business community. Their relationship was marked by collusion and corruption, which was evident in the awarding of charters for transit facilities, the procurement of city equipment and supplies, and contracts for municipal public works. In addition, the political machine flourished because of several systemic failings, among them, a weak-mayor system, a divided and unwieldy city council, a patronage bureaucracy, and an uneducated citizenry. In spite of its weaknesses, the political machine served several positive purposes, including the effective coordination of city government, the integration of newly arrived immigrants, the development of improved public services, and the creation of myriad jobs and opportunities. Famous political bosses included William Marcy Tweed (Tammany Hall, New York), Jim Pendergast (Kansas City, Missouri), Frank Hague (Jersey City and Hudson County, New Jersey), James Michael Curley (Boston, Massachusetts), and Richard J. Daley (Chicago, Illinois).

Political Party **(71)**
A group of individuals, many of whom share a general economic and social philosophy, who organize to contest elections, administer the government, and shape public policy. A political party differs from an interest group, in having as its primary goal winning control of and operating the government. Scholars differ as to the nature and design of political parties, but the most widely accepted definitions can be subsumed under three main categories: (1) those that define parties in terms of commonly shared principles, values, and stands; (2) those that define parties in terms of voters, candidates, and activists; and (3) those that view parties in terms of role, function, and activities. In his book *Party Government*, political scientist E. E. Schattschneider argues that "responsible parties" perform six major functions.[11] Ideally, they (1) develop and clarify policy alternatives for the electorate; (2) edify the voters about the issues and simplify the choices before them; (3) recruit candidates for elective office based on the parties' policy stands; (4) organize and direct their candidates' political campaigns; (5) ensure that their elected officials implement the parties' policy positions once elected; and (6) organize legislatures to guarantee party control of the policy-making apparatus. *See also* EXTRALEGAL POLITICAL ORGANIZATIONS, 56; PARTY ACTIVISTS, 64; PARTY COMPETITION, 65; PARTY REALIGNMENT, 66; PARTY REFORM, 67; POLITICAL SOCIALIZATION, 72.

Significance   Political parties are diverse and decentralized. For example, the Democratic parties of Alabama, California, Massachusetts, and Nevada possess little in common other than the same party label. Depending on the state and its political history, parties vary in terms of ideology, competition, and organization. Despite popular misconceptions, there is no one Democratic party or Republican party—rather, there are 50 state Democratic parties and 50 state Republican parties. Parties in the United States are, to a large extent, semi-independent units at the main levels of government (national, state, and local). Nationally, the party surfaces every four years, when it holds its convention and nominates its candidates for president and vice-president and drafts its platform. Although both major parties boast a national committee and national chairperson, the real power of the party system exists at the state level. Indeed, the most important party officials are probably the state and county chairpersons, who, in consultation with the state and county central committees, administer the affairs of the party. Political scientist Frank J.

Sorauf contends that political parties resemble "three-headed giants" in that they comprise: (1) the party organization (e.g., party committees, officials, workers); (2) the party in government (e.g., party candidates for public office and state, local, and national officeholders); and (3) the party in the electorate (e.g., voters with loyalty to and identification with the party).[12]Despite the controversy surrounding Schattschneider's "responsible party" model, most experts agree that, pragmatically speaking, parties recruit candidates, contest elections, promote party ideology, and guide elected officeholders. Their success in these areas, however, varies from year to year, state to state, and election to election.

Political Socialization   (72)

The process by which individuals acquire their beliefs and attitudes, often including their party identification, about politics and political life. Political socialization is a lifelong process, one that continues to evolve from childhood to old age. It takes place both formally (e.g., school) and informally (e.g., family). In many ways, informal learning is more important than formal, in-class learning about politics. It is acquired, absorbed, and acted upon in ways that determine one's political loyalties and partisan attachments. Political socialization occurs through several major agents, among them, family, school, peers, race, religion, economic status, political events, opinion leaders, the media, and sundry demographic factors. Of these agents, the family is clearly the most important, owing to its pervasive impact in terms of time and emotional content, especially in the formative years. Studies show that the majority of children are socialized to embrace their parents' political party. This does not mean, however, that familial influence is impenetrable. Indeed, parental rebellion and generational slippage often serve to undermine family values and beliefs. Although children often mirror their parents' views about parties, the presidency, and political issues, as they encounter other influences at school, through peer groups, and from the mass media, they are likely to deviate from their parents' opinions and loyalties. *See also* PARTY COMPETITION, 65; PARTY REALIGNMENT, 66; POLITICAL PARTY, 71; THIRD PARTY, 80.

Significance   Political socialization is a fluid concept; that is, it evolves over time. It is influenced by numerous agents, with mixed and often contradictory results. One such agent is the school. At the primary and secondary school levels, children are taught the importance of authority, respect, and loyalty, as well as discipline, conformity, and obedience. At the college level, however, students are exposed to a wide variety of stimuli, many of which encourage critical thinking. As a result, students are more likely to ask questions, weigh evidence, and challenge popular conceptions. Political socialization is critical to the future of political parties, as most children's party identification coincides with their parents'. In this regard, most parents inculcate partisan attachments through informal learning; few parents lecture their children about the respective virtues and evils of the Democratic and Republican parties. As a result of parental influence, children form strong partisan loyalties. Once they reach adolescence, however, their ideas begin to change. Indeed, party identification has been steadily declining among young people as well as older citizens. Clearly, the percentage of U.S. citizens who classify themselves as independents has steadily increased for all age groups. Most noticeable are the increasing numbers of adults who, over the last 30 years, have become less partisan. This trend has affected both major parties, which have lost support in roughly comparable degrees. These trends pose important challenges to the two major parties. If they are to survive, they must devise new ways to influence youth and to maintain their party loyalty throughout life.

Poll (73)

A device to gauge public opinion or forecast an election. Polling is a major subindustry in campaign management, second only to media advertising. Polls have evolved from the early newspaper straw-vote surveys of subscribers, to the current in-depth personal interview, based on scientifically controlled sampling techniques. For the political candidate, polls serve several important functions. The candidate is not only interested in who is ahead and who is behind, but also in various other answers that polls can yield. Louis Harris, one of the major U.S. pollsters, contends that polls can reveal (1) how various social groups view the race, in order to build a winning coalition; (2) how the voters perceive the candidate's personal qualities; and (3) what issues are important to the voters, and what they think about those issues.[13] Polling has become a highly technical craft—one that involves selecting a representative sample of people to question, designing questions that will generate the desired information in an unbiased manner, summarizing the results by computer, and interpreting the findings. *See also* INCUMBENT'S ADVANTAGE, 60; POLITICAL CAMPAIGNING, 69; VOTING BEHAVIOR, 82.

Significance   Polls are only as good as the techniques they employ. There are dozens of professional pollsters, among them, Gallup, Harris, Roper, Yankelovich, and Cadell. A valid poll can be extremely expensive. For example, a survey for a large-state gubernatorial candidate by an established firm will run between $15,000 and $20,000 (which often excludes follow-up samplings). Despite their limitations—and there are several—polls can be extremely useful to candidates. For example, in 1974, Democrat Ella Grasso aspired to become Connecticut's first woman governor. In her race, she was forced to address the issue of sex discrimination if she hoped to prove successful. Her pollster, Peter D. Hart, helped her to overcome this obstacle by identifying the sources of the bias, as well as by formulating an effective strategy to neutralize the disadvantage. Although polling has, in many ways, become a science, relying upon widely accepted empirical tools, many polls are fundamentally flawed, owing to improper construction, execution, and interpretation. For example, many surveys, including *straw polls* (in which people are questioned on street corners, at shopping centers, or by mail), are of dubious validity. Political scientists Harry Holloway and John George have compiled a list of important questions that one should answer when assessing a poll.[14] These include: (1) Who took the poll? (2) Who paid for the poll? (3) How many respondents were contacted? (4) How many were interviewed? (5) How many refused to be interviewed? (6) How were the respondents selected? (7) What was the exact wording of the questions and how many questions were asked? and (8) Does the interpretation in the article accompanying the poll follow from the data? Armed with the answers to these questions, political candidates and, for that matter, interested citizens, should be better able to interpret the validity of a poll.

Poll Tax   (74)
A levy to be paid as a qualification for voting. The poll tax was prevalent throughout the South, where it was used to prevent blacks and poor whites from voting. In 1964, with the ratification of the Twenty-Fourth Amendment, poll taxes were abolished in national elections. However, several states tried to retain them for state elections. In 1966, the United States Supreme Court declared these attempts to be an unconstitutional denial of equal protection of the law (*Harper v. Virginia State Board of Elections*, 383 U.S. 663). The poll tax originated in the late 1800s, when the political establishment in the South became increasingly alarmed about a possible alliance between blacks and poor whites. To prevent such an alliance, many

southern states enacted poll tax legislation. This tax, as conceived, would impose an economic hardship on these two groups and, in the process, preserve the white power base. The poll tax requirement was instituted in Tennessee in 1879, where it was written into the state constitution. However, it was not officially enforced until 1890. Virginia experimented with the poll tax between 1875 and 1882, but discontinued the practice for fear that it would encourage widespread corruption. Florida initiated the poll tax in 1889, followed by Mississippi in 1890, Arkansas in 1892, South Carolina in 1895, Louisiana in 1898, North Carolina in 1900, Alabama and Virginia in 1901, Texas in 1903, and Georgia in 1908. All told, the poll tax was made a qualification for voting in eleven states—all in the South—by 1920. The amount of the poll tax varied. It was $1 per year in three states, $1.50 in two, $1.75 in one, and $2 in two. In Arkansas, the $1 tax was doubled in case of failure to pay. Sometimes receipts were required not only for the current year but for previous years. Virginia required receipts for three years preceding the election. Alabama often required the would-be voter between the ages of 21 and 45 to show receipts for every year that had elapsed since he or she was 21. The only persons commonly exempted from poll taxes were veterans, the disabled, and the aged. In South Carolina, the requirement applied only to men. *See also* GRANDFATHER CLAUSE, 59; LITERACY TEST, 62; POLITICAL ACCESS, 68; WHITE PRIMARY, 83.

Significance   The poll tax was established to dilute the potential power of black voters and, to a lesser extent, that of poor white voters. For example, in Alabama, the poll tax was a direct response to the race situation. At the time, the black vote would have been negligible in the northern part of the state. However, in southern Alabama, it could have been the deciding factor in many elections. To prevent this from occurring, the white power structure enacted a poll tax. The results of the poll tax were striking. From 1896 to 1916, the combined vote of the eleven states with poll taxes shrank 18 percent, while the adult male population increased 50 percent. When North Carolina, for example, repealed its poll tax in 1920, the result was an immediate increase in the popular vote. Between 1916 and 1932, the vote actually increased 140 percent in that state.

Precinct (75)

The smallest unit in the election process and political party organization. The precinct, as a miniature voting district, facilitates electoral participation and party activity. Counties and cities are divided into precinct polling districts, each containing from 200 to 1,000 or more voters and a polling place. There are approximately 178,000 precincts, or voting districts, in the United States. Political parties elect or appoint a precinct captain or chairperson who serves as the party leader in the precinct. Party organization, at the precinct level, can take one of two forms. Most often, the precinct captain is elected by a precinct caucus or by voters in the party primary. This person becomes a member of the county committee, which elects the county chairperson. In the other form, the city or ward (city council electoral district) is the lowest level of organization. If precincts are organized, as in Chicago, it is accomplished by appointment from the ward level. *See also* COUNTY CHAIRPERSON, 54; COUNTY COMMITTEE, 55.

Significance   Precincts are the hub of party organization in the United States. Despite their importance, however, large numbers of precinct captain positions remain unfilled. In other cases, thousands of individuals are simply assigned the position on organizational charts, but fail to perform the requisite duties. Precinct captains are, in a real sense, the workhorses of the party system. They are charged with three major tasks: (1) voter canvass (maintain an accurate list of precinct residents, especially party supporters); (2) voter registration (ensure that party loyalists are registered); and (3) voter turnout (guarantee that the party's registered voters actually vote on election day). Precinct captains vary, both in terms of attitudes and behavior, depending on several factors. For example, in one study, political scientists M. Margaret Conway and Frank B. Feigert compared the beliefs of precinct captains in an affluent suburb of Washington, D.C., and a rural county in Illinois.[15] In the affluent suburb, precinct officials were motivated, in large part, by ideological incentives (e.g., issues and principles), while in the rural county, they were attracted by concrete political objectives (e.g., winning elections, exercising influence, developing contacts). Overall, the study suggests that while party activists may be drawn to the party because of issues, it is more likely that those who stay will do so because of the pragmatic rewards associated with winning elections. Finally, in recent years, attendance at precinct caucuses has, with few exceptions, been quite low (usually, under one percent of those eligible). However, in some states, such as Iowa, participation has increased noticeably. This can be attributed, in part, to heightened media attention to the caucus in presidential election years.

Primary Election   (76)
A preliminary contest in which voters of each party nominate candidates for office. Primary elections, as conceived by the progressives

early in this century, were devised to remove the candidate selection process from party bosses and allow party members to directly choose their own candidates. The *direct primary* (an election in which a party's rank-in-file select candidates who will run in the next general election) is the main device by which party candidates are nominated for state and local office. There are three types of direct primaries: open, closed, and blanket. Thirty-nine states use the closed primary, in which voting is restricted to party members. Eight states use an open primary, in which the voter can request both party ballots, but may only vote on one. Three states—Alaska, Louisiana, and Washington—use blanket (or "crossover") primaries, in which a voter may choose a candidate from one party for one office and a candidate from another party for another office. *See also* AT-LARGE ELECTION, 52; GENERAL ELECTION, 57; NONPARTISAN ELECTION, 63.

Significance   Primary elections are administered much like general elections (statewide contests, held following a primary election, to fill various state and national offices). Voters cast a secret ballot for the candidates of their choice in accordance with the state's primary laws. State-run primary elections are generally limited to Democratic and Republican party nominees, since only a party whose gubernatorial candidate received a minimum percentage of votes in the previous election may nominate a candidate through primaries. In most states, the candidate who wins a plurality (the largest number, as opposed to a majority) of the votes in a primary election becomes that party's nominee in the general election. Eleven states employ a run-off primary when a candidate fails to receive a majority of votes in the regular primary. Some states provide for nonpartisan primary elections by which the number of candidates for certain types of positions, especially judgeships, are reduced to two to ensure majority rule. Many primaries are noncompetitive, with incumbents routinely securing renomination. Primary elections can be distinguished from general elections in the types of voters who participate. Generally, primary voters are older, wealthier, better educated, more politically astute, and more ideologically committed than the general electorate. While primary elections are frequently praised for placing the candidate selection process in the hands of the voters, critics contend that this has served to erode the function of the political party, as candidates appeal directly to the public, and build their own support independent of party leaders. Finally, primary election campaigns are extremely costly, and if no candidate enjoys an overwhelming advantage, most of the primary campaign tactics must be repeated in the campaign for general election.

Racial Districting (77)

The legal use of racial quotas in drawing election boundaries where such plans do not disfranchise either the majority or minority population. Racial districting won United States Supreme Court approval in 1977, when, in *United Jewish Organizations of Williamsburgh, Inc. v. Carey* (430 U.S. 144), it upheld the constitutionality of a controversial New York State redistricting plan. In 1974 the New York Legislature, in an effort to increase the voting strength of blacks and Puerto Ricans, passed a redistricting plan that rearranged existing assembly and senate boundaries in the borough of Brooklyn. The area in question—Williamsburgh—included about 35,000 Hasidic Jews, a small, tightly knit orthodox religious sect. Until 1974, their neighborhood was part of the 57th Assembly District and the 17th Senate District; it was all included in one assembly district and one senate district. The state legislature, acting under what it saw as compliance with the federal Voting Rights Act, moved to assure blacks and Puerto Ricans in that area of the borough a "visible majority." Under their plan, the Hasidic minority wound up in different districts, with 15,000 residing in the 56th Assembly District and 20,000 in the 57th Assembly District. Similarly, the Hasidic community was broken up into two senate districts. The Hasidic community, led by United Jewish Organizations, Inc., took the plan to court, charging that the new boundaries would weaken Hasidic voting power and thus amounted to "reverse discrimination." In reviewing the complaint, the appeals court found no evidence of political discrimination. United Jewish Organizations, Inc., appealed that decision to the Supreme Court, which, on reviewing the evidence, affirmed the lower court ruling in a 7–1 decision. *See also* GERRYMAN-DERING, 58; POLITICAL ACCESS, 68.

Significance   Racial districting, as adjudicated by the Supreme Court, raises a number of important questions. The Court's decision was extremely complicated. Indeed, each of the seven justices in the majority wrote a separate opinion, with no two agreeing with the exact language of the others. In brief, the Supreme Court held that a state may, under certain circumstances, employ racial quotas to assure that blacks and other nonwhites secure majorities in certain legislative districts. The Court concluded that such districting may, in some cases, be constitutional when the state does so in an effort to comply with the 1965 Voting Rights Act. Supporters of the decision hailed it as a major civil rights advance, particularly in the area of affirmative action, with important implications for employment discrimination and education. Critics argued that the decision was extremely narrow, and that similar situations were likely to be infrequent in the future. Although the long-range implications of the decision are unclear, the Supreme Court did, in fact, approve the use of race-conscious remedies in order to implement the spirit and intent of the Voting Rights Act of 1965. Still, future redistricting plans cannot, regardless of this decision, violate the United States Constitution or the principle of "one-person, one vote," upon which all reapportionment schemes must be based.

State Central Committee (78)

The main governing body of a political party within a state. State central committees consist of party members representing congressional districts, state legislative districts, or counties. These committees vary markedly among the 50 states, in terms of function, organization, and composition, and range from a dozen to over a hundred members. In some states, such as California, membership is fixed by state law. Although state central committees, because of their role in the election process, are governed by statute their operations are, for the most part, dictated by their own bylaws, customs, and traditions. Generally, members of the state central committee are elected in party primaries, by lower party committees, or by party convention. Today, most state central committees provide equal membership for men and women. Indeed, there is a chairman and chairwoman at virtually every level of the party hierarchy. *See also* COUNTY CHAIRPERSON, 54; COUNTY COMMITTEE, 55; STATE PARTY CHAIRPERSONS, 79.

Significance State central committees have suffered a major loss of power in recent years. In theory, they were supposed to coordinate election campaigns for statewide office and serve as the principal fund-raising arm of the party. Today, that is no longer the case, as most candidates now run their own campaigns and raise their own funds. The power of the state central committee has been further eroded by the rising importance of party primaries and the advent of public financing of elections. These and other developments have altered the role of the state central committee, which largely attempts to implement party decisions arising out of the party's state convention. It is only peripherally involved in formulating campaign strategy and disseminating party funds (in many cases, it has few funds to distribute). Although it may advise the party's state chairpersons (the principal leaders of the party at the state level, chosen by the state central committee), it possesses scant influence with the party's state legislators and executive department officials. In most cases, the state central committee only plays a nominal role in state party affairs, often meeting only once or twice a year, and delegating formal authority to the party's state chairpersons. In spite of its waning power, the state central committee continues to exert influence at the state level, particularly in terms of the party's official organization.

State Party Chairpersons   (79)

Top elected or appointed officials who administer the party organization and promote the party's program. State party chairpersons, male and female, exercise sundry roles, depending on the state and its political dynamics. In some cases, state chairpersons view themselves as political emissaries of the governor; that is, they simply execute gubernatorial directives. In other cases, party chairpersons are independently powerful—they act on their own initiative, make decisions, and assume responsibility. Usually, chairpersons of the party out of power enjoy greater authority and independence than chairpersons of the party in power. The latter, in many instances, are politically eclipsed by the governor. In most states, the party chairpersons are selected by the state central committee (the main governing body of a political party within a state) or the state convention, usually with the approval of the governor (if he or she is of the same political party). *See also* COUNTY CHAIRPERSON, 54; COUNTY COMMITTEE, 55; STATE CENTRAL COMMITTEE, 78.

Significance   State party chairpersons play a pivotal role in determining the future of the party. The party chairpersons are, in many cases, the symbols of the party. As such, they must create a positive public image for the party. Where the party does not control the governorship, the party chairpersons may serve as spokespersons for the party. Apart from these tasks, the party chairpersons must raise funds, recruit candidates, influence patronage decisions, and strengthen the party organization, particularly, at the local level. Despite their success, state chairpersons enjoy a limited tenure in office—typically, less than three years. Some party chairpersons resign to seek elective office, while others simply tire of the position, finding it frustrating, expensive, time-consuming, and unrewarding. There are several types of chairpersons. Some are former politicians, who exercise influence through patronage, pork barrel, and political campaigning. Other chairpersons are younger, less wedded to the old-style politics, and place special emphasis on demographical studies, public opinion polls, campaign consultants, and sophisticated fundraising techniques. Prior to assuming their position, most state chairpersons held high-level positions in business, law, or public relations. Many state chairpersons serve with little or no remuneration, simply out of personal interest and desire. Overall, most state party chairpersons possess considerable influence and, at times, genuine power, depending on their personality, party strength, and relationship to the governor.

Third Party (80)

A new political party, often comprised of independents and disgruntled members of the two major parties, whose members hold a similar view on specific issues and who use their influence to affect the outcome of a state or national election. Third parties boast a long and checkered political legacy. The term *third party* is often used interchangeably with *minor party*. However, the two differ noticeably, both in purpose and impact. Generally, minor parties (e.g., Socialist Labor, American Independent, Prohibition, People's) are built around a single principle or idea, and attract little voter support because they are either localized or widely scattered. On the other hand, a third party (e.g., Bull Moose, Dixiecrat, Libertarian) typically develops out of a protest movement and succeeds in garnering sufficient votes to influence a specific election outcome. *See also* PARTY COMPETITION, 65; PARTY REALIGNMENT, 66; POLITICAL CAMPAIGNING, 69; POLITICAL PARTY, 71; POLITICAL SOCIALIZATION, 72; VOTING BEHAVIOR, 82.

Significance Third parties have fared rather poorly at the state level, although they enjoy ballot position in several states. Still, a Libertarian was elected to the Alaska legislature in 1978; their 1978 candidate for governor of California (running as an independent) received 378,000 votes; and the 1978 Right to Life candidate for governor won 120,000 votes in New York. Generally, third-party candidates fail to receive more votes than the difference between the two major party candidates, which is usually defined as the margin necessary for determining an election outcome. In many cases, third parties serve as propaganda organs. They are both isolated and irrelevant, disorganized and ineffectual. Frequently, they are creations of small handfuls of political malcontents, who exploit them for their own personal and political objectives. Certainly, this is not true of all third parties. In New York, for example, the Liberal and Conservative parties enjoy both influence and respectability and have, on occasion, either elected their own members to public office or affected the outcome of elections. Other third parties have experienced similar successes: the Farmer-Labor party in Minnesota, the Progressive party in Wisconsin, and the Socialist party in a number of cities. In these cases, success was made possible by effective leadership, a unique ethnic group base, and a popular local or state issue. A third-party movement achieves its greatest success when it replaces one of the two major parties, as, for example, when the Republican party replaced the Whig party in the 1850s by offering a clear antislavery platform. Third parties face sundry political obstacles, among them, the two-party tradition, discriminatory election laws, inexperienced leadership, inadequate finances, meager press attention, a negative public image, ideological intransigence, insufficient numbers, and poor organization. Still, third parties have performed an important political service in U.S. politics. They have sparked increased voter interest, advanced numerous reform proposals, forced the two major parties to address salient issues, provided alternative avenues for political expression, and encouraged the electorate to vote on the basis of issues and not simply by party affiliation.

Voter Qualifications   (81)
The legal criteria to register and vote in the election process. Voter qualifications have changed substantially since the promulgation of the United States Constitution. With the passage of the Fifteenth Amendment in 1870, the Constitution made it unlawful for any state to deny a person the right to vote because of race, color, or previous condition of servitude (having been a slave). This measure, one of the most important in the struggle for political access, gave blacks and other ethnic groups the right to vote. Suffrage was further broadened in 1920, when the Nineteenth Amendment extended the right to vote to women, who had previously been disfranchised in national, state, and local elections. Together, these two amendments broadened the original definition of suffrage, as conceived by the framers of the Constitution, who limited this right to white, male property owners. *See also* POLITICAL ACCESS, 68; VOTING BEHAVIOR, 82.

Significance   Voter qualifications have reflected historical shifts in the attitudes of the U.S. electorate. Despite efforts to broaden the franchise, not everyone may vote. To do so, prospective voters must meet certain legal requirements. All states require that new voters be United States citizens, be at least 18 years of age (for all elections since the adoption of the Twenty-Sixth Amendment in 1971), and satisfy minimal residency requirements (the Voting Rights Act of 1970 provided a 30-day residency period). According to the Constitution, the states may not impose (as they once did) literacy tests, poll taxes, property qualifications, or lengthy residence requirements. They are, however, able to exclude various groups of individuals, including mental incompetents, prison inmates, election law violators, and transients. Although individuals may not be denied the right to vote on grounds of race or ethnicity, they may be disfranchised in other ways. For example, they forfeit their right to vote if their citizenship is revoked, if they fail to register when required, or if they are found guilty of certain crimes. Many people are disfranchised temporarily when they move, either within the state or from state to state, until they establish new residences. Groups may also be disfranchised through political corruption when their ballots are either counted or not counted depending on the intent of local election officials. Or they may lose the power of their votes through political subterfuge, such as gerrymandering.

Voting Behavior (82)
The ways in which people vote and participate in the political process. Voting behavior is a central concern of political scientists and the subject of myriad studies. Overall, less than half the U.S. electorate votes in state and local elections. Voting, like other forms of political participation, is closely linked to socioeconomic status (income, occupation, and education). Clearly, the higher the social and economic status of the prospective voter, the more likely he or she is to participate in the election process. This is because those who rank high on the socioeconomic ladder are more likely to be familiar with political issues, believe that election results will affect their personal lives, and view voting as an ingrained civic obligation. Generally, voter turnout is greater in state elections than in local elections. State elections, unlike local contests, are usually partisan, which tends to increase participation among those with lower socioeconomic backgrounds, who vote infrequently in local elections. *See also* POLITICAL SOCIALIZATION, 72; VOTER QUALIFICATIONS, 81.

Significance　　Voting behavior is influenced, in large part, by such important variables as family, friends, party affiliation, race, sex, income, region, nationality, occupation, education, personality, ideology, and the mass media. In addition, suffrage (voting) requirements also affect voter turnout. For example, all states (with the exception of North Dakota) require citizens to register before they can vote. Some states, such as Minnesota, Wisconsin, Maine, and Oregon, permit voters to register on election day. Although registration by mail is more convenient, research indicates that it does not necessarily increase voter turnout. Overall, registration laws play a salient role in determining the percentage of the population who vote. However, such proposals as assigning additional registrars, permitting individuals to vote in their own neighborhoods (as opposed to city or county offices), and allowing voters to remain on the election rolls even if they had failed to vote for the previous eight years have little or no effect on voting behavior. Generally, voter studies indicate that rates of turnout are lowest among southerners, blacks, poor people, the less educated, and rural dwellers, while they are highest among males, whites, those with higher incomes, white-collar professionals, and the better educated. In addition, voting behavior is influenced by the type of election (whether it is national, state, or local), the composition of the electorate, the degree of party competition, the intensity of issues, the styles and personalities of candidates, and the level of media coverage. Sadly, the low rate of participation among the poor and uneducated is an interesting paradox, in that these groups are most in need of governmental assistance and intervention. According to political scientist John J. Harrigan, this is best explained by four main factors: (1) individual psychological and skill barriers; (2) political obstacles; (3) the lack of organizations to mobilize them; and (4) indifference of the governing institutions to their demands.[16]

White Primary   (83)
A discriminatory device used to exclude blacks from voting in primary elections on the ground that party primaries are private affairs. The white primary was, until its abolition in 1944 (*Smith v. Allwright*, 321 U.S. 649), a powerful legal barrier to black participation in the election process. Although the Fifteenth Amendment forbids states from denying the right to vote on the basis of race, several states argued that party primaries did not come under the protection of this amendment, that the Democratic primaries in the South were "private" affairs and that the states could legally forbid black participation. The white primary was fairly widespread following Reconstruction, during which time the South was largely a one-party (Democratic) region. Thus, if blacks could be prevented from voting in Democratic primaries, they could be effectively disfranchised by law. *See also* GRANDFATHER CLAUSE, 59; LITERACY TEST, 62; POLITICAL ACCESS, 68; POLL TAX, 74; PRIMARY ELECTION, 76.

Significance   The white primary remained intact until the mid-1940s. In 1940, for example, only 250,000 blacks had been registered in the entire South; after the *Smith v. Allwright* decision, however, the number had doubled. By 1960, it had increased to 1.4 million. In *Smith v. Allwright*, the Supreme Court held that since primaries were an integral part of the candidate selection process, by certifying nominees chosen in white primaries for the general election ballot, the states had violated the Fifteenth Amendment. In essence, the Court rejected the states' argument that the Democratic party was a private organization and thus immune from the Fourteenth and Fifteenth Amendments. However, the deep South was not the only region that sought to disfranchise black voters. In 1923, for example, the Texas legislature passed a law that prevented black participation in Democratic primary elections. However, in 1927 the Supreme Court held that the statute violated the equal protection clause of the Fourteenth Amendment (*Nixon v. Herndon*, 273 U.S. 536). Following the Court's ruling, the Texas legislature repealed the law and enacted another measure that allowed the executive committee of each party to determine the qualifications for party membership. Again, the Supreme Court ruled that this provision violated the equal protection clause (*Nixon v. Condon*, 286 U.S. 73: 1932). Later, the Democratic state convention voted to limit the primary to white voters, insisting that the party was a private association that organized its own primaries. This time the Supreme Court ruled that the Democratic party could exclude black citizens without violating the equal-protection clause (*Grovey v. Townsend*, 295 U.S. 45: 1935). However, the Supreme Court reversed itself in *Smith v. Allwright* and later invalidated the "preprimary," organized by a Texas association and comprised of all eligible white voters in a county (*Terry v. Adams*, 345 U.S. 461: 1953). Shortly thereafter, a United States circuit court declared unconstitutional South Carolina's attempt to maintain the white primary by repealing all statutory references to primaries.

4. The Legislative Branch

Appropriation   **(84)**
The allocation of funds for agencies and programs authorized by the legislature. No funds may be appropriated before authorization, but the actual money granted may be less than that authorized. The state legislatures exercise control over the purse strings, a power derived from each state's constitution. Their impact on government programs is threefold: they allot the amount to be appropriated; they control its use; and they influence a program's progress with the threat of funding cutbacks. An appropriation committee specifies how money is to be used, and is concerned only with spending bills. Appropriation bills originate in the lower house of state and federal legislatures. New programs are first authorized, then financed. An appropriation may be either lump sum or segregated, the former allowing administrative personnel greater discretion in expenditures. *See also* AUTHORIZATION, 85; VETO, 140.

Significance   Appropriation is a major control exercised by the legislature over the executive branch of government. An appropriation bill can make or break an agency or program by providing or withdrawing money. This power enables an appropriation committee to shape the objectives of agencies dependent on its support. To prevent an agency or program from exhausting its budget before the fiscal year ends, money is provided quarterly, and governors or state comptrollers are advised accordingly. In the United States, no expenditure of public funds can be made without the authorization of the state or federal legislature. In each state the legislature controls the executive branch's spending, considering its own goals and objectives as well as of the executive branch. Most states give governors control over the appropriation laws through the *item veto* (the power of governors to veto parts of an appropriation bill).

Authorization (85)

A legislative action that permits the executive branch to undertake a specific program and determine the appropriate level of funding. An authorization is usually enacted before the appropriation bill covering the program; it is the first step in a two-part budgeting process. The authorization committees review measures to fund government agencies and programs, as well as to limit their cost. The United States Congress, the state legislatures, and the local governments all require authorization prior to the appropriation of funds. Typically, an agency will request more money than it expects to be allocated. As there are no independent authorization committees, standing committees are always designated as authorization committees. The legislative procedure that precedes funding is a multistep process. It begins in the legislative committees, which consider the proposed authorization and recommend appropriations. The bill produced is authorized, and then funds are appropriated. *See also* APPROPRIATION, 84.

Significance   Authorization may be annual, biennial, multiyear, or permanent. To be funded, a government agency must receive legislative authorization. Authorization bills establish certain rules and amounts for spending. This permits the legislature to monitor more carefully the agencies' performance. Without such a system it would be virtually impossible to assess their effectiveness when reviewing requests for a renewal of funds. Lengthy assessments sometimes force the government to begin its new fiscal year without funding for many programs. The legislatures circumvent this problem by adopting *continuing resolutions* which allow agencies to spend funds, as in the previous fiscal year, for a specified period. Complications can arise with biennial or multiyear authorizations if the legislature is required to approve funds for more than a year without understanding the issue. Therefore state legislatures, like the United States Congress, require governmental agencies to justify their requests and show tangible proof that their goals have been met. Any agency that fails to provide such evidence may find the legislature unwilling to approve additional appropriations.

Bicameralism (86)

Having a two-house legislature. Bicameralism was drafted into the state constitutions following the example of the United States Constitution. Nebraska replaced its bicameral with a unicameral (one-house) legislature in 1934. Bicameralism developed out of the Connecticut Compromise, which emerged from the Constitutional Convention of 1787. This established a balanced legislature for the United States, with a House of Representatives organized on the basis of population and a Senate based on equality of states. But in the states, both houses are based on population. In a bicameral legislature, a bill must pass in identical language in both houses before it becomes law. The two houses perform similar functions and have adopted similar procedures in many cases. However, there are differences between the two bodies. One is that revenue bills must originate in the lower house, which most states call the house of representatives; another provides that the upper chamber, which each state calls the senate, must approve certain apportionments made by the state's governor. *See also* LOWER HOUSE, 99; UNICAMERALISM, 113; UPPER HOUSE, 114.

Significance   Bicameralism provides representation for varying interests. It is also consistent with the principle of checks and balances. Bicameralism serves many purposes: it gives representation to the constituent elements, such as states and counties; assures rural and urban areas fair representation; permits participation of economic and cultural groups; and diffuses power within the legislature. Supporters of bicameralism further contend that it is well suited to a federal system, respecting state equality as well as population. The U.S. Supreme Court, in a landmark decision, *Reynolds v. Sims* (377 U.S. 533: 1964), maintained that under the equal protection clause of the Fourteenth Amendment both houses of a bicameral state legislature must be apportioned on the basis of population. Supporters also point out that the debate and deliberation in two houses result in better legislation. Critics of bicameralism cite an overlapping of the lawmaking process and duplication of responsibility that wastes the time and efforts of legislators. Bicameralism, with more legislators, costs more. Opponents also maintain that if Nebraska can function effectively with a unicameral legislature others can too.

Bill   (87)

The draft of a proposed law at the time of its introduction into a legislative chamber. A bill must go through several stages including introduction, committee consideration, debate, and vote. Once a bill is passed by both houses, in identical language, and approved by the chief executive (or enacted over his veto), it becomes law. Among the states, only the governor of North Carolina does not have veto power. Only members of the state legislature can introduce a bill. A bill is introduced, numbered, referred to the appropriate committee with the sponsor's name, and copies are distributed for study. Legislators may introduce as many bills as they wish, and thousands are introduced, but only a small percentage become law. Many bills are killed by committee. In most state legislatures the mortality rate of bills is about 70 percent. During a recent session of the New York legislature 15,021 out of 15,916 bills died (94 percent). *See also* COMMITTEE SYSTEM, 91; LAWMAKING PROCESS, 94.

Significance   Bills must be drafted with precision; otherwise, if enacted, the courts may refuse to enforce them. Only some bills receive serious consideration, which depends on (1) the nature of the bills, (2) the interest groups affected by it, (3) its sponsors, (4) the cost, (5) its impact, (6) the support that it enjoys with party leadership and executive officials, (7) public interest and backing, (8) its merits, (9) the extent to which it differs from existing policies in the country, and (10) the attitudes of influential individuals. Bills do not pass on merit alone. Success lies in a solid base of support for the bill among legislators, party leadership in and out of the legislature, the president, governors, governmental agencies, and the general public. Bills that pass promise the greatest dividends for the greatest number. Many lawmakers introduce bills knowing that they will be killed by committee; yet they do so to satisfy their constituents.

Committee Chairperson (88)

The head of a legislative committee. A committee chairperson gives leadership that may result in almost decisive control over bills in committee. In most state legislatures, the chairpersons in the lower houses are appointed by the speaker; in the upper houses the presiding officer also make the selection, although in some states a committee on committees (a body of persons empowered to create other committees) selects the chairpersons. Committee chairpersons at one time had virtually absolute power, but changes have since been introduced that limit their role. Their authority is evident in establishing priorities and managing the affairs of the committee, and they are still the key figures in the legislative process. The formal powers of the chairpersons and the support they receive from committee members often determine the fate of a legislative proposal. *See also* COMMITTEE SYSTEM, 91; LAWMAKING PROCESS, 94.

Significance   A committee chairperson plays a crucial role in the consideration of bills assigned to a committee. Normally the chairperson controls if and when the committee meets, allocates time for hearing, decides which bills the committee will consider, and whether or not a public hearing will be held. The chairperson typically is best informed on the bills brought before the committee. In recent years chairpersons have been more accountable to their committee members, but along with the speaker of the lower house, the president of the senate, and the majority leaders in both houses, chairpersons still exercise great influence in lawmaking. An effective chairperson can often expedite bills and overwhelm opposition. The effectiveness of a chairperson depends on the ability to achieve consensus among legislators and to be accountable to colleagues, and success is measured by the harmony of committee members and the overall performance and effectiveness of the committee.

Committee of the Whole   (89)
The membership of a deliberative body meeting informally to transact business. The committee of the whole procedure is utilized by a state legislature to consider bills and other legislative matters less formally than is possible during regular proceedings. The committee chairperson mentioned in the bill is the bill's spokesperson, while the ranking minority member mentioned in the bill manages the opposition. In some states, when considering bills upon second reading (especially revenue and appropriation bills), it is customary for the lower house to resolve itself into a committee of the whole. Like the United States House of Representatives, the lower houses of state legislatures are thus able to bypass the formal rules of debate. *See also* COMMITTEE SYSTEM, 91.

Significance   The committee of the whole is a procedure used to expedite legislation. It is advantageous in that a quorum is easily formed and it dispenses with such formalities as roll calls. The committee considers only legislation that deals directly with appropriations, taxation, or any important measures. In practice, the small quorum required to do business is most beneficial. Almost all important bills are considered by the committee of the whole, with those not on calendar considered on motion. Because of the small quorum, many laws are made by a minority of representatives, and critics contend that it is deceitful to bypass the normal procedures and that this furthers vested interests. The only notable difference between the regular session of a legislature and the committee of the whole is that the regular presiding officer (speaker) is replaced by a temporary chairperson of the committee. The committee of the whole procedure in the state legislatures does not play as vital a role in lawmaking as it does in the House of Representatives of the United States Congress.

Committee Staff   (90)

Professional aides who provide research and technical assistance to legislative committees. Committee staff are experts in legislative and other matters and perform background work during legislative sessions. Their functions include drafting bills and amendments, organizing hearings, conducting investigations, working on conference committees, lobby liaison, preparing reports, liaison with the executive branch, preparation of floor action, and press relations. Most staffers are appointed by the chairperson as a perquisite of office (privileges and benefits received by members of legislatures). Their tenure depends on political patronage, but some make a career of it. Because senators serve on more committees, they have larger staff than the members of the lower house. Staffers are relatively young and overwhelmingly male. *See also* COMMITTEE CHAIRPERSON, 88; COMMITTEE SYSTEM, 91.

Significance   Committee staff have a self-determined sphere of influence. They initiate legislative ideas, conduct necessary research and investigation on proposed bills, and brief the legislators on their findings. Many staffers are more knowledgeable than the legislators, and their expert opinion is valuable in the lawmaking process. They provide legal, investigative, public relations, and technical services for the committee. Lawmakers often do not have the time to read and scrutinize bills; thus there is an increasing need for staff support. This has given rise to a vast number of unelected bureaucrats in the legislative process. There is no exact definition of how committee staffs are to function; their roles, responsibilities, and influence vary, but they must perform their duties so the committee's work can flow evenly. Sometimes committee staff provide access to interest groups and individuals. Because staff members are mostly anonymous and neutral, they remain unrecognized, but they are an essential part of the legislative machinery.

Committee System   (91)

Organization of legislative groups that study proposed legislation and oversee executive agencies and their administration of policy. The committee system is an integral part of the legislative process both in the United States Congress and in state legislatures. Committees study and consider legislation. The four principal types of committees are (1) standing or permanent committees, (2) select or special committees, (3) joint committees, and (4) conference committees (always joint committees). Standing committees are permanent bodies with specified jurisdiction over stated policy areas. Select committees are temporary (ad hoc) panels for the study of important issues that do not fall within the jurisdiction of the standing committees. Joint committees are composed of members of both houses to study specific problems; they preclude the necessity of bills being considered separately by both houses. Conference committees are created to reconcile differences when a bill passes in different forms in the two houses. There are also many subcommittees that function as specialized subgroups. Through hearings, a committee obtains information and solicits government and public opinion on proposed legislation. *See also* COMMITTEE CHAIRPERSON, 88; COMMITTEE STAFF, 90.

Significance   The committee system is an indispensable part of the legislative process. No legislature can hope to act effectively as a whole throughout the legislative process because of its size. It must be divided into various committees along functional lines so as to provide for specialization. The committee system has resulted in legislatures within legislatures, each quasi-independent with mostly self-determined rules and procedures. In the committees the legislature learns the breadth and depth of various interests. Facts, interests, sentiments, and politics are blended at the committee level. Committee hearings allow expression of these phenomena and provide feedback. Additionally, hearings can advance a legislator's political career by demonstrating his or her skill as a lawmaker. The committees also test public opinion and pave the way for future legislation.

Conference Committee (92)

A special joint committee of the two houses of a legislature established to iron out differences between versions of bills. The conference committee is an ad hoc joint body composed of members from both houses. State constitutions require chief executives to receive legislation in the exact same language from both houses before signing it. The committee consists of conferees (managers) appointed by the speaker of the house and the president of the senate, usually drawn from the standing committees in each house that considered the bill originally. In the conference committee process there is a request for a conference, a selection of conferees, conference committee bargaining, a report, and consideration by both houses. The version of the bill that emerges from the conference committee is usually passed by the two houses, without further amendments. The recommendation must be fully accepted or rejected, and a majority vote of the managers in both houses, voting separately, is required for agreement. If the compromise version is then rejected by either chamber, the bill will likely be renegotiated by the conference committee. *See also* COMMITTEE SYSTEM, 91.

Significance   Conference committees substantially rewrite bills after they receive them and wield great power in determining the fate of legislation. Conference committee meetings are often held in secret. Supporters of secret conferences maintain that in open meetings members play to the galleries and their constituents, but opponents emphasize that constituency pressure is required in order to reach compromise. Amendments may be added to bills simply as a bargaining ploy. Sometimes legislators evade the conference process in order to expedite passage of a bill. In a bicameral legislature log rolling and compromise prevail to achieve common goals, especially toward the end of a session when the legislation's fate becomes critical.

Joint Committee   (93)
A special legislative panel composed of members of both houses. A joint committee is created by statute or legislation, and the number of members appointed is usually divided equally between the two chambers. The procedure is the same on the federal and state levels. The joint committee is established to inform the legislature on matters of special concern to both houses. It studies and investigates legislation, as well as monitors and supervises administrative agencies. Several subtypes of joint committee exist, such as standing, select, and conference. The chairmanship and vice-chairmanship rotate between the two houses. When a senator is a chairperson, a representative is vice-chairperson. *See also* COMMITTEE SYSTEM, 91; CONFERENCE COMMITTEE, 92.

Significance   Joint committees usually depend on the standing committees to frame legislative proposals. As special joint conference committees, with members from both houses, they make it possible to iron out differences and compromise on bills. The passage of important legislation is expedited through shared responsibility. It has been suggested that all standing committees be joint committees, so that overlapping of existing committees could be eliminated. This would save time, money, and other resources. Unlike the United States Congress, in some state legislatures nearly all standing committees are joint committees. Ideally, joint committees provide a means of coordination in the lawmaking process, but sometimes members of the lower house are intimidated by the senators, who enjoy greater prestige. This creates roadblocks to effective cooperation in joint committees. Interparty, interhouse, and personality clashes may also hinder the joint committee process. But supporters of joint committees maintain that they eliminate the need for duplicate testimony before separate committees. The passage of legislation can be expedited through shared resources and manpower, and legislative costs can be reduced.

Lawmaking Process (94)

The manner in which a legislative body passes legislation. The lawmaking process begins with the introduction of a bill. Then it goes through a committee stage, the calendar, the floor procedure, voting, and executive approval. A bill may originate in the legislature, introduced by a member of either house. However, much of the legislation originates in the executive branch. When the presiding officer in either house receives a bill, he or she numbers and assigns it to an appropriate committee. A bill considered important by a committee is assigned for hearing by a subcommittee, although the full committee may immediately consider the bill if it so chooses. The committee then requests input from interested parties. This may include testimony of government officials, experts, scholars, and other interested groups. When a bill is reported out of committee, it is placed on a calendar. Floor debate may then begin at the convenience of the legislature. Approval requires a simple majority vote of the members present. A bill must pass in identical language in both houses before it is sent to the chief executive. He may sign or veto it. If vetoed, the bill is sent back to the legislature, which may override the veto by a two-thirds vote in each house. *See also* BILL, 87; COMMITTEE SYSTEM, 91.

Significance The lawmaking process involves stages that all bills must go through. Each stage presents an obstacle that may kill the bill. Often, in order to satisfy their constituencies, members may introduce bills that are either trivial to other members or the state and the nation. Normally, these bills die in committee. The lawmaking process has grown in size and complexity, and it is decentralized in that each bill must pass in both houses. No bill can become law without a cumulative affirmative action at every stage of the process; a negative action at any level in either house can kill a bill. The process is not perfect, and usually slow to respond, and often majority rule is difficult to obtain because of the power of minority opponents to kill or modify a bill.

Legislative Branch   (95)
The lawmaking body of government, which enacts the majority of bills. The legislative branch in each state can make laws except in areas specially denied by the federal or state constitutions. Most states hold biennial sessions, but New York and five others have annual sessions. About three-fourths of the state legislatures convene in regular session in January of the odd year. Special sessions of the legislature may be convened by the governor in almost every state; in some states the legislators themselves can demand a special session. All state legislatures follow the federal model of a bicameral (two-house) system except Nebraska, which has a unicameral (one-house) legislature. The membership in the upper house varies from 17 in Delaware and Nevada to 67 in Minnesota. The lower houses have more members, from 35 in Delaware to 400 in New Hampshire. About two-thirds of the upper houses have four-year terms; the remaining have two years. Most lower houses have two-year terms; the four exceptions have four-year terms. State legislatures are primarily concerned with their powers to police and regulate the health, safety, common convenience, and general welfare of the people. In addition to lawmaking, the state legislatures propose amendments to state constitutions, define the state's responsibilities, investigate public issues, confirm executive appointments, oversee judicial functions, and impeach and try civil officers of the other branches of government. *See also* LAWMAKING PROCESS, 94; LEGISLATIVE POWERS, 97.

Significance   The legislative branch speaks for the people; it guides and protects cities, alters the social structure, and controls the chief executive. The rationale of bicameralism supports the principle of checks and balances between the two houses of the legislatures. The history of state legislatures emphasizes their leadership in the struggle against British colonialism. What the legislatures were immediately before and after the revolution in 1776 and what they are today seem poles apart. From a dominant position the state legislatures succumbed to the need for strong executives. The governor's position was strengthened, and new executive offices were created to augment the power of the state administration.

Legislative Drafting Service (96)

Assistance for legislators in the preparation of bills. Legislative drafting requires specialized skills and qualifications. It offers legislators pertinent, reliable, and concise information on any subject. Its personnel can receive the desired material quickly from reports, articles, books, newspapers, pamphlets, and interviews. Among the oldest forms of legislative assistance are a central secretarial pool and a bill-drafting service. In 1901, Charles McCarthy opened a legislative information service for the Wisconsin legislature. They liked it so much that they made provision for it by law. It gave birth to the Legislative Bureau or Legislative Drafting Service in many states. At the national level, the Library of Congress maintains a reference library for congresspersons and a Congressional Research Service to aid them. Today, most legislatures provide for a legislative drafting service. Data gathering is a year-round job that reaches its height during legislative sessions. As most of the questions are common in many state legislatures, the Council of Governments acts as the clearing agent for all state legislative drafting services. This avoids duplication and overlapping of resources among them. The staff also coordinates and integrates the activities of legislative committees, legislators, the two houses, the executive branch, and the citizenry. *See also* LAWMAKING PROCESS, 94.

Significance The legislative drafting service has become an essential part of lawmaking. For much of the states' history, legislators have been sadly deficient in the art of drafting bills. The service saves legislators time in which to accommodate constituents and act on legislation. A law should be carried out as intended. Despite alterations the statute should still convey the original thrust and meaning of its authors. Laws must be written in precise, legal language else the courts may refuse to provide enforcement action. Lacking certain techniques, many legislators rely upon lawyers and lobbyists to draft desired statutes. It is one thing to be politically astute and something else to form legislation. The professional staff not only draft bills but also suggest policy ideas and alternate solutions to problems. Ultimately, much of what becomes law may originate with staff members.

Legislative Powers (97)

The lawmaking authorities of a legislature or a chief executive. Legislative powers usually refer to the lawmaking authority of the state or federal legislatures. The basic function of a legislature is to enact laws. It also has many nonlegislative functions. All the powers of the federal government are delegated or implied by the United States Constitution. All other powers are reserved to the states, subject to prohibition by the federal constitution. The main powers of a state legislature are those to: (1) deal with taxing and spending, that is, the collection of revenue and the appropriation of funds; (2) establish the machinery of state government; (3) enact state laws to regulate those of local governing bodies in cities, counties, and municipalities; (4) pass civil laws to regulate relations between and among citizens; and (5) protect the public through law enforcement. *See also* STATE LEGISLATURE, 111.

Significance   Perhaps the most important set of legislative powers are those that deal with taxation and other actions that generate revenue for the state, and those that involve how these revenues will be spent. By approving a budget the legislature keeps government functioning. Most state legislatures are constrained by their state constitutions and by political differences. A common constitutional restriction is to forbid the passage of special laws for certain purposes, especially those that relate to the powers of local government. Governors and courts set policies as well as the legislatures. In some states, such as South Carolina, the legislatures are the predominant policy makers, but in New York the governor controls much of the policy making. Although the scope of the power of a state legislature to pass laws is theoretically broader than that of the United States Congress, the states like to defer to the federal government in such crises as inflation and pollution control, unemployment, and welfare benefits. While the powers of the federal government are detailed, those of the states are general in scope; the legislatures have residual or inherent powers. Often legislatures fail to exercise their powers. Many critics consider state legislatures as drawbacks. According to the Citizens Conference on State Legislatures, "Legislatures are the main 'drag' upon the capacity of states to function as full partners in the federal system."[1] The great debate over legislative authority goes on, sometimes heatedly.

Legislator Characteristics (98)

The dominant traits that influence the election and decision making of lawmakers. Legislator characteristics include education, age, social background, religion, race, sex, and political acumen. A legislator is the index of his or her constituency and usually hails from a high stratum of society. In general, the 7,500 state legislators enjoy higher social, economic, educational, and professional status than those they serve. The 435 United States representatives and 100 senators enjoy even higher social status. A legislative candidate must meet certain requirements beyond the formal demands in order to be elected. These may include having no well-organized opposition on social, political, or racial grounds. Characteristics of legislators may vary slightly from session to session, but the overall composition of the legislature remains steady. Most legislators are college graduates, and many have law degrees. *See also* STATE LEGISLATURE, 111.

Significance   Legislator characteristics are a critical factor in nominating a candidate. Personal popularity, fortune, and family background are quite relevant. Many candidates contribute part of their personal wealth to the campaign to augment party resources. Media-dominated politics demands an attractive appearance, as success depends somewhat on a candidate's television image. Incumbency also strengthens a person's candidacy. In the legislatures, minorities are more fully represented than women, who make up a greater percentage of the population. Blacks are relatively well represented in the North, although they have been underrepresented in the South and in the United States Congress. An overwhelming number of white, male, Anglo-Saxon, Protestant Americans dominates the country's legislatures. Obviously, such a situation favors the interests of a dominant group to the disadvantage of ethnic minorities such as blacks and Hispanics. This minority underrepresentation points up the stratified composition of legislatures, which critics decry as a failing in a representative government.

Lower House   (99)

The house of representatives in a bicameral (two-house) legislature. The lower house is called the house of representatives in most state legislatures and at the national level. State lower house membership averages about 113, while the upper house has an average membership of 40. New Hampshire has the largest lower house (400 members), which is almost as great as the United States House of Representatives (435 members). The median biennial pay of the members of a state lower house is more than $20,000. The leadership in the house includes the speaker, the floor leaders, the whips of the two major parties, the Rules Committee, and the committee chairpersons.

State lower house terms are two years, as is the case with the United States House of Representatives, with no limit on the number of terms members may serve. The terms of members expire simultaneously so that the lower house may originate anew every two years. Members of the lower house are often called representatives, sometimes assemblypersons. The 49 state lower houses have 5,500 members. The age requirement for members is 21 in most states, although some states have reduced the minimum age to 18. They must be United States citizens and must have resided in their state and county for a certain length of time for eligibility. The lower houses have two unique functions: (1) they must originate money bills, and (2) they possess the power of impeachment. *See also* STATE LEGISLATURE, 111; UPPER HOUSE, 114.

Significance   Lower houses have little prestige in the states. The pay is low because legislative expertise is frequently poor. The low age limit for members helps open legislative doors to young people, but their understanding of legislative affairs is sometimes embarrassing. Most legislatures meet so infrequently that legislators remain inexperienced in their jobs. Time needed to campaign for reelection and secure financial backing is time lost from carrying out legislative duties, but this has advantages. By maintaining close contact with the voters, a member increases the chances of reelection. Frequent contact with the electorate is an invaluable political asset. Many Americans tend to regard the lower house of representatives as their most direct contact with government.

Majority Leader   **(100)**
The floor leader of the majority party in the senate or the lower house. The majority leader, second in command to the speaker in the house and the president of the senate, controls the legislative schedule and programs, leading the majority party in floor debate. The majority leader forms strategy with the speaker of the house and the president of the senate, and serves as party spokesman, nominating members of party committees and appointing ad hoc groups. The majority leader implements the decisions of the party and is aided by party whips. *See also* MINORITY LEADER, 101; PRESIDENT OF THE SENATE, 102; SPEAKER, 109; WHIPS, 115.

Significance   The majority leader is the undisputed leader of the majority party in the house or senate. A skillful leader can exercise considerable influence on legislative matters. Members of the majority party in each house elect the majority leader. Election depends on (1) popularity, (2) ability to forge a winning majority, (3) skills at presenting the party's position, (4) ability to unite dissenters, and (5) courage to oppose the other party when necessary. The majority leader in each chamber guides legislation to the floor, usually consulting the party's policy committee before setting the schedule for debate. In the house, the majority leader is groomed for the speakership, since the two leaders work closely on the floor. A majority leader, who is usually an able organizer, can exercise influence on legislation. The majority leader, with the aid of colleagues, helps establish a legislative schedule by securing unanimous consent agreements beforehand. The cooperation of the majority leaders in the two houses is of crucial importance to the governor for the passage of his or her legislative programs. Because they hold critical positions in the legislature, governors respect their influence and court their support.

Minority Leader (101)

The floor leader of the minority party in either house of a legislature. The minority leader is the most important legislator of that party, mobilizing minority opposition to the majority party's legislative programs and marshaling support for minority positions. Duties are similar to those of the majority leaders, except that he or she cannot schedule legislation. The minority leader is that party's spokesperson and promotes party unity. He or she is assisted by a party whip and other assistants, consulting with ranking minority members on committees and encouraging them to follow party positions. The minority leader is not usually involved in committee hearings but is prepared to deal with bills as they come to the floor. *See also* MAJORITY LEADER, 100; STATE LEGISLATURE, 111.

Significance   The minority leader is the titular head of that party on the floor of the legislature but is disadvantaged in terms of office space and staff. He or she lacks the votes necessary to translate minority party programs into law. The minority leader, like the leader of the opposition in a parliamentary system, is top critic of proposals of the majority, defending the rights of those opposed to the legislation. The minority leader preserves his or her party's rights against a majority that at time ignores the established rules and procedures. If the governor is of the same party, the minority leader may speak for him or her. If there is not enough support for the minority party's position in the legislature, the leader may offer alternatives to programs of the majority or cooperate with them. Like the majority leader, the minority leader is usually an experienced legislator and is instrumental in formulating the party's legislative strategy. If the party supports a bill, the minority leader's job is to garner enough votes to secure passage.

President of the Senate   (102)

The presiding officer of the upper house of the state legislature. The president of the senate in 27 states is the lieutenant governor. Where there is no lieutenant governor, the senate elects its presiding officer from among its members. If the president is absent, the senate chooses a *president pro tempore* or temporary president. The president of the senate or the stand-in appoints various assistants; some are legislators and some staff. The president of the senate has the power to recognize a member of that body for debate and the introduction of bills, to decide points of order, to appoint senators to conference and select committees, to enforce decorum, and to administer oaths of offices. The president of the senate's power does not equal that of the speaker of the house, who presides over that body. The senate withholds significant political power from its presiding officer. Like the vice-president, who presides over the United States Senate, the lieutenant governor does not participate in debates and can vote only to break a tie. See also PRESIDENT PRO TEMPORE, 103; SPEAKER, 109.

Significance   The president of the senate holds several of the formal powers of the Speaker of the House, but cannot directly influence legislation. However, many bills depend on his or her interpretation of the rules and procedures, and he or she can also abort bills by his choice of consideration. The senate president is considerably freer than the Speaker of the House and is less subject to rules and restrictions. Like the speaker, the president of the senate is an active leader in the legislature. Unlike the Speaker of the House, the senate president is not the chosen leader of the majority party in the senate or a member of that body. Still, the position of the presiding officer of the senate is regarded as a symbol of authority, toward which debate is directed.

President Pro Tempore   (103)

The temporary presiding officer of the senate during the absence of the president of the senate. In those states that have no lieutenant governor, the senate elects the presiding officer and the president pro tempore. The president pro tempore is chosen from the ranks of the majority party and is ordinarily the senior member of that party. The United States Senate also selects a president pro tempore. *Pro tempore* means "for the time being," to act in the absence of the presiding officer of the senate. The powers of the president pro tempore are (1) to recognize members who wish to speak; (2) to decide points of order; (3) to appoint senators to conference committees; (4) to enforce order; (5) to administer oaths; and (6) to appoint special committee members. The president pro tempore holds office as long as he or she serves in the Senate and his or her party maintains control over the senate. *See also* PRESIDENT OF THE SENATE, 102; SPEAKER, 109.

Significance   The president pro tempore has many of the formal powers of the speaker of the house, but is not as influential. As a partisan leader he or she uses the position to support the party's programs. The role is of considerable importance as it is awarded to the senior member of the party. Elected by the senate, the president pro tempore enjoys the confidence of that body, and is usually the chairperson of the Rules Committee. His or her primary power comes from the position as a top leader and from the power to appoint committees. Although not as politically powerful as the speaker of the house, the president pro tempore belongs to the inner circle of the party and influences what bills are passed. The legislative leadership often consults with the president pro tempore on policies and actions of the party. Like the speaker of the house, the president pro tempore is a partisan officer who may use his or her position to aid the program of the party.

Quorum   (104)
The minimum number of members of a legislative body who must be present to validly conduct official business. A quorum is usually a majority, just over half of the members of a legislative chamber. Thus, 51 members of a 100-member legislative body would constitute a quorum. The federal and state constitutions impose the same requirement for a quorum. It is often difficult to obtain a quorum. Rarely are more than a few dozen members in attendance at one time, and the leadership must often go to great lengths to summon the requisite number of members. Sometimes legislatures conduct business without a quorum until challenged. Legislators have numerous other responsibilities, such as committee meetings and visits to their constituencies, but their attendance is recorded and noted by their opponents in the next election. *See also* ROLL CALL VOTE, 105.

Significance   The quorum requirement is essential to the legislative process. It can be positive or negative by advancing or retarding progress. Quorum calls can be used to stall or obstruct a key vote that influences legislation. Most members dislike quorums, which interfere with business, meetings, speeches, appearances, and trips in order to be present on the floor. However, the public expects legislators to represent them in the lawmaking process for which they were elected. Although there are many nonlawmaking responsibilities, they are secondary to lawmaking in the public's view. Many deals are made off the floor of the legislatures, and some members prefer to exploit those areas for personal gain, shunning duties that are not self-serving. Normally, in the absence of a quorum, no serious business is conducted.

Roll Call Vote   (105)
The method of calling by name individual legislators to ascertain their vote. A roll call vote is separately recorded and is used to determine a quorum. It is also used to record votes on controversial legislation, for example, the vote to override a veto. Like the state legislatures, the United States Congress requires roll call votes on important measures or whenever one-fifth of the members of a chamber demand it. Roll call votes are cast in one of three ways: yea, nay, or present (if a member does not wish to vote). Every member present is expected to respond and be recorded. Most state legislatures stipulate a specific number of members to require a roll call vote on an issue. The statutory purpose is to put how members vote on public record. Electronic voting devices are used in most state legislatures as well as in the United States Congress. A scoreboard shows the result in such a way that a member can verify his or her vote before a photograph is taken for a permanent record. A roll call vote is also known as a *record vote*. *See also* QUORUM, 104.

Significance   A roll call vote is demanded on almost all major and controversial bills. This assures a member's accountability, as his or her vote is recorded and publicized. It is difficult to "speechify" one way and vote another, and nothing is veiled in secrecy. The legislation publicly passed is most useful to the news media, scholars, and others interested in research, writing, and publishing. Roll call votes are often close on controversial issues, particularly when lawmakers are undecided. Often, members pass the first time to determine the outcome from others' voting. In the past, roll calls were time-consuming, but electronic devices have alleviated this problem.

Rules Committee (106)

A rule-setting legislative body under which the lower house of a state legislature operates. The Rules Committee is charged with developing and administering rules or procedures by which bills are to be debated and voted. A standing committee determines the outcome of a bill. The Rules Committee recommends rules and makes necessary amendments thereafter. The committee usually includes the majority leader and the speaker of the house. This committee's reports take precedence over other business. The Rules Committee controls the legislative calendar and can influence the progress of a bill, especially toward the end of the session when bills pending will die without the committee's favorable priority ranking. *See also* COMMITTEE SYSTEM, 91.

Significance The Rules Committee functions like a legislative traffic director, assigning the fate of bills. For example, it can reject a bill by requiring further study by the committee that reported it for consideration. Having custody of the bill, the Rules Committee can virtually veto bills reported out by other committees. Most members of the Rules Committee are from the majority party, and the speaker of the house is the chairperson, a position of considerable power. This committee has become an instrument of legislative oligarchy, and an example of the partisan rule of the majority. Outsider members of the majority party and those from the minority party watch in frustration as their bills die while measures favored by the Rules Committee are promoted. However, there is one remedy: a bill can be forced out of the Rules Committee after seven days by means of a *discharge petition* signed by a majority of members. The Rules Committee is a procedural body, dealing with rules and not the subject matter of proposed legislation, but this committee can determine the shape and scope of legislation, as well as its chances for passage.

Seniority System (107)

The process of selecting legislative leaders based on length of service and party membership. The seniority system is used to award committee chairperson positions to the majority party in many state legislatures as well as in the United States Congress. Both major parties assign their members to committees on the basis of length of service in the legislature. Unlike the United States Congress, state legislatures do not use seniority as the sole criterion of leadership. Political considerations and personal factors modify the seniority rule in many state legislatures. When members are sworn on the same date, it is customary to favor those with prior important political experience. Once assigned to a committee, a legislator usually maintains the position; otherwise it would be impossible to build up seniority. Traditionally, the system has stood as a means of distributing favors and perquisites. *See also* COMMITTEE CHAIRPERSON, 88; COMMITTEE SYSTEM, 91.

Significance   The seniority system is favored by older members and disapproved of by younger legislators. Older members like the system and prefer the status quo; it guarantees them powerful committee positions. Younger members argue that the system retards persons of ability and maintain that longevity is not necessarily synonymous with effective leadership. Supporters counter that the system has produced legislators of stature, and obviously, the older members enjoy the powers and benefits of committee chairmanship and the attractive perquisites. Although there is a movement to decentralize legislative authority, it is unlikely that the seniority system will be changed substantially. However, as Elliot and Ali argue, "a system that generates power and influence for some at the expense of others will likely remain open to criticism and further reform as members vie to establish themselves in the political arena."[2]

Session   **(108)**
The period during which a legislature meets to transact its regular business. State legislatures assemble biennially (every two years), although some have annual sessions. Most states' regular sessions begin in January and last two or three months. The United States Congress assembles at least once a year and may be summoned into special session by the president. In most states the governor may convene special sessions of the legislature to deal with emergencies, and in some states the legislatures, by greater than majority vote, may ask the governor to convene a special session to discuss a specified topic. During the depression in the 1930s many special sessions were held on economic issues. Forty-three states have annual sessions. At least three states—California, New Mexico, and West Virginia—have tried split or bifurcated sessions. Under this system the legislature meets for about 30 days, when bills are introduced, then later returns for deliberation on the bills. *See also* GOVERNOR, 123; STATE LEGISLATURE, 111.

Significance   Special sessions of state legislatures have been called more frequently to solve increasingly difficult problems. Since the reapportionment of the 1960s, many restrictions on the frequency and length of sessions have been removed. Colonial days and the post-Revolution era saw many farmers as state legislators who took the job as a winter pastime. But gradually many professionals (e.g., lawyers, doctors, engineers, educators, businesspeople, and labor leaders) have sought a lawmaking career as a full-time avocation. At the same time, legislative councils (interim committees employed by some legislatures between sessions to study state problems and to plan legislative programs) are increasingly used by state legislatures to provide better preparation for their sessions. Today, many sessions are held round the clock and even during weekends and holidays in order to cope with the complicated lawmaking process.

Speaker (109)

The presiding officer of the lower houses, state and federal. The speaker is elected by fellow members at the beginning of the session, usually on a party vote following recommendation by the caucus of the majority party. Occasionally the leaders of the two major parties reach an understanding about the speakership. In addition to presiding over legislative sessions and appointing committees, the speaker's powers include (1) the right to rule on motions, points of order, and procedure, (2) the recognition of members on the floor, and (3) the authority to assign bills to committees. The powers and functions of the state speaker are comparable to those of the Speaker of the U.S. House of Representatives. An additional power of the speaker of the state legislature is to appoint members of the standing committees. The speaker may participate in debate and vote, and is the chairperson of the Rules Committee, which in many states is the most powerful committee. As the leader of the majority party, the speaker shapes party policy and implements decisions; he or she is the chief strategist of his or her party and the lower chamber of the legislature. *See also* PRESIDENT OF THE SENATE, 102; RULES COMMITTEE, 106.

Significance The speaker, chosen from among the most experienced members of the majority party, is invariably the power behind the scene as well as the presiding officer of the lower house. The speaker has considerable freedom to interpret rules and procedures because legislators are often uninformed on the rules. In a typical state legislature the speaker is considered more powerful than his or her counterpart in the United States Congress. Powers vary with states, but the California speaker is notably powerful. This legislator appoints the chairperson and members of all standing and select committees, refers all bills to committees, presides over the committee of the whole, recognizes members on the floor, serves as ex-officio member of all committees, participates in debates, occasionally votes, interprets rules and points of order, and performs other duties. The speaker can delay a vote on legislation while seeking support for its passage.

Special Interest Groups   (110)

Persons or agents who seek to persuade legislators to vote for or against a bill. Special interest groups may also attempt to convince officials of the merit of a bill. These are called interest groups, pressure groups, lobbyists, and sometimes the "third house" of the legislature. The term *lobbyist* arises from the fact that they are usually active in the public lobbies and corridors of the legislature, through which members must pass. They also testify with expertise at committee hearings to support their clients. Lobbying is directed toward federal and state legislatures and their committees—lobbyists seek to sway all who have influence in lawmaking. Interest group activity is a time-honored form of participation in U.S. politics. Many states, however, require the registration of lobbyists, the disclosure of information about their employees, their pay and other benefits, and the money spent to influence legislation. Lobbyists at the state level are part-time amateurs, while at the national level they are full-time professionals. *See also* POLITICAL PARTY, 71.

Significance   Special interest groups are usually more powerful than individuals in the U.S. political process. These groups affect government at every stage, from establishing party platforms to actual lawmaking. Almost everybody belongs to some interest groups—church, social club, labor union, professional association, cultural organization, and the like. Lobbyists are frequently reliable persons on whom legislators depend for information, and although most state legislators have access to reference libraries, it is often easier and quicker to obtain free information from the lobbyists. Lobbying is criticized because it serves particular interests rather than the general interest of the electorate. The process seems corrupt and at times lobbyists resort to bribery to influence legislators and others. The government, particularly the courts, restrict lobbying cautiously, as restraint could be construed as an abridgement of freedom of speech and the right to petition the government under the First Amendment to the United States Constitution.

State Legislature   (111)

The lawmaking branch of state government. The state legislature, within constitutional limits, decides on policies and programs for the state and where money to implement them will come from. All state legislatures are bicameral (two-house body) except Nebraska's, which is unicameral (one-house legislature). The generic term is *state legislature,* but they are also called the assembly, the legislative assembly, or, in the case of Massachusetts, the general court. The upper house in all states is called the senate, while the lower house is known as the house of representatives, the assembly, or the house of delegates. In unicameral Nebraska, the single house is called the senate. Forty-six states have two-year terms for legislators in the lower house; the others allow four-year terms. Forty states provide four-year terms for senators, and the remaining ten states hold to the two-year terms. The membership in the upper house varies from 17 in Delaware and Nevada to 67 in Minnesota. The lower house membership varies from 35 in Delaware to 400 in New Hampshire. The main duties of the legislature include lawmaking, budgeting, taxing, spending, visiting constituents, amending federal and state constitutions, supervisory functions, and judicial duties (to impeach executive and judicial officials). *See also* LAWMAKING PROCESS, 94; LEGISLATIVE BRANCH, 95; SESSION, 108.

Significance   The state legislature symbolizes the U.S. belief that a government closer to home is more reliable, more cognizant of local needs, and less likely to abridge people's rights. The state legislature is charged with reflecting the people's will. However, only a small percentage of the population is knowledgeable about the state legislature, and many feel that the legislature wastes time. Their criticism is also directed at interest group influence, excessive party politics, inefficiency, corruption, favoritism, nepotism, financial scandal, and misuse of power by many legislators. Still, since colonial days the state legislatures have been the cornerstone of the U.S. democratic tradition. The state legislatures, the direct forerunners of the United States Congress, set much of the pattern for the national legislature and for legislative procedures.

Statute   (112)

A law passed by a legislature. A statute differs from common law and equity law in that it is legislative-made and not judge-made law. The legislative process in the states is much like that at the federal level. A bill is introduced into each house (except in Nebraska, which has a one-house legislature), referred to committees, passed by a majority in both houses, sent to the governor for approval or veto (except in North Carolina, where the governor does not have the veto power). Statutes take two major forms: public laws and private laws, with the former of general concern to the public and the latter concerned with a particular problem affecting private persons that public laws created or ignored. A statute may be real, personal, or mixed. A real statute is a law that deals directly with property, while a personal statute concerns a person. A mixed one affects both. Other than the state legislatures, lawmaking powers have been conferred upon cities, counties, townships, and school districts by statutes. The date of the passing of a statute is the date when it receives the chief executive's assent or the time fixed for its commencement. A breach of a statutory law is indictable. *See also* COMMON LAW, 143; EQUITY, 160; LAWMAKING PROCESS, 94.

Significance   Statutes are written and collected in volumes of law as record, but state laws are not codified regularly. Today, statutory law is the main source of regulations that govern citizen behavior at all levels of government—federal, state, and local. Many areas once covered by common law are now treated by statutes. In every session the state and federal legislatures approve hundreds and thousands of enactments, but most of these are administrative directives. The number of statutes dealing with property, contracts, crime, and other basic concerns is small. No matter how carefully a statute is drafted and drawn, there is need for judicial interpretation. Should a legislature disagree with the court's interpretation of a statute, it can enact new legislation clarifying its intent.

Unicameralism   **(113)**
A one-house legislature, found only in Nebraska. Unicameralism is also practiced by local governmental bodies such as county boards, city councils, and township boards. Ten states proposed constitutional amendments for unicameral legislatures between 1910 and 1934. The Nebraska legislature (senate) has 43 members elected by districts upon nonpartisan nomination. The preceding bicameral legislature had 133 members. The transition from a bicameral to a unicameral legislature met with overwhelming approval. Since 1937, when the Nebraska innovation became operative, the National Municipal League sponsored the unicameral system as part of its Model State

Constitution, but to no avail. *See also* BICAMERALISM, 86; STATE CONSTITUTIONS, 26; STATE LEGISLATURE, 111.

Significance   Unicameralism has succeeded in Nebraska, and is easy to understand. The main arguments for unicameralism are (1) efficiency of operation, (2) economy, (3) elimination of deadlocks, (4) reduction of duplication, (5) absence of buck passing, (6) less interest group influence, and (7) greater responsibility and prestige. The arguments against unicameralism include: (1) hasty and ill-conceived legislation may result; (2) more legislators may be susceptible to popular passions; and (3) the system is inconsistent with the principle of checks and balances. A nationwide movement for single-chambered legislatures failed, as bicameralism proved stronger in U.S. politics. Nebraska adopted unicameralism during the depression years, when the economy argument proved persuasive. Many reformers argue that because representation is based on population there is hardly any need for bicameralism, which owes its continuing existence to tradition and the existence of more jobs for political patronage. Opponents of unicameralism maintain that it is not suited to a federal system of government because it does not allow representation based on state equality and population. Proponents contend that, if Nebraska can function with a unicameral legislature, other states and the United States Congress could also. They believe that unicameralism will eliminate deadlocks resulting from the rivalry and friction between two houses in bicameralism.

Upper House   (114)

The higher chamber in all state legislatures, except Nebraska's. The upper house is the smaller body of a bicameral legislature. Representation in the United States Senate is based on state equality, while in the state senates it is based on population. The membership numbers only 17 in Delaware and Nevada and as many as 67 in Minnesota; the average is about 40. The lieutenant governor is normally the presiding officer of the state upper house. In his or her absence, a state senator fills the position as president *pro tempore* ("for the time being"). The houses are relatively equal in power. Most state senators serve longer terms (four years), although a number of states, such as New York and North Carolina, have equal terms for all legislators. Originally, the upper house was patterned after the British House of Lords, which represented the aristocracy and not the masses. The upper house confirms appointments of officials and holds trials of impeached officers. *See also* BICAMERALISM, 86; LEGISLATIVE BRANCH, 95; LOWER HOUSE, 99.

Significance   The upper house has long been more prestigious than the lower. Aside from lawmaking and representational functions, the upper house enjoys certain special powers, including the power to confirm appointments and to try impeachments. Because of the upper house's small size, its members can more easily win recognition for their talents. It resembles a small club based upon close personal relationships; such intimacy may, at times, breed conflicts of interest. However, many maintain that the upper house is more conducive to serious business than the crowded lower house. Although the term *upper house* is inherited from the British Parliament, it is unofficially used in the United States. Class distinction is not recognized in the United States as it has been traditionally in Britain.

Whips   **(115)**
Assistant floor leaders who aid the majority or minority leader in the legislature. Whips perform in state legislatures and in the United States Congress. The term *whip* refers to the man who "whipped in" the hounds in the hunt to keep them in line. Whips of both major parties monitor party members and induce them to vote the party line. Party whips are selected in caucuses, usually on the recommendation of the floor leaders. The whips appoint assistants to help them in the management of the floor. A whip serves as the acting floor leader in the absence of the majority leader. The whips keep in touch with their party legislators, canvass their views, remind legislators of meetings, and arrange "pairs" for absent members. (Absent members agree to cancel each other's votes.) They make certain that party legislators are present to vote on important issues, and maintain party discipline. The whips and their assistants review and sometimes form legislative strategy. They assess how members are likely to vote and attempt to counteract the other party's strategy. *See also* MAJORITY LEADER, 100; MINORITY LEADER, 101.

Significance   Whips are like lobbyists working for their party, and they mobilize members to support the party position. They act as a liaison between their party's leaders and the members, and on crucial votes the passage of legislation depends on their persuasiveness. Effective whips acquire name and fame and sometimes advancement. A majority whip may become the leader and finally the speaker. Although sometimes frustrating, the whip role is desirable for its possibilities. Whips have a difficult time promoting party unity. At times, they have openly defied stands taken by their party leaders, and this has made party leaders reluctant to share power with them.

Many legislative party leaders and whips affect legislation to the detriment of the party and the electorate. Although the job of whip can be mechanical at times, competition for the position is keen. Candidates for whip campaign vigorously, take advantage of past favors, and are quick to promise future help in exchange for support.

5. The Executive Branch

Agriculture, Department of (116)

An agency of state government that provides services for farmers, regulates various aspects of agriculture, and coordinates many of its activities with the United States Department of Agriculture. Most states have a department of agriculture, with the state secretary of agriculture either elected or appointed by the governor. At the national level, the secretary of agriculture is appointed by the president with Senate approval. In every state the United States Department of Agriculture has established committees of farmers and agricultural experts. Although there is no formal relationship between these committees and the state department of agriculture, county and state officials frequently serve on them. Like their federal counterpart, the state department of agriculture conducts research, collects data, publishes information, and assists in weed control, food production, milk production, and the eradication of plant diseases. It also inspects and labels seeds and marketed grains, and grades honey, maple syrup, apples, and corn. With few exceptions, states have an agricultural college that conducts scientific and social research and shares its findings with individual farmers. *See also* HUMAN RESOURCES, DEPARTMENT OF, 128.

Significance   The department of agriculture in each state is responsible for promoting agribusiness and furnishing legal protection for consumers. Promoting agribusiness includes expanding agricultural markets and maintaining stability in the farm economy. Consumer protection includes inspection of poultry, eggs, and milk; assuring the accuracy of weight and measures; controlling plant and animal diseases; and regulating the use of chemicals and pesticides. The

121

county agricultural extension service, established by federal funds, serves as a rural educator, publishing and distributing informational materials on agriculture. Some state programs overlap and even conflict with federal programs. For example, state efforts to boost farm productivity and levels of production tend to foster overproduction, which the federal government attempts to deal with through its various loan/purchase subsidy programs. Agriculture department activities vary from state to state. Colorado farmers, for example, face irrigation and dry farming problems, while New York and Wisconsin farmers are concerned mainly with dairy farming.

Appointment Power   (117)

The authority of a governor or an administrator to fill a nonelective position. The power to fill about 400 high state positions is vested in the governor, but most require senate confirmation. The governor also appoints members to advisory boards and commissions. Nationally, the president performs the same function, but he or she can also remove appointees, except those whose terms are specified by law. The governor in many states cannot remove officials except for "cause"—nonattendance of office and nonperformance of duty. In Alaska, Iowa, and Pennsylvania both houses of the legislature must confirm appointments. In Maine and New Hampshire, the governor and an elected council jointly appoint officials. Most governors appoint those in charge of accounting, finance, administration, revenue collection, budget, planning, personnel, purchasing, health, employment security, corrections, labor, conservation, natural resources, environmental protection, agriculture, public works and buildings, information systems, transportation, public safety, insurance, civil defense, and many others. The appointment power is sometimes derived from constitutional provisions, but frequently it comes from statute. *See also* GOVERNOR, 123; GUBERNATORIAL POWERS, 126.

Significance   The appointment power of governors in many states is limited. The governor's power of removal is delineated in state constitutions or statutes. Under administrative reorganization many states now empower governors to remove appointed public officials, but elected ones can be removed only by impeachment. Like the president, the governors choose officials who are personally loyal and have the ability to supervise the operations of the government. Appointments made for party loyalty and patronage, however, often produce inferior results. The types of individuals appointed may greatly affect decisions made by governors in their control of the bureaucracy. Although a merit system is favored by reformers, the recent trend is to grant governors increased powers of appointment so as to strengthen their control of the state's bureaucracy.

Attorney General (118)

The head of the state department of justice and a member of the governor's cabinet. The attorney general is the chief legal officer of the state and serves as a legal advisor to the governor and to all state agencies. Each state has an attorney general, who represents the state in legal proceedings and oversees a legal staff. In many states the attorney general gives legal advice to local officials and often advises the legislature, particularly on bills under consideration. The attorney general helps draft and prepare contracts, bond forms, and other legal documents for the state. It is a constitutional position in 40 states, and in the others the position is a statutory one. In 42 states the attorney general is elected by popular vote, in 7 appointed, and only in Maine elected by the legislature. Duties are mainly prescribed by statute, and the attorney general serves as the chief law enforcement officer. Legal opinions rendered by the attorney general set precedents and become the law of the state. Opinions cover all subjects, and in one year in Ohio there were as many as 1200 opinions given by the attorney general. The attorney general's opinions are published collectively. *See also* CABINET, 119; JUSTICE, DEPARTMENT OF, 130.

Significance   In many states the attorney general is second in importance only to the governor. Legislative acts are not self-defining, and the attorney general spends considerable time preparing opinions and interpreting laws. The attorney general has a dual responsibility: as an elected official responsible to those who voted for him or her, and as a member of the cabinet in providing advice to the governor. The attorney general is apt to be motivated by the desires of the voters in deciding what laws will be enforced aggressively. The office can be used to great advantage toward higher political goals. An ambitious attorney general can enhance his or her image and gain prominence by investigating irregularities and corruption. Critics contend that the attorney general should be appointed since the governor should have full confidence in the chief legal advisor, whose opinions ordinarily have the force of law. His or her advisory relations with the governor frequently depend on similar party affiliation.

Cabinet   **(119)**
An advisory body elected by the people to aid the governor in making
decisions. The cabinet members are heads of their respective departments and coordinate and implement policy. The cabinet usually
consists of the heads of the departments of agriculture, correction,
education, human resources, interior, justice, revenue, state, and
transportation, among others. In 1912, influenced by President
William Howard Taft's Efficiency and Economy Commission, several
states implemented plans of administrative reorganization. New
York, under the governorship of Alfred E. Smith, introduced the
cabinet idea. California, Connecticut, and Kentucky followed suit by
also installing cabinets. At the national level, the cabinet is appointed
by the president with Senate approval. The president can remove
cabinet members if he or she chooses to do so, but most governors do
not have this power. In states where cabinet members are appointed,
the governors have greater control over them. *See also* GOVERNOR,
123; GUBERNATORIAL ROLES, 127.

Significance   The cabinet is an extraconstitutional development
both at the national and state levels. It helps the chief executive form
policy. One of the governor's most difficult tasks is to maintain cordial
relations with the legislature and the public, and the cabinet helps to
defend and explain administration policy. Many political scientists
believe that the governor's cabinet should be established for the same
general purposes as the presidential cabinet and should be appointed
in order to maintain harmony between the governor and cabinet
members. The governor is the chief state executive, elected by the
people. To administer effectively, he or she needs sound advice, and
this can best be accomplished by a cabinet of experts answerable
directly to the governor rather than to the electorate. One may ask, if
appointed cabinet officers perform efficiently at the national level,
why cannot the states follow suit? However, unlike the presidential
cabinet, members of the gubernatorial cabinet are elected and are
therefore responsible to the voters rather than to the governor, and
thus many state administrations suffer from a lack of cooperation.

Comptroller   **(120)**
A state official who has responsibility for establishing an accounting
system. A comptroller or officer of similar title was set up by the
constitutions of most states to oversee the state's finances. The word
comptroller stems from the fact that this official controls and checks the
accuracy of bookkeeping dealing with income and expenditures. The

job is not always performed by one official. For example, in Ohio it is done by the director of administrative services and the director of the Office of Management and Budget. Many states use the title *auditor* because of the authority vested in the office to audit accounts and to see that funds are lawfully disbursed. Some states have given the comptroller the authority to require a uniform accounting system, and in others, to supervise the accounts. The comptroller ensures that expenditures have been made in accordance with law and audits government accounts to keep them within the limits prescribed by the legislature. *See also* GOVERNOR, 123; TREASURER, 139.

Significance   A comptroller's main duty is to guard the expenditure of state funds to ensure honesty and accountability by preauditing as well as postauditing. Proper auditing of the budget is a legislative act, but its execution is the responsibility of the comptroller, who guarantees that funds are spent in accordance with the legislature's intent. The comptroller performs duties independent of the administration and is expected to report irregularities in expenditures to the legislature. Because the governor and the comptroller are independently elected state officials and are not responsible to each other, sometimes their differences erupt in personal warfare and public debate. Many political scientists doubt the wisdom of electing or appointing the comptroller. Selection through the civil service system or by the legislature seems more desirable because the comptroller is a technocrat, not a policy maker.

Correction, Department of   (121)

The state agency responsible for the care, custody, and supervision of persons convicted of crimes. The department of correction handles individuals convicted of a felony or a serious misdemeanor. State laws direct the department to provide custodial care, educational opportunities, and psychological treatment for all prisoners. The state also provides community-based supervision and various social services to individuals on probation or parole. The secretary of the department, appointed by the governor in most states, is responsible for the supervision and administration of departmental activities but cannot release incarcerated prisoners, which is the responsibility of the parole commission. At the national level, the Bureau of Prisons in the Department of Justice provides care and custody of those convicted of federal crimes. The federal government gives financial assistance to state authorities for many correctional programs and for law enforcement. *See also* CORRECTIONS, 267.

Significance   The department of correction provides safety to citizens by operating and maintaining prisons and by supervising probationers and parolees. Many programs try to rehabilitate offenders, but few are successful. According to political scientist Robert S. Lorch, "Eighty percent of all felonies are committed by repeaters who were previously in contact with the corrections system and were not corrected by it."[1] Statistics indicate that a high rate of recidivism persists—ex-convicts repeat their criminal activity and are returned to prison. Criminologists are not sure which rehabilitation programs are effective. Usually rehabilitation is not taken seriously, and many vocational skills, such as barbering, are not always marketable because many communities do not allow convicted criminals to work in certain occupations. Rehabilitation programs, long sentences, parole, and punishment have all failed to markedly reduce recidivism. Although capital punishment has been reinstated, the current trend is toward longer and more rigorous sentences.

Education, Department of   (122)

An agency of state government established to promote public education. A department of education fixes the minimum standards for public schools, including in some states institutions of higher education, and exercises general supervision to maintain these standards. At the national level, the U.S. Department of Education supports and coordinates educational assistance programs. It is responsible for ensuring compliance in programs and activities receiving federal assistance, and it provides financial and technical assistance to meet federal mandates to eliminate racial discrimination and segregation. The typical state department of education grants subsidies for the support of the districts' schools, and leaves the remainder to local initiative. Although most elementary and high schools are administered by local districts, the state sets the curriculum and dictates teacher qualifications. The state board of education, appointed in some states and elected in others, carries out the state's policy. The state superintendent of schools, appointed by the state board of education in many states and elected in others, directs the education department.

Significance   The department of education determines to a large extent the state's educational policy. This policy falls under four general categories: (1) legislation establishing and regulating a system of public schools; (2) supervision and control of local schools through state administrative agencies; (3) financial support for elementary and secondary schools; and (4) the maintenance of state colleges and universities. Nevertheless, the primary responsibility for public education remains with the local school district, although centralization at the state level has increased. Many state legislatures have forced small districts to consolidate. The U.S. Department of Education has historically played a very small role in public education. Its largest impact on public education is felt in three areas: (1) desegregation; (2) special programs for the disadvantaged; and (3) encouragement of special curricula, such as science and mathematics.

Governor (123)

The chief executive in state government. The governor is elected in all 50 states and serves for four years in most states and two years in some. Most state constitutions stipulate that the governor shall be a citizen of the United States; that he or she shall have resided in the state, usually for five years; and that he or she shall be at least 30 years of age. In most states the candidates for governor are nominated in a direct primary; the convention system is used in the others. The governor's constitutional authority includes the power of appointment and removal, financial powers, law enforcement powers, legislative powers, and the power to pardon or reprieve. In some states, the governors appoint judges at all levels, from the lowest district court to the state supreme court; when necessary the governor declares emergencies and requests federal aid. Governors command the national guard, except when it is called into national service. All governors, except in North Carolina, can veto legislation. The governor plays many roles—chief of state, chief legislator, chief administrator, military chief, chief of party, and chief leader of public opinion. The governor's salary is fixed by the constitution in some states and decided by the legislature in others. In case of impeachment, death, or resignation of a governor the lieutenant governor becomes chief executive in many states. In others, the president of the senate or the speaker of the house fills the vacancy. *See also* GUBERNATORIAL POWERS, 126; GUBERNATORIAL ROLES, 127.

Significance The governor is usually designated by the constitution as the chief executive, responsible to see that the laws are faithfully executed. The governor is, in a sense, a mini-president. However, the governor is not the only executive officer of the state; the executive authority is divided among the governor, attorney general, secretary of state, and many others. Unlike the president, a governor's administrative powers are limited. Many of the cabinet members are elected and not directly responsible to the governor but rather to the electorate and to the legislative and judicial branches. Thus, the governor's office is weaker than that of the president. Recent trends in most states suggest the need to strengthen the appointive power of the governor and expand the office's financial and legislative authority. Despite public expectations to the contrary, governors often lack the legal authority to provide strong leadership.

Governor's Staff   (124)

Aides to the governor. The governor's staff usually includes a personal secretary, press secretary, administrative aides, legislative liaison, budget analysts, policy specialists, and legal counsel. Governors also use staff from various state agencies and departments. The latter facilitate and maintain communication with the legislature, executive departments, the information media, and the general public. The staff often help the governor campaign for office and share his or her policial ideology, and the govenor depends on their loyalty and devotion to duty. The staff confer with the governor whenever necessary, and have direct access. They serve as the governor's chief confidants, and it is on their performance that the governor's administrative success depends. *See also* APPOINTMENT POWER, 117.

Significance   Members of the governor's staff can become a power in their own right. They provide information to the governor and analyze issues and problems. In the past the governor's staff, like other governmental employees, served in a simple manner devoid of public scrutiny, but demands for reform have forced governors to engage professionally qualified help. Under the patronage system, the governor and his or her party were responsible for filling positions. Today, the governor uses the appointment power to reward party faithful only at the highest levels of administration. With the rise of the merit system, the state civil service commissions have taken control from the governor in the appointment of most state workers. Governors, of course, continue to appoint their personal staffs. The staff assists the governor by collecting and disseminating information and serving as an instrument in the formulation and execution of gubernatorial directives. Personal and political pressures have not only forced governors to expand the size of their staffs but also to recognize their growing influence in policy making. The belief that critical local, state, and national problems require that experts aid and assist the governor has caused the governor's staff to grow. It is through their help that governors have increasingly emerged as leading figures in most state governments.

Gubernatorial Characteristics   **(125)**
The traits or qualities of a governor. Some gubernatorial characteristics are formally prescribed by state constitution. Other informal
characteristics increase a candidate's ability to become elected. These
may include such factors as having no large, well-organized opposition
bloc of voters. State constitutions stipulate that a governor shall be a
citizen of the United States; shall have resided in the state for at least
five years; and usually shall have attained the age of 30, although some
states have a minimum age of only 21 or 25. Most governors have been
white, male, Protestant, Democratic, and lawyers. In 46 states the governor's term of office is four years; in the remaining 4, two years. In
the mid-1980s, the median salary was $35,000; 44 states provide the
governor with a mansion, and most states provide an expense allow-
ance. *See also* GUBERNATORIAL POWERS, 126; GUBERNATORIAL ROLES, 127.

Significance   Gubernatorial characteristics refer to the electability
of a candidate for governor. Most likely candidates are middle-aged
(35–55), and have a common racial, religious, and ethnic background
with the majority of their constituents. Electoral statistics show that
white, male, Protestant, and Democratic aspirants have a distinct advantage over females, Republicans, blacks, and Hispanics. The successful candidate is an accomplished politician, well educated and
financially independent. Many candidates have served in lesser state
offices. To be successful a governor must be a leader. Professor Larry
Sabato, in a study of 312 governors, found that the key leadership
qualities included competence, dedication, and ability to meet the
needs of the people.[2] The personal popularity and the governor's
family background are also relevant. Although their lifestyle is costly,
they are not particularly well paid. Prominent governors must maintain a high standard of living and be able to meet the cost of enter-
taining legislators and dignitaries. Several of them have become
national figures—Jimmy Carter and Ronald W. Reagan are two
recent examples of governors who were elected president of the
United States.

Gubernatorial Powers   **(126)**
The authorities of the state's chief executive. Gubernatorial powers
usually include supervision of administration, appointment and removal of officials, legislative influence, law enforcement, preparation
and execution of budget, issuance of executive orders, and the power
to pardon and grant reprieves. The governor is usually designated by
the constitution as the "supreme executive" of the state and is charged

with seeing "that the laws are faithfully executed." Gubernatorial power is divided among many secretaries of departments and an attorney general. The governor can only remove the secretaries he or she appoints; those appointed by him or her with the consent of the senate may be removed only with approval of the senate. In every state the governor may propose legislation and call the legislature into session. In all states, except North Carolina, the governor can veto legislation. The governor is the chief law enforcement officer. He prepares the budget and, when passed by the legislature, executes it. The governor can also declare a state emergency. In most states the governor can grant pardons and reprieves; in others, a pardon may be granted only upon the recommendation of a board of pardons. *See also* GOVERNOR, 123; GUBERNATORIAL ROLES, 127.

Significance   Gubernatorial powers are comparable to the presidential authority, but the governor is a weaker executive since the president has control and jurisdiction over more areas. Whereas the United States Constitution (Article II, Section 1) delegates the executive power to the president, in the states the executive power is divided among the governor and a diverse group of elected officials. U.S. governors are not always held in high esteem, and in political prestige a governor is sometimes outflanked by United States senators. As the nation faces additional future crises, the public will demand that state governments take a more active approach toward meeting public needs. Many governors themselves led the movement for reform and constitutional changes by removing limitations on their authority to deal with desegregation, crime, riots, prison unrest, drug addiction, urban renewal, and other problems. Contemporary trends suggest the need for increased powers for governors, including longer terms and greater authority over legislative, financial, and personnel matters.

Gubernatorial Roles   (127)

Activities carried out by the governor in administering state affairs. Gubernatorial roles are many and varied. He or she is the chief of state, chief legislator, chief administrator, chief of the state militia, chief of party, and chief leader of public opinion. As head of state, the governor participates in various ceremonial functions and represents the state in official matters of many kinds. As chief legislator, the governor can introduce bills and can convene special sessions of the legislature and veto bills (except in North Carolina). As head of the state administration, the governor appoints many officials, and can remove most of them. The governor is responsible for supervising the state administration and can activate the national guard to maintain peace and order. By communicating with the media, the governor may be able to cultivate favorable public opinion for plans and programs. The governor may grant paroles, pardons, reprieves, and rendition. *See also* GOVERNOR, 123; GUBERNATORIAL POWERS, 126.

Significance   Gubernatorial roles have evolved through practical needs and are also specified in state constitutions. Like the president, the governor plays many overlapping and varied roles. Many duties are routine. A governor is limited to one state, while the president is head of the federation of states. As commander-in-chief of the national guard or state militia, the governor can mobilize and direct them, but the national guard is largely financed by federal funds and can be nationalized at any time by the president. Like the president, governors function as chief executives, supreme lawmakers, party leaders, and major policy makers in their states. The governorship, like the presidency, is an institution—it includes personal staff and many other government officials who function in the governor's name and under his authority. Today, many governors function increasingly as chief executives, wielding effective authority over state administrations.

Human Resources, Department of   (128)

A state agency that helps individuals, families, and communities achieve adequate levels of health and economic and social well-being. The department of human resources provides services through various county-operated agencies; in a typical state more than 200 programs exist. One of the goals of the department is to offer prevention services to reduce human suffering and costs. The department offers care for individuals such as children, older adults, and alcohol and drug abusers. The U.S. Department of Health and Human Services determines the overall structure of the social welfare program. Each state department of human resources implements most of these programs. Both departments seek to expand and improve the range of human services that foster the sound development of children, youth, and families. The counties often run homes for the elderly and for children. The department is headed by a secretary or director who is elected or appointed. *See also* COUNTY, 199.

Significance   The department of human resources drafts rules and regulations to implement policies established by the legislature, and it oversees the implementation of programs by the county agencies. These county agencies not only administer state programs, but also implement the federal Aid to Families with Dependent Children (AFDC). Benefit levels vary depending on the economic situation of a state; New York, for example, offers eight times as many benefits as Mississippi. However, it is not always the economic situation of a state that determines the difference in benefit levels but often political and other social conditions. The recipients are mostly underprivileged people, from 25 to 35 million U.S. residents. The most troublesome problem for the federal and state departments of human resources is that the impoverished have become a permanent component of our society. Poverty in the land of plenty could destabilize the socioeconomic fabric of the society unless the situation is controlled. Generally, people in the United States agree that without governmental, social, and humanitarian programs the problems of hunger, disease, and poverty would worsen.

Interstate Rendition   (129)
Return by one state to another of a person accused of a crime. The process of interstate rendition resembles extradition, which is a practice of rendering up individuals accused of crime on the international level. Article IV, Section 2 of the United States Constitution requires that "A person charged in any State with Treason, Felony, or other Crime, who shall flee from Justice, and be found in another State, shall on Demand of the executive Authority of the State from which he fled, be delivered up, to be removed to the State having Jurisdiction of the Crime." Procedurally, a governor who demands the return of a fugitive from justice conveys his or her request to the governor of the state in which the suspect was apprehended and subsequently dispatches an agent to return the fugitive to that state. All costs are borne by the demanding state. Nations may enter into extradition treaties with one another for the return of international fugitives. *See also* RENDITION CLAUSE, 22.

Significance   Interstate rendition is considered a moral rather than a legal obligation by the United States Supreme Court. The language of the Constitution in Article IV, Section 2 appears clear when it uses the word "shall," which makes the return of the fugitive to the demanding state mandatory, but in a leading case on the subject at the outbreak of the Civil War, the U.S. Supreme Court questioned the lack of powers of the federal government to compel governors to return suspects: the governor of one state may not ask for a *writ of mandamus* (a court order to a public official to perform an act that is legally required). In most cases a governor will comply with a proper request but is not obliged to do so. Normally, the governor returns a fugitive because of the fear of public criticism and similar reprisals and because he or she is unwilling to harbor criminals. Still, a governor may decline to return someone he or she feels should not face criminal charges. Depending on the circumstances, this rare refusal to return an accused person usually will not jeopardize relations between states and governors.

Justice, Department of   (130)

The principal state law enforcement agency. The department of justice represents the state in legal disputes and its head, the state attorney general, is the legal adviser to the governor and other state officials. The agency represents the state in court. The functions and responsibilities of the department are to render legal services and enforce the law. Typically, legal services are organized into the following areas: consumer protection; legislative services; energy and utilities; education, labor, and correction; state agencies and local government; state highways; special prosecution; special investigations; antitrust; and a department of administration. The law enforcement sections consist usually of the state bureau of investigation, the state police department, and the criminal justice division. The attorney general is elected in 42 states by popular vote, appointed by the governor in 7 states, and in Maine is elected by the legislature. The attorney general is a constitutional position in 40 states, and in the others his or her position is a statutory one. *See also* ATTORNEY GENERAL, 118.

Significance   The department of justice, in the public interest, may intervene in proceedings before any courts, regulatory offices, agencies, or bodies on behalf of and representing the public. It also has the authority to institute and originate proceedings before courts, offices, agencies, or bodies on behalf of the state. Through the attorney general's office, the department charges and prosecutes violators of state law. In most states, the attorney general's opinion has the force of law unless challenged in court. The department is one of the most powerful organizations in the state, with the power to initiate prosecution in civil and criminal cases. Although law enforcement is primarily the responsibility of state and local authorities, the U.S. Department of Justice is playing an increasingly large role in civil rights issues. Both state and federal departments of justice play a key role in protecting citizens through crime prevention and detection, prosecution, and rehabilitation of offenders.

Legislative Address   (131)

A message to the legislature in which the governor discusses state problems and proposes legislative programs to meet the needs of the state. The legislative address sets the lawmaking agenda and serves as the basis for the formulation of state policy. The governor may address a regular or special session of the legislature in a joint session. He or she does so to approve or to veto acts and to make his or her influence felt among members. The governor can call the legislature into special session whenever it is in the public's interest. At the national level the president proposes legislative programs to the Congress. Like the president's messages to Congress, the governors also send messages regularly to the legislature. To supplement these messages, governors usually submit fully drafted bills for legislative action. Many governors present their legislative program in an inaugural address. Some states require governors to prepare a budget to be presented in a legislative address. *See also* GOVERNOR, 123; GUBERNATORIAL POWERS, 126; GUBERNATORIAL ROLES, 127.

Significance   The legislative address offers the governor an opportunity to highlight and dramatize his or her legislative agenda. The message focuses on major problems facing the state (and sometimes the country), and proposed solutions. Many governors view their legislative efforts as their proudest achievement. Governors follow the presidential model, reporting on the overall condition of the state. Many times a governor can expedite passage of a desired legislative action quicker than a president because state assemblies are of shorter duration. The governor's message is often followed by lobbying by aides and supporters to ensure passage of favored bills. These messages receive media attention and public notice, and the threat of a veto (except in North Carolina) helps to secure passage of the governor's legislative program. Governors do not always elicit a favorable response from the legislature, but they can and do dramatize their legislative agenda.

Legislative Council   (132)

An interim body established to study state problems and to develop a legislative program for consideration by the legislature. The legislative council studies, during legislative breaks, subjects likely to command the legislature's attention. The council reviews proposals from legislators, the governor, and the public, collects information, and holds discussions. It may publish its research findings and may draft bills for legislative action. The legislative council is composed of members selected by the two houses of the legislature. In several states the governor is represented by staff. The number of members varies from five to the entire legislature. Normally, the council is a joint bipartisan body with a professional staff and director, and this staff is sometimes called the legislative council. The council meets when necessary. Thirty-seven states have legislative councils or council-type agencies. *See also* LEGISLATIVE BRANCH, 95.

Significance The legislative council enjoys the confidence of the legislature, and its recommendations receive special consideration. It is a means by which state legislatures develop their own leadership and planning facilities. This reduces their dependence on the executive branch and promotes the principle of separation of powers by checks and balances. As the lawmaking process becomes more intricate and the workload heavier, legislatures are becoming more dependent upon legislative advance planning. The Model State Constitution of 1948, drafted by the National Municipal League's Committee on State Government, provides for a legislative council. The legislature may delegate to the council authority to supplement existing legislation by general orders. If the states had adopted the model, the legislative council would have been able to recommend such legislation as it deemed necessary, and the council would have had more powers in several respects than the legislature itself.

Lieutenant Governor (133)

The second highest executive official in many states. The lieutenant governor succeeds to the governorship in case of the resignation, death, or removal of the governor. In a number of states the lieutenant governor acts as governor during the latter's temporary absence from the state. In most such states, the lieutenant governor presides over the senate. In the seven states—Arizona, Maine, New Hampshire, New Jersey, Oregon, West Virginia, and Wyoming—that have no lieutenant governor, either the secretary of state or the president of the senate is eligible to succeed the governor. Like the vice-president of the United States, who presides over the United States Senate, the lieutenant governor is not a member of the body over which he presides, does not participate in the debate, and only

casts the deciding vote in the event of a tie. *See also* PRESIDENT OF THE
SENATE, 102.

Significance   Many consider the office of lieutenant governor
unnecessary. It may be more desirable to have the secretary of state or
an officer closely associated with the administration succeed to the
governorship when a vacancy arises. The state senate could, as is done
in some states, choose its own presiding officer. While most lieutenant
governors have few duties, the lieutenant governors of Alabama,
Mississippi, North Carolina, and Texas are heavily involved in the
senate work of assigning bills to committees and appointing members.
Robert S. Lorch, in *State and Local Politics,* maintains, "Lieutenant
governors are, characteristically, split between two branches of government more than any other elected officers."[3] This negates the
concept of separation of powers, as the same official has duties and
responsibilities in both the executive and legislative branches of
government.

Pardon   (134)

The power of a governor to grant clemency from punishment to
those convicted of crimes. A pardon is granted by the governor in
some states; in others, he or she may do so only with the recommendation of a board of pardons of which he or she is sometimes a
member. There are two kinds of pardons—absolute and conditional;
the former restores the person outright to the position he or she
enjoyed prior to conviction, whereas the latter requires that certain
obligations be met before the pardon becomes effective. Closely
associated with pardon is *commutation,* which is the reduction of
punishment, and *reprieve,* which delays the execution of a prisoner.
About three-fourths of the states grant the governor the absolute
power of pardon, while in the remainder it is based on the recommendation of a board of pardons, whose advice the governor need
not follow. This quasi-judicial power is attached to a governor by the
constitution or by custom and gives the governor the authority to
mitigate sentences imposed by courts. Usually, pardons are granted to
correct mistakes made in convictions or to release offenders who are
considered rehabilitated. *See also* GOVERNOR, 123; GUBERNATORIAL
POWERS, 126.

Significance   Pardons have decreased markedly in recent years,
owing to widespread public criticism. Greater knowledge of civil
rights, criminology, psychology, and psychiatry leads many governors

to depend on the advice of specialists in the matter of pardons. Most governors, like the president of the United States, regard a pardon with distaste. They are often criticized by the public for pardoning or commuting sentences because of political favoritism. Governor John C. Walton of Oklahoma pardoned 698 prisoners in 11 months and was impeached and removed for accepting bribes to do so. It is argued that the pardon is often granted to influential persons. Studies have shown that the effect of pardon upon prisoners is, at times, negative, because they are frequently only interested in obtaining the pardon, not in changing their criminal conduct. To avoid problems, most governors would prefer to turn this responsibility over to pardon boards.

Plural Executive (135)

The authority of the government shared by many officials who are popularly elected. Plural executive means that the executive power of state government is shared with the governor by various state officials, such as the lieutenant governor, secretary of state, attorney general, treasurer, auditor, and others. These elected officials are primarily responsible to their constituents and not directly to the governor nor any other authority. They are individually elected and often are from different parties. The governor, like the president, cannot always count on their support. Sometimes governors spend more time maintaining harmony than developing plans and programs for the state. In the counties the mode of government has been traditionally based on a commission plan, which is a form of plural executive. In many counties, no single person is recognized as overall county administrator, and so the governing board shares power and responsibility with persons elected to perform specified duties, such as the sheriff and county treasurer. *See also* GUBERNATORIAL POWERS, 126; GUBERNATORIAL ROLES, 127.

Significance The plural executive system is a weak form of government because the executive authority of the government is diffused. The lack of a single chief executive can lead to inefficiency in delivering services. While all governors are popularly elected, 42 states also elect their attorney general, 40 the treasurer, 38 the secretary of state, and 43 the lieutenant governor. Besides these, most states elect many other officials including the comptroller, insurance commissioner, and auditor. Since these officials are elected and have independent constituencies, their willingness to cooperate with the governor may be limited. Unlike the president, who can both hire and remove cabinet officers, the governor must depend on the will of a much more independent cabinet to administer effectively. Some of the governor's cabinet officers may aspire to become governor and conspire against him. Political scientist Robert S. Lorch notes, "It may be a great show to watch, but it does impair the governor's ability to mobilize his administration and political party into accomplishing his goals."[4] This weakens the state government and adds to the public's confusion.

Revenue, Department of   (136)

A state agency that collects taxes for use by state and local governments. The department of revenue is accountable for these funds, and it attempts to ensure equitable tax laws. In general, there are four sources of state revenue: commerce, administration, taxes, and transfers. Commercial revenues arise from operations in which the state acts as a proprietor, such as public industries and agricultural lands. Administrative revenues include fines, fees, and special assessments. A fine is a punishment for a violation of criminal law, while a fee is charged for recording deeds and other legal documents. A special assessment is a proportional contribution levied upon land to defray the cost of improvement. Taxes are collected from individuals or corporations and are levied on the income, sale, or valuation of property. The major sources of state revenue are income and sales taxes. Property taxes provide the great bulk of income for local governments. Intergovernmental transfers are another source of state revenue. The department of revenue is headed by a secretary, usually appointed by the governor. *See also* INCOME TAX, 250; PROPERTY TAX, 255.

Significance   The department of revenue is the chief administrative agency of the state government for procuring funds. It advises taxpayers, attorneys, accountants, and tax preparers on interpretation of laws; it issues legal documents necessary to effect collection; and it receives audits and processes applications for licenses. The department also deals with taxpayers on controversial matters and protested assessments. As the financial needs of governments have increased with the expansion of services, federal, state, and local governments have become competitive for revenue sources. This involves taxation of the same individuals, corporations, and properties by all three levels of government. State governments carry the heaviest burden because they must support themselves in addition to supporting local governments. Moreover, many states have allowed local governments to raise taxes but lack the power to levy import, export, and tonnage taxes. State governments today receive more than 30 percent of their revenue from the federal government, and local governments garner almost half of their revenue from the federal and state governments.

State, Department of (137)

A state agency responsible for the preservation of official documents, issuance of business licenses and certificates of incorporation, registration and issuance of motor vehicle licenses, and the administration of elections. The department of state is keeper of the state seal and discharges miscellaneous statutory duties. Other functions include countersigning all commissions issued by the governor; attesting all documents issued in the name of the state; assigning seats to members of the general assembly; and receiving and preserving original laws of the general assembly and furnishing certified copies to interested parties. The department compiles and publishes information useful to the legislature, state agencies, and the general public. It also notarizes certain documents. All states have a department of state headed by a secretary, usually elected. Most charters of incorporation of private companies and municipalities are filed with the office. The secretary is usually present when the legislature convenes in joint session. Titles of state property and official measurements of public buildings and public lands are kept on file by the agency. *See also* COUNTY CLERK, 202.

Significance The department of state has some supervisory powers over election returns, and it may be able to delay or expedite special elections as political considerations may dictate. Several of the department's functions are prescribed by the state's constitution, but most are provided by the legislature, with the result that many of the department's functions are unrelated. The secretary of the department has few policy-making responsibilities. In states where the secretary is elected, the governors have little control over this office, and in states where appointed, the governors often install political allies. In most states the department enjoys prominence because its name is affixed to numerous documents. Political scientists differ on whether this office should be elective or appointive by the governor.

Transportation, Department of (138)

A state agency that regulates highways and air, rail, and water transportation. The department of transportation is responsible for centralizing most of the state's public transportation system under one authority. It does not regulate common carriers, which is the province of the utility commissions. The department of transportation has numerous divisions, including highways, motor vehicles, air, rail, and coastal. The highway division constructs, maintains, and operates an efficient, economical, and safe transportation network consisting of roads, streets, highways, and ferries. The division of motor vehicles administers the laws applying to drivers and vehicles. The division of aeronautics sees to the development of airports and airways. The railroad division studies the need for federal and state support for the system's improvement. The coastal division looks after the operation of the state ferry system. *See also* INTERSTATE HIGHWAY SYSTEM, 277.

Significance   In the mid-1980s, the states spent more than $12 billion a year on transportation. The federal government has brought relief by providing highway funds to the states on a 50-50 matching grant basis and, in the case of the interstate highway system, on a 90-10 basis. The federal government has spent over $270 billion in highway construction. Although the main transportation concern of most of the states is highways and motor vehicles, they are also involved in other forms of transportation, particularly mass transit. Many states are now planning and coordinating air and urban mass transit, but highways remain the top priority.

Treasurer   **(139)**
A state official responsible for the safekeeping of state funds and the payment of bills. The treasurer is elected in most states and chosen by the governor or legislature in others. He or she is one of the four most common constitutional officers of the state (the other three are secretary of state, comptroller, and attorney general). The treasurer's approval is required for expenditures authorized by the legislature. In the past, when the property tax was the main source of state revenue, the treasurer had no important tax-collecting functions to perform. Today, in many states he or she is responsible for the collection of taxes. As a custodian of state funds, the treasurer's authority is limited to the investment of funds and the floating of state bonds. In recent years, the treasurer has become an investment counselor and acts as financial adviser to the state government. Many decisions are financial in nature, not political, and are often dictated by financial houses in New York and Chicago. *See also* COMPTROLLER, 120.

Significance   The treasurer is, in many ways, an office manager. He or she has little authority beyond choosing the banks in which state funds should be deposited. First established as an appointive position by state constitutions, it was later made elective. In most states, the treasurer receives and disburses all state taxes and monies. The work of the treasurer's office is checked by another state official, the comptroller. A treasurer is not involved in controlling but in keeping and investing state funds. Treasurers cash checks and issue warrants after they have been preaudited by the comptroller. They collect funds only in accordance with state law, which is interpreted by the comptroller. Still, treasurers have considerable influence. For example, they decide where state funds will be deposited. At one time, a treasurer might choose banks offering kickbacks, but this practice has been outlawed. Many political scientists view the election of a treasurer as unnecessary; they believe the position should be filled by gubernatorial appointment. This would make the treasurer responsible to the governor, as is the case with the secretary of the treasury of the United States, who is responsible to the president.

Veto (140)

The authority of a governor to nullify a bill passed by the state legislature. The veto power is a mechanism used by governors in every state except North Carolina to quash legislation that threatens their policies or is considered unwise or politically dangerous. The president uses the same power to defeat legislation. When the state legislature passes a bill, it is sent to the governor, who has from three to ten days to consider it. Most governors have the power to veto items (certain portions) in budget, appropriation, and other bills. A few states allow governors to use the *pocket veto* (burying a bill in his or her pocket, not signing it until the legislature adjourns). Unlike most governors, the president does not have an item veto; he or she must either approve or reject a bill in its entirety. A gubernatorial veto can be overridden by the legislature by a vote of two-thirds or three-fourths in both houses (except in Nebraska, which has a one-house legislature). Sometimes the legislature, anticipating a veto, may withdraw a bill. *See also* GOVERNOR, 123; GUBERNATORIAL POWERS, 126.

Significance Veto power was used sparingly in the past, chiefly as a means of preventing unconstitutional legislation. Now veto power is increasingly used to political advantage. Does the veto kill a bill? Usually, because the legislature cannot always call itself back into session. Even if it could reconvene, it would be difficult to muster a two-thirds or three-fourths vote of the two houses to override the veto. The mere threat of a veto is often more effective than its actual use. The veto power of the typical governor is stronger than that of the U.S. president. The president and only seven governors lack the item veto. To avoid problems and expedite legislation, three states— Alabama, Massachusetts, and Virginia—give the governor a choice between vetoing a bill or returning it to the legislature with changes. In case of acceptance by the legislature, amended bills go back to the governor for his or her signature. This process reduces the chance of frequent use of the veto in those states. Politicians, like a governor or president, dislike the use of the veto because it creates conflict even within a party. However, sometimes a minority governor or a minority president can exercise great power through the use of the veto. Resort to the use of the veto may also give a chief executive sufficient clout to form a winning coalition in the legislature.

6. The Judicial Branch

Civil Law (141)

The code regulating the conduct of private disputes between persons or corporations. Civil law does not provide punishment but makes remedy available to the complainant. A divorce suit or discrimination case involves civil law. The word *civil* is derived from the Latin *civilis*, "a citizen or relating to the citizenry of the state." Civil law has traditionally existed in Europe, from which it came to the United States. It designates Roman "jurisprudence" as applied and enforced by civil courts, and can be distinguished from criminal law, which regulates individual conduct. The body of civil law in force in a particular state depends upon the heritage of common law (judge-made law). Civil law provides settlement of disputes between private parties in such matters as property (real and personal), inheritance, torts, contracts, family relations, and business conduct. Sometimes a case may be both civil and criminal. For example, if a negligent driver injures a person, the state may prosecute him or her for a criminal offense and the injured person may sue the driver for civil damages. *See also* COMMON LAW, 143; CRIMINAL PROCEDURES, 159.

Significance Civil law designates all rules of law governing the members of society. In this sense, it becomes synonymous with the concept of law itself. All crimes are civil wrongs, but the reverse is not true. Civil law governs the relations between individuals and defines their legal rights. A party bringing suit under civil law seeks legal redress in a personal conflict, such as breach of contract or defamation of character. Yet, while most civil law suits are between private individuals, some involve the government either as plaintiff or defendant. Both federal and state governments, especially the federal, under the Sherman Anti-Trust Act of 1980, have more frequently brought civil rather than criminal actions when either type of case is permissible under the law. The main reason for this preference is that under civil actions the rules of evidence needed to win a case are more easily satisfied.

Civil Procedures   (142)

Modes of dealing with litigation. Civil procedures differ from state to state, but in all cases include the following: (1) pleadings, (2) trial, (3) verdict, and (4) appeals. Pleadings are initial presentations to a court. A party to a civil suit may retain an attorney and tell his or her story; then the attorney asks a court to issue a writ of summons calling the defendant to appear in court at a specific time to answer suit. Next, the plaintiff sets forth his or her cause of action in a complaint. The defendant may admit the facts but deny their validity. The case is then prepared for trial. The case may be tried before a jury with a judge presiding. The jury is screened and must be mutually acceptable. In a jury trial, the jurors are sworn, and the attorney for the plaintiff argues the case. He or she may make an opening statement and examine witnesses, including the plaintiff. Then the attorney for the defendant may cross-examine the witnesses to expose falsehoods or inconsistencies in the testimony. The judge explains the law applicable in the case, and the jury decides the facts and presents its verdict. If the jury disagrees, the case may be tried again (the majority of the states require a unanimous jury verdict). The losing party may appeal the verdict to a higher court. Not all cases can be appealed, but important civil cases involving high awards and constitutional questions may be appealed. *See also* CIVIL LAW, 141 CRIMINAL PROCEDURES, 159.

Significance   Civil procedures are steps through which a civil action must normally pass. The government may be a plaintiff or defendant in a civil suit. In civil cases, it is not necessary for attorneys to appear in person, although they may do so. In major cases that originate in municipal courts, it is usual for an attorney to appear for the litigants. Civil litigation is handled either by a single judge or, in more serious cases, by a panel of three judges. Most civil cases in both state and federal courts are tried without a jury. Because of the absence of a jury, relatively few exclusionary rules of evidence have been developed; the court considers the evidence offered, so long as it is neither irrelevant nor simply cumulative. Where juries are used, some states permit trial by a jury of fewer than 12 persons, and decision by less than unanimous vote.

Common Law (143)

Judge-made law that originated in England based on custom, precedent, and legal commentaries. Common law is a body of judicial decisions that serves as the source of other laws. The legal systems of England and the United States are partly based on common law. It is distinguished from statutory or legislature-made law. The idea of common law goes back to the Constitution of Clarendon (1164), which established the supremacy of the king's courts in England. This customary law has been administered by the common law courts of England since the middle ages. The concept of common law was brought to America by the English colonists. With time, much of the common law has been embodied in legislation. Trial by jury and cross-examination of witnesses are part of English common law. Common law forms the basis of legal procedures in most of the United States except in Louisiana, where French legal traditions and the Napoleonic code are preserved. *See also* EQUITY, 160; JURY, 170.

Significance　Common law permits judges flexibility to adjust law to community needs, thereby making judicial decisions more credible. In a broader sense, common law designates many positive laws of general and universal application. The introduction of equity (flexible law that provides a remedy where the common law does not apply) enriched the English legal system, stimulating the growth of common law, but it created conflicts between different systems. Common law also had to adapt itself to statutory law. In England as well as in the United States, legislation supersedes common law. Yet common law serves a purpose in many countries of the world where the English have settled or ruled. Today a large portion of common law applies in countries outside England, such as the United States, Canada, Australia, New Zealand, India, Pakistan, Bangladesh, Nigeria, Ghana, and most other Commonwealth nations (former British colonies).

Court System (144)

The network of the judicial branch of government responsible for interpreting authoritatively the laws in a particular jurisdiction. The court system interprets laws enacted by the legislative branch and administered by the executive branch when disputes arise as to their meaning and constitutionality. The court system exists at the national and state levels. These are mutually independent except that the United States Supreme Court may, under special circumstances, review a state court's decision. The jurisdiction of a particular court system is determined by either federal or state constitutions. In both national and state systems, the courts consist of professionally trained judges, either appointed or elected. The state court system includes (1) county court; (2) courts of original jurisdiction; (3) general trial court; (4) intermediate appellate court; (5) justice of the peace; (6) juvenile court; (7) municipal court; (8) probate court; (9) small claims court; (10) state supreme court; and (11) traffic court. The state court system tries over three million cases per year, while the federal courts handle approximately 140,000 cases annually. *See also* COURT SYSTEM: COUNTY COURT, 146; COURT SYSTEM: COURTS OF ORIGINAL JURISDICTION, 147; COURT SYSTEM: GENERAL TRIAL COURT, 148; COURT SYSTEM: INTERMEDIATE APPELLATE COURT, 149; COURT SYSTEM: JUSTICE OF THE PEACE, 150; COURT SYSTEM: JUVENILE COURT, 151; COURT SYSTEM: MAGISTRATE, 152; COURT SYSTEM: MUNICIPAL COURTS, 153; COURT SYSTEM: PROBATE COURT, 154; COURT SYSTEM: SMALL CLAIMS COURT, 155; COURT SYSTEM: STATE SUPREME COURT, 156; COURT SYSTEM: TRAFFIC COURT, 157.

Significance   The court system yields a complex variety of arrangements and names. The U.S. judicial system is a dual system, consisting of both federal and state courts. Although such a system is inherent in the federal scheme of government, it invariably leads to confusion. Many legal experts believe that the multitude of courts within states has resulted in much wasteful litigation. Federal and state courts are characterized by independence and localism. Recent reform measures have eliminated many differences, but despite progress, the major drawback of the court system is delay in the administration of justice. There is also a need for improvement in the organization of the courts, in judicial procedure, and in methods of selection of and tenure of judges. At the state level, there is a need for a unified court system in which all state courts would be organized as branches of a single judicial bloc.

Court System: Appeals Court   (145)

A higher judicial body, also known as an appellate or intermediate court, that can review questions of law in lower-court decisions. The appeals concept requires the existence of a judicial hierarchy, which at the state level may include an appellate court above the county, municipal, and supreme courts. The highest state court is called the supreme court, except in Kentucky, Maryland, and New York, where they are called the court of appeals, and in Maine and Massachussets, the supreme judicial court. In the state and federal judicial systems, any higher court having jurisdiction can serve as a court of appeals of decisions by lower courts. A lower court or trial court is presided over by one judge, while an appeals court usually has three or more judges. At the federal level, there are 13 courts of appeals, each with 4 to 23 judges. These courts hear appeals from the district courts within its circuit (a geographic area), which includes several judicial districts. The larger states have an elaborate appellate court system. In New York, for example, there are 152 appeals courts; above them are 10 appellate judicial districts, and finally, the court of appeals (supreme court). Smaller states have only one appellate court. *See also* COURT SYSTEM, 144.

Significance The appeals court serves as a review body, and except in special cases where original jurisdiction is conferred, it does not function as a trial court (court of first instance). As a rule, only the party aggrieved by a judgment of a court is entitled to seek review of that order in appellate court. The appeals court reviews cases by lower courts that are unsatisfactory to one of the parties. In all states, the decision of the highest appeals court is final unless a "federal question" is involved. In such cases, an appeal based on a writ of *certiorari* can be filed with the United States Supreme Court. If at least four of the nine Supreme Court justices agree that the case should be heard by the Court, then the Court will accept the case for review. Generally, in an appellate court, only points of law, not questions of fact, are at issue. An intermediate court may sustain or reverse the judgment of an inferior court, sometimes directing the lower court to hold a new trial.

Court System: County Court (146)

A court of original jurisdiction in the county. A county court is sometimes called a district court, superior court, circuit court, or court of record. These are all trial courts with judges elected in 37 states and appointed in the others, usually for four-year terms. Original jurisdiction is exercised in virtually all criminal cases other than misdemeanor cases handled by justices of the peace or magistrates. In some states separate county courts exist for civil and criminal cases, and in others as separate divisions of the same court. In many states the same judge who sits in the same court handles all types of cases. In Pennsylvania, separate civil and criminal courts exist, although the same judge sits in both courts. In Arkansas the power of county courts are entirely administrative and financial. Generally, county courts perform some administrative duties, such as management of estates of deceased persons and the appointment of certain county officials.

See also COURT SYSTEM: JUSTICE OF THE PEACE, 150; COURT SYSTEM: MAGISTRATE, 152; COURT SYSTEM: PROBATE COURT, 154.

Significance   County courts are state rather than local courts. A county court's jurisdiction extends to all civil and criminal offenses, and it has jurisdiction over both original and appellate cases. In serious cases, juries are frequently used. Cases from peace court and magistrate court can be appealed to the county court. The number of judges assigned to a court varies with the volume of litigation, but at least one judge is required. If a court does not exist in a county, several counties are consolidated into one circuit, and a judge holds court in each circuit at fixed intervals. County court or district court has been a vital unit in state judicial systems ever since colonial days, and its organization and structure has changed very little. Considering the relatively low judicial salaries in most counties, their short term of office, and the necessity of running for office every few years, county court judges perform relatively well.

Court System: Courts of Original Jurisdiction   (147)

Courts where cases are initiated and heard in the first instance. Courts of original jurisdiction, as a class, are often referred to as trial courts. The jurisdiction of these courts may be divided into four categories: civil, criminal, probate, and equity. In some states the court may handle all types of cases; in others, several types of courts may be established. Illinois has circuit courts (county courts) of original jurisdiction in civil and criminal cases. Below the courts of original jurisdiction, there are minor courts that have original jurisdiction in petty cases. Courts of original jurisdiction have elected judges, commonly for four-year terms. Every state has these courts, and they have unlimited jurisdiction in both civil and criminal cases. Although cases can be appealed to an intermediate appeals court or to the state's highest court, most remain in the courts of original jurisdiction, where trials are frequent. *See also* COURT SYSTEM: COUNTY COURT, 146; COURT SYSTEM: GENERAL TRIAL COURT, 148.

Significance   Courts of original jurisdiction hear and decide all but the most minor cases. Appeals taken from the inferior courts to higher courts of original jurisdiction are heard *de novo* or "in the first instance," since they involve a new trial. Permanent records are maintained. Justice in the United States is defined essentially by the courts of original jurisdiction. Appeals in criminal convictions are rarely accepted, and this tendency has steadily increased. For many people, the courts of original jurisdiction are the first and last contact with the judiciary. Therefore, it is vital that these courts merit credibility and that people respect their decisions. Society perceives judicial decisions as an objective force for fairness and justice, and the courts of original jurisdiction are principally responsible for upholding this image.

Court System: General Trial Court (148)

A court with the authority to hear a case in the first instance. General trial court is the place of original jurisdiction for all criminal cases regardless of the seriousness of the offense. It is also authorized to try civil cases without limitation as to the amount involved. In this court, major civil actions and criminal prosecutions for felonies are heard for the first time, and questions of fact as well as law are decided. In many states general trial courts are called county, district, circuit, or superior courts. These are courts of record; that is, they keep a full transcript of their proceedings. In some states a single court handles criminal matters. Although it is possible to try cases without juries, general trial courts almost always use *petit* (trial) juries. The judges of the general courts are elected. At the federal level all judges are appointed including those of the general courts, known as district courts. Like the general trial courts, they hear both civil and criminal cases. The right to trial by jury in federal criminal cases is guaranteed by the Sixth Amendment to the United States Constitution. The Fourteenth Amendment has been interpreted as guaranteeing trial by jury in most criminal cases. *See also* COURT SYSTEM: COUNTY COURT, 146; COURT SYSTEM: STATE SUPREME COURT, 156.

Significance   General trial courts serve as the first judicial contact of the litigants, juries, and the judiciary. Most important cases come before a general trial court, where final decisions are made. The quality of justice meted out and the image the court conveys depend upon how this court functions. Thus it is vital that a general trial court be effectively administered in order to maintain credibility and respect for law and the judicial system. The general trial court is often called the backbone of the U.S. judicial system.

Court System: Intermediate Appellate Court (149)

A place of appeal below the level of the state court. An intermediate appellate court is found in 20 states, and in 25 others the county court functions as the intermediate appeals court. These intermediate appeals courts are called by various names—courts of appeal, district courts of appeal, and superior courts. There may be one intermediate court of appeals, as in Pennsylvania, or several such courts, as in California. Each court has three to nine judges, who constitute a body and render judgment by a majority vote. The jurisdiction of these courts varies, but generally they handle cases on appeal from lower courts. Their decisions are final in some cases, but subject to appeal to the state's highest court in others. Few states confer trial or original jurisdiction to these courts on controversial matters such as election results or *writs of mandamums* (an order of a court to compel performance of an act) proceedings against a state elected officer. Intermediate courts of appeal simply review written and oral arguments received from trial courts. Law and fact are not considered, and usually there is no need for juries in these courts. Typically, the judges of these courts are elected, but in a few states they are appointed by the governor. *See also* COURT SYSTEM: COUNTY COURT, 146.

Significance   Intermediate appellate courts exercise general appellate jurisdiction with further appeal possible to the highest court. Many states have found it necessary to interpose courts of appeal between the trial courts and the highest state court in order to lighten the burden of the highest court. In an appellate court, the case begins from written transcripts of the trial testimony. Personal credibility, variability, and the human element that can influence trial situations are absent from the appellate court. Intermediate court is a place for lawyers, who customarily present their arguments in dignified style, to evidence their professionalism.

Court System: Justice of the Peace   (150)

A local judicial officer empowered to hear minor civil and criminal cases, such as traffic offenses or breaches of peace. Justices of the peace are elected in towns, townships, or counties, usually for a two-year term. In several states, they are appointed by the governor. A justice of the peace rarely has formal legal training, although a few states require a law degree. The justice of the peace is authorized to try petty civil and criminal cases and, in some states, to conduct preliminary hearings on serious criminal charges. In such hearings, the justice of the peace does not determine the guilt or innocence of a suspected person. If the evidence presented in the hearing is sufficient to warrant prosecutorial action, the next step is action by a grand jury or a prosecutor. The justice court originated in England and has existed in the United States since colonial days to handle minor quarrels informally and to prevent formal litigation. The justice of the peace is dependent upon fees collected from parties and cases coming before the justice court. In misdemeanor cases, justices of the peace receive fees from the fines they assess on guilty persons. The jurisdiction of this court is fixed by statute in most states. It is not a court of record, and except where a jury trial is demanded, no jury is provided. Outside their judicial duties, in some states the justice of the peace is authorized to perform marriages and to attest to formal documents. *See also* COURT SYSTEM: MUNICIPAL COURT, 153.

Significance   A justice of the peace was once a prestigious person in his or her area, but not today, and the justice of the peace's office has been widely criticized in recent years. This person is commonly untrained in the law, responsible to no one for his or her decisions, and has a vested financial interest in the outcome of cases, which can lead to corruption and prejudice. Another frequent criticism is that justices use their homes to hold court. In many urban areas, the justice of the peace has been replaced by municipal or district courts. The disappearance of the justice of the peace may spell the end of inexpensive justice in the United States, with the exception of small claims courts. The United States Supreme Court has condemned the fee system, but it has somehow managed to survive. The old agrarian U.S. society has transformed itself into a giant industrial nation requiring a more sophisticated system of justice, and the justice of the peace has become obsolete.

Court System: Juvenile Court   (151)

A specialized court that processes cases of delinquent, neglected, or dependent children. Juvenile court seeks to determine the causes of misconduct and to recommend reform. The jurisdiction of juvenile court is limited to persons between the ages of about 7 to 18. Some states allow juvenile courts to hear cases involving adults (over 18 years) who contribute to juvenile delinquency. State laws provide that juvenile courts shall handle youngsters who are alleged to have engaged in behavior that may be grounds for an adjudication of delinquency. Violation of criminal statutes is the criterion for juvenile courts to try children who are felt to be potentially delinquent or morally questionable. Youngsters are brought before the court, where the judge speaks with them about their problems. The judge tries to elicit a frank statement of the details of the act committed. On the basis of the investigation the child may be placed on probation or committed to a detention center. In serious felony cases, such as murder, the juvenile court may waive its jurisdiction, thereby permitting the youngster to be tried as an adult subject to the much stiffer penalties of the law. *See also* COURT SYSTEM: MUNICIPAL COURT, 153.

Significance   Juvenile court is a recent development, with most established since the 1960s. Eliminating juvenile delinquency is difficult. Juvenile delinquency is viewed as a civil rather than a criminal matter because a child may not be fully responsible for his or her conduct, and it is essential that the juvenile court be sympathetic to the problems of children. The courtroom formality of a criminal trial is dispensed with so that the youthful offender need not feel he or she is a criminal. However, a fair trial requires due process of law, which means, among other things, the right to counsel and cross-examination of witnesses. The United States Supreme Court held *In re Gault* (387 U.S. 1: 1967) that the right to counsel, protection against self-incrimination, and the right to confront witnesses apply to juveniles accused of offenses. Despite rising public concern and experimentation with rehabilitation, youth services in most states are extremely limited. Thus, the remedies available to the juvenile court are limited because of the lack of treatment facilities. Probation from the court, following release from a correctional institution, is handicapped by staffs that are inadequate in numbers and training.

Court System: Magistrate   (152)
A minor official, elected or appointed, with judicial or executive powers. A magistrate is authorized to try cases involving traffic violations, civil suits, and criminal offenses. He or she may pass arraignments, issue warrants, or exercise judicial control over police. The term *magistrate* is derived from the Latin *magister* or "master," the holder of a public office. The duties of a magistrate often include: (1) acting as a judge at trials of minor criminal matters; (2) determining the sufficiency of evidence to hold an accused for trial or to hold grand jury proceedings; (3) determining the amount of bail; and (4) issuing warrants for arrest and for search. A magistrate may also conduct preliminary hearings in serious criminal cases and commit the alleged offender for trial in a higher court. At the national level, magistrates are appointed under a merit selection system by federal district court judges for eight-year terms. They hold jury and nonjury trials in civil and criminal misdemeanor cases. *See also* COURT SYSTEM: JUSTICE OF THE PEACE, 150.

Significance   A magistrate is a lower-court officer with power to handle misdemeanor cases in urban areas; his or her rural counterpart is the justice of the peace. Magistrate salaries are low— often so low as to attract only low-level politicians. The typical magistrate is not a lawyer, and the intricacies of complex legal situations present them with difficulties. Magistrate court is commonly held in a police station or in a small office. There is often no dignity to the proceedings, and little justice may result from them. A lack of order in the courtroom, lateness of hearings, and improper disposition of cases are frequent complaints. Short shrift is often made of civil cases, and intimidation is not uncommon in criminal cases. On top of this, bail irregularities and political influence in determining cases are widespread. A right of appeal from magistrate court exists in almost all cases, but appeals are expensive and the outcome uncertain, so justice or injustice is often accepted in the magistrate's court. Magistrates have been indicted, tried, and jailed on charges of corruption, irregularities, and mismanagement; studies have found that they are often inefficient and, at times, dishonest. However, magistrates dispose of large numbers of cases and provide relief for the overburdened higher courts.

Court System: Municipal Court (153)

A minor court of justice authorized by charter or state law. Municipal court enforces local ordinances and exercises civil and criminal jurisdiction similar to that of a justice of the peace. The justice of the peace has been replaced in many states by municipal courts. In large cities such as Detroit, Chicago, and Cleveland the municipal courts are organized with several divisions for the disposition of specific cases. Most municipal court cases include traffic offenses. Municipal courts have jurisdiction over criminal and civil cases but do not have as broad jurisdiction as do general trial courts. Sometimes the jurisdiction of the municipal court is concurrent with the general trial courts so that a plaintiff may bring a case to either. Municipal courts are organized in specialized divisions such as night court and family court; the former tries petty criminal cases, and the latter deals with family relations and divorce. Cases can be transferred from one judge to another for expediency in what is often referred to as "unified" municipal courts. *See also* COURT SYSTEM: GENERAL TRIAL COURT, 148.

Significance　　Municipal court exists only in a few places, as municipalities usually do not wish to assume the expenses. Where there is no municipal court, violations are tried by a county court. The overlapping of the general trial court and the municipal court is objectionable because it may induce the litigants to bring a case to one of the courts for reasons not directly related to its merits. There are also special county or circuit courts in some cities, and their jurisdiction is confusing and overlapping. The solution to this problem may lie in a unified municipal court system. Proponents of the unified court system claim it will promote uniformity in decision making, will relieve court dockets from congestion, and will encourage a more efficient use of money and personnel.

Court System: Probate Court   (154)
A court to establish the authenticity of wills. Probate court's jurisdiction has been expanded to include all matters and proceedings relating to administration of estates and guardianship. In many states judges of the general trial court perform probate work, but in about one-half the states a separate probate court exists. In some areas probate court is called surrogate court. The Latin term for probate is *probatio*, meaning "proof," and in English *probate* refers to the proof of will, that is, the testament of a deceased person. Probate court has original jurisdiction to consider the validity of wills and the disposal of property of deceased persons, to assign executors (where the deceased has not named an executor) to carry out the provisions of the will, and to dispose of property left by persons without a will (intestate). Much of the work of the probate court is administrative in nature. This court also protects estates pending the settlement of disputes among the heirs. *See also* JUDICIARY, 169.

Significance   Probate court is a specialized place and is usually set apart from the ordinary court structure. The probating of a will is a technical task, and sometimes the amount of property and money that falls under the probate court's supervision is large. The court exercises supervisory control over the administration of trust funds by the trustees who have been appointed. The naming of trustees or administrators is sometimes used as patronage, helping the probate judge win reelection by distributing favors to the influential. Occasionally, being a trustee is a lucrative job—a fee as high as 10 percent of the estate is charged. Unlike other courts, probate court exists to help people rather than to punish wrongdoers.

Court System: Small Claims Court   (155)
A special court that handles cases under a designated sum, up to about $2,000. Small claims court provides for informal, inexpensive, and expeditious settlement of petty claims. These courts are often a

division of courts of general jurisdiction. Jurisdiction is usually limited to collection of small debts and accounts, and litigants are encouraged to represent themselves. Where small claims courts are not found, such cases are handled by a justice of the peace or magistrate court. The court procedure is simple but varies from state to state. A written complaint is filed with the clerk of the court on payment of a small filing fee, normally $5 to $10. Most cases are settled by default, as the defendant fails to appear. Cases may be appealed and, in such instances, the appellate court hears them *de novo* (starts anew). In the appeal court parties to the dispute can have attorneys, a jury, and witnesses. Small claims courts were originally established for businesses and collection agencies to collect overdue bills. *See also* COURT SYSTEM: JUSTICE OF THE PEACE, 150; COURT SYSTEM: MAGISTRATE, 152.

Significance   Small claims courts were created in many states owing to a widespread movement to make justice affordable and expeditious. The relatively high cost of going to the standard courts led to the creation of small claims courts. Rent, small bills, and neighborhood disputes are settled in small claims courts. These courts have often disappointed those who supported their creation. Instead of helping the poor to receive quick, inexpensive, and simple justice, the small claims courts are frequently bogged down with large case loads, cumbersome procedures, and lengthy formalities. Another problem is that small businesses cannot collect unpaid bills from those who lack funds. The small claims court is virtually useless in resolving important monetary disputes among the poor, but this court is often a satisfactory solution where small amounts are involved. Poor organization has prevented these courts from attaining maximum efficiency in most of the states where they have been established.

Court System: State Supreme Court   (156)

The court of last resort in most state judicial systems. Each state supreme court, for the most part, fulfills an appellate function. Its purpose is to maintain statewide uniformity in the interpretation of law and to correct mistakes and conflicts in the decisions of lower courts. The state supreme court uses a simple majority vote to decide cases, and the chief justice has no greater vote; he or she is first among equals. The chief justice is usually elected or appointed to the court and serves as its administrative head. State supreme court judges are generally chosen by the people, and their terms of office are long—more than half of the states provide at least eight years. Massachusetts, New Hampshire, and Rhode Island provide their supreme court judges lifetime tenure, subject to good behavior. The procedures for state supreme courts are similar to those of the United States Supreme Court. When a judge or judges find themselves in the minority, they may write a minority opinion. An appeal from the state supreme court goes directly to the United States Supreme Court and not to any inferior federal court. The state supreme court consists of from three to nine judges. Like the United States Supreme Court, the state supreme court hears cases in original jurisdiction in which the state is a party or on the issuance of certain writs. In New York, Maryland, Kentucky, and West Virginia, this court is called the court of appeals. *See also* COURT SYSTEM, 144; JUDICIARY, 169.

Significance   The state supreme court is the final state interpreter of the state's constitution and laws. No appeal from its ruling can be taken to the U.S. Supreme Court unless the matter hinges upon the meaning of the United States Constitution or federal law. The state supreme court differs in some ways from the U.S. Supreme Court. For example, in half the states, dissents occur only in 5 percent of the cases, while in the U.S. Supreme Court it occurs in more than two-thirds of the cases. In Maryland, judges of the state supreme court who do not agree on a case are expected to accept the majority opinion. Although not comparable with the U.S. Supreme Court, the state supreme court also has great public policy-making power. This court often determines the final meaning of legislative acts and administrative decisions.

Court System: Traffic Court   (157)

A special court that handles cases of alleged violations of motor vehicle laws. Traffic courts vary widely from state to state, and in many instances they have no similarity within a state. In New Jersey, as many as ten different courts handle traffic cases, and prosecutors use any court that is convenient. Traffic cases arise out of a violation of state law, county regulation, or municipal ordinance. They include felonies, misdemeanors, summary offenses, and civil actions to collect damages. Traffic court may serve any territorial area established by law, be it a state court, county court, or a court designed to serve any municipality or other political or administrative unit. Judges who sit on these courts are known by various names: municipal judge, city judge, police judge, county judge, criminal judge, magistrate, municipal magistrate, county magistrate, trial magistrate, reader, city-county judge, superior judge, trial magistrate, circuit judge, district judge, justice, justice of the peace, juvenile court judge, general session judge, alderman, mayor's court judge, and traffic court judge. *See also* COURT SYSTEM: JUSTICE OF THE PEACE, 150; COURT SYSTEM: MUNICIPAL COURT, 153.

Significance　　Traffic court tries to secure prompt and uniform treatment of offenders. It is a misnomer, as there are only a few courts in the United States set aside specifically for the trial of traffic cases. Traffic offenders are tried by courts of general criminal jurisdiction such as the justice of the peace court, municipal court, county court, and other state courts. Traffic court is a descriptive term that applies to any court, irrespective of name, that has the authority to hear, determine, and adjudicate traffic cases. Effective traffic courts contribute immeasurably to the accident prevention programs of many communities. Almost all courts treat traffic cases apart from their normal business. Ideal traffic law enforcement would involve the expeditious trial of traffic cases on a uniform basis in special courts before a judge trained for that purpose. A statewide traffic court system may be suitable for economically dispensing justice.

Criminal Law (158)

The codes that describe offenses committed against the state and regulate the conduct of individuals. Criminal law refers to state and federal statutes that define offenses and specify corresponding punishments. The state and federal governments have enacted statutory definitions of major crimes, and these codes make provisions for trying those accused of committing the acts prohibited by law. Criminal offenses are classified as to seriousness, be they felonies or misdemeanors, the former being major. A criminal suit grows out of a public wrong—an offense against the state. A person may be arrested with or without a warrant, depending on circumstances. The next stage is to produce the prisoner before a court for a determination of the crime. The third stage is to accuse the person formally of the alleged offense. In case of a serious offense, this is done by a grand jury indictment. In minor crimes the prosecuting attorney files a complaint or indictment against a criminal suspect. The final stage is the trial and punishment of the person if found guilty. *See also* CIVIL LAW, 141; CRIMINAL PROCEDURES, 159.

Significance　　Criminal law ensures the protection of society from the wrongful acts of individuals. The quality of enforcement affects not only the crime rate but, sometimes, the provisions of law itself.

The criminal justice system in recent years has functioned under great stress. Rising crime rates, drug abuse, and child abuse have aroused public demand for effective enforcement of criminal law. The first difficulty with law enforcement is that there can be no crime without a criminal law to define it. Second, only legally prescribed punishment can be imposed for a crime. Third, there cannot be an *ex post facto* (retroactive) law to try or punish a criminal. Finally, a criminal statute must be interpreted strictly—any ambiguity is considered unconstitutional, as it violates legal due process. Those accused of crimes have rights, and criminal actions can only be punished except on the basis of existing law, after a fair trial and treatment of the criminals.

Criminal Procedures   (159)

The legal processes of apprehending, charging, trying, and convicting suspected offenders. Criminal procedures permit the challenging of the legality of conviction after judgment is entered. Challenges that may involve a denial of due process include arrest, search, arraignment, confession, entrapment, grand jury, *habeas corpus*, immunity, plea bargaining, public trial, right to counsel, and self-incrimination. An arrest warrant is a court order to detain a person. Search is the method adopted by a police officer to gather evidence to make arrests. Arraignment is to bring the accused before a court to hear the formal charges. Confession is an admission of guilt by an alleged offender. Entrapment is to lure a person into self-incrimination by inducing him or her to perform an illegal act. A grand jury is a body, usually consisting of 12 to 23 laypersons, that hears evidence presented by the state's attorney and decides whether or not to indict the accused. *Habeas corpus* is a judicial order to present a prisoner in court. Immunity is a privilege granted a witness that exempts him or her from prosecution for any self-incriminating testimony. Plea bargaining is negotiation between a prosecutor and an accused to secure a guilty plea in exchange for lesser charge. Public trial is the right to a trial open to the public. Right to counsel is the privilege to have the assistance of an attorney. Self-incrimination is the disclosure of facts that make a person liable to criminal prosecution. *See also* BILL OF RIGHTS, 1; CIVIL LAW, 141; CIVIL PROCEDURES, 142; CRIMINAL LAW, 158.

Significance   Criminal procedures are primary concerns of criminal law. The law attempts to advance and reconcile the interests of society. It must contribute to public peace and order. Violations of criminal law are prosecuted by government at all levels—national, state, and local. Prosecution brought under criminal law involves an accusation that the defendant has violated a specific provision of law, for which a penalty is provided. The defendant's rights are protected by the state constitution's bill of rights and by the Fourteenth Amendment to the United States Constitution. Together these provisions of the state and federal constitutions forbid a state to deprive any person of life, liberty, or property without due process of law, or to deny to any person the equal protection of the law. The largest volume of criminal law is enacted at the state level and thus is enforced by state officials. At all levels the courts render decisions in criminal cases.

Equity   (160)

Authority to decide cases according to fairness as contrasted with the strictly formulated rules of common or statutory law. Equity is used to render justice in cases where specific laws are lacking. It is a branch of remedial justice that arose in England in the thirteenth century out of petitions to the king to redress wrongs for which there was no remedy. Equity was based on abstract principles of justice but has since developed its own body of rules and procedures. Some states have equity courts, sometimes called chanceries. The chancery court originated because the English common law (judge-made law) courts largely limited the relief available in civil cases to the payment of damages and to the recovery of the possession of land. Common law refused to grant relief in complex situations. Unsatisfied litigants turned to the king with petitions for justice. The petitions were referred to the lord chancellor, the prime minister. This resulted in the development of equitable remedies. Both British and U.S. courts have a wide area of lattitude in equity cases to provide solutions to litigation. *See also* COMMON LAW, 143.

Significance   Equity, which is synonymous with fairness, plays a vital role in the work of judges, legislators, and administrators. By supplementing common law, equity has been a creative force in U.S. law. The English colonists carried their system of law to the New World, and the independence of the United States did not change the law in the states. Under equity procedures, a jury is seldom used, except in a few states where the right of jury trial in equity cases is granted. Equitable principles are formulated to do justice according to the principles of ethics. For this reason equity power is sometimes called a power of conscience, that is, to settle a controversy according to the dictates of conscience. Such decisions or decrees may often become part of common law, having established procedures. Equity courts render their decisions in the form of decrees. Failure to comply with these decrees constitutes contempt of court and is punishable by fine or imprisonment.

Grand Jury   (161)

A panel of citizens selected according to law to examine certain facts and determine if a crime has been committed and if an individual should be charged and bound over for trial. A grand jury is traditionally composed of 23 persons in many state and federal courts. The grand jury's function is to decide whether there is probable cause to believe that a crime has been committed and whether an indictment or *true bill* should be returned against anyone for such a crime. The accused then must stand trial before a *petit* (trial) jury, whose duty is to determine guilt. The Fifth Amendment to the U.S. Constitution declares that "No person shall be held to answer for a capital, or otherwise infamous crime, unless on a presentment or indictment of a Grand Jury." The grand jury does not determine guilt or innocence but only decides whether evidence presented warrants bringing the accused to trial. It is empowered to subpoena witnesses and records and can compel testimony under oath. The grand jury may also conduct investigations on its own when official misconduct is suspected or when a prosecutor fails to do his or her duty. It meets in secret and decides the matter by majority rather than unanimous vote. *See also* JURY, 170.

Significance   A grand jury exercises vast powers under the common law. In some states, if a crime is very serious, a grand jury indictment is required before the alleged criminal can be brought to trial. In politically serious cases the grand jury is used as a buffer for the prosecutor. At other times he or she may dominate the grand jury. More than half of the states have abolished or limited grand jury indictment to capital cases replacing it with the "information" that permits the prosecutor alone to bring charges. In a few states, such as Michigan, the traditional grand jury has been abolished, but a one-person grand jury can still be used to investigate conditions of political corruption, employing the traditional investigating powers of a grand jury. The U.S. Supreme Court has held that the Fourteenth Amendment to the U.S. Constitution does not require indictment by a grand jury in the states. Still, the grand jury is useful and, when composed of capable persons, safeguards the interests of law and citizens.

Injunction (162)

An order of a court in an equity proceeding directing a person or institution to perform or refrain from performing a particular act. An injunction is issued by a court on behalf of a party forbidding the defendant from violating the plaintiff's personal or property rights. There are several kinds of injunctions: A mandatory injunction requires the specific performance of an act; a preventive injunction commands a person to desist from an act already commenced; a preliminary injunction is issued when a court is unable to determine the rights of the parties; and a permanent injunction is the final court decree. Violation of an injunction constitutes contempt of court and the guilty party is liable to summary punishment. Injunctions are issued in connection with labor disputes, government regulations, and the protection of constitutional rights. An injunction is a common remedy for unlawful strikes. When an employer fears that strikers may cause serious damage to his or her business or property interests he or she has the right to seek protection from a court. If the court agrees with the contention, it may issue an injunction ordering the workers to desist. *See also* COURT SYSTEM, 144.

Significance The use of injunctions has been the subject of many criticisms because the courts have often invoked their powers to restrict labor or union activities. As a result, unions brought pressure to bear on state legislatures to restrict the use of injunctions in labor disputes, and the legislatures passed such laws in many states. Still, judges in all states wield great power to determine the scope of injunctions. Another problem involves the use of injunctions against acts of public officials, such as the regulation of business. These and other problems led the U.S. Congress in 1910 to prohibit the issuance of such injunctions except by a court of three judges. The Norris-LaGuardia Act of 1932 outlawed the use of labor injunctions when labor pursues lawful ends by legitimate means. The most famous injunctions in recent years have been those under the Taft-Hartley Act of 1947 banning labor strikes that threaten the national welfare for a period of 80 days.

Judge (163)

An official appointed or elected to preside over a court and to administer the law. A judge is charged with the control of proceedings and the decision on questions of law. Judge, justice, or court are often used interchangeably. By common acceptance most judges are now lawyers, although there is no constitutional requirement that this be so.

Federal judges are appointed; in the states judges are selected by partisan election, appointment, nonpartisan election, and merit plan. A judge maintains a "legal atmosphere" in which arguments and evidence can be presented according to the rules of judicial procedure. He or she also instructs the jury regarding the law and pronounces the sentence. Just as the selection procedures vary widely, so, too, do the titles of judicial officers. In most states the supreme court members are called justices, the presiding officer being known as chief justice. The lower state courts are staffed by judges rather than justices in the same manner as the federal courts. The exception is that in New York and Maryland, for example, in the highest state court (court of appeals) judicial officers are called judges, and the lower court officers are designated as justices. *See also* JUDICIAL SELECTION, 167.

Significance   A judge serves as a catalytic agent to balance various interests involved in litigation that comes before the courts. His or her own philosophy and the sociopolitical and economic conditions of the litigants may affect the outcome. Although a judge is supposed to impart "equal justice under the law," he or she is sometimes stymied by laws that are not equal. Ethnic, religious, racial, and social background may also affect certain judicial decisions. Although judges must be color-blind, a realistic view belies that ideal. They are human and susceptible to the glare of publicity that a sensational case receives. A judge may decide a case by common sense as long as this is not outside legal norms and guidelines set by precedent, especially those set by higher courts.

Judicial Qualifications   (164)

The requirements for appointment or election of a judge. Judicial qualifications vary among the states and from the state to the national level. Most states require that judges be lawyers, except justices of the peace. While most states make no formal requirement for judicial appointment or election, many hold that judges must be of good character. At the federal level, Article III, Section 1 of the United States Constitution states, "The Judges, both of the supreme and inferior Courts, shall hold their Offices during good Behaviour." In selection of judges, the qualifications required differ in accordance with the traditions and needs of the state. While most judges in the United States (federal, state, and local) are generally trained in the law, they are not trained to be judicial officers and need not have courtroom experience before becoming a judge. The qualifications sought in judicial aspirants are character, intelligence, legal knowledge, patience, objectivity, diligence, compassion, dignity, courage, morality, and resoluteness. *See also* JUDGE, 163; JUDICIARY, 169.

Significance   Judicial qualifications should ideally be set to select individuals from the highest level of the legal profession. Unfortunately, this is not always the case. Many state judges are elected and are politicians rather than legal scholars. While the nation's federal and state courts have attracted many brilliant legal minds, the judges in lower courts who actually handle the overwhelming majority of cases may be barely competent or even mediocre. Many municipal judges and justices of the peace do not have a college background, much less a law degree. Small salaries are a major deterrent. Although judges are well paid by public standards, many experienced and able lawyers make several times as much. Obviously, many talented lawyers prefer private practice.

Judicial Removal   (165)

Dismissal of a judge or justice from his or her duties. Judicial removal, in a number of states, provides that the governor may remove a judge upon address by the legislature, which is available in ten states. Judges may be removed in every state and in the federal system by impeachment, which requires a trial and a conviction for a specific offense. Nearly half of the states authorize removal of judges by a majority of both houses of the legislature; in seven states the people may recall a judge by a special election held when a stipulated percentage of the electors or the voters in a previous election request it. In New Jersey, the state supreme court certifies to the governor that a particular judge is believed to be incapacitated; the governor then appoints a three-person commission to inquire and on its recommendation may remove the judge. Where the state supreme court or court of appeals has the power to remove judges, the court is assisted by a judicial commission that investigates complaints against judges. Upon the commission's recommendation, the state's highest court may remove, retire, suspend, or censure a judge. Thirty-one states have commissions, tribunals, or special boards for disciplining or removing judges. *See also* GUBERNATORIAL POWERS, 126; LEGISLATIVE POWERS, 97.

Significance   Judicial removal by the ordinary processes of law is very difficult. Impeachment, the universal means of removing a judge, is a highly politicized procedure. In practice, an impeachable offense is defined by whatever a two-thirds majority of the state senate decides at a given time. Judges in the federal system enjoy life tenure, and it is almost impossible to remove them, although five judges have been removed through impeachment and conviction. The most recent conviction occurred when Harry E. Claiborne, the chief U.S. district judge for Nevada, was found guilty of tax evasion by the United States Senate in October 1986. It is not easy to remove state judges, although several have been convicted and removed by state legislatures. The judges interpret law and may at times have to rule against the interests of the lawmakers and the chief executives. The U.S. judicial system, both federal and state, guarantees some security so that judges can, if necessary, make unpopular decisions.

Judicial Review   (166)

The power of the courts to interpret laws and rules, and to declare a statute or governmental action unconstitutional. The power of judicial review was used by several state courts during the confederation, and was declared to be inherent in the judiciary by the United States Supreme Court in *Marbury v. Madison* (1 Cranch 137: 1803). A state court, for example, may void state laws and provisions of state constitutions by holding them contrary to the United States Constitution. State courts may declare a statute to be unenforceable because it is in conflict with a section of the state constitution. The state courts, like the federal courts, pass upon the constitutionality of an act only when deciding a controversy in a formal case. When a constitution has conflicting provisions, the state supreme court (or court of appeals as is the case in New York, Kentucky, and Maryland) is inevitably requested to determine what the constitution actually means. *See also* STATE SUPREME COURT, 156.

Significance   Judicial review is based on the assumption that the constitution is a contract between the people and their government and functions as the supreme law of the land. Any act contrary to the Constitution, therefore, is null and void. U.S. citizens have accepted the court's power of judicial review as an integral part of the constitutional system. Since Chief Justice John Marshall and the U.S. Supreme Court struck down an act of Congress in 1803 as unconstitutional, more than 110 federal laws and several hundred state laws have been declared unconstitutional by the federal courts. Judicial review is a far-reaching restraint upon legislative and executive powers. Courts are reluctant to use their judicial review power since it may create controversy among the three branches of government, and since constitutions are susceptible to different interpretations. The approach of the Supreme Court is to try to resolve cases by statutory interpretation and other means, invoking the power of judicial review to resolve a case only when absolutely necessary (for example, *Ashwander v. Tennessee Valley Authority* (297 U.S. 288: 1936). State courts generally exercise similar restraint in invoking the power of judicial review.

Judicial Selection (167)

The process of electing or appointing judges to fill vacancies. The judicial selection process differs from state to state and between the state and federal systems. At the federal level all judges are appointed by the president with the consent of the Senate. The following methods are most commonly practiced among the states for selecting judges: (1) all are elected either by partisan ballot, as in Pennsylvania and Texas, or by nonpartisan ballot, as in Michigan and Ohio; (2) all are appointed by the governor with state senate approval, as in New Jersey and Delaware; (3) all are appointed by the governor from a list of candidates considered qualified by a judicial nominating commission and then approved or rejected by the voters, as in Iowa and Nebraska; (4) some are appointed by one of the preceding methods and some are elected, as in Florida and New York; and (5) all are elected by the legislature, as in Connecticut and South Dakota. In addition, the system adopted in Missouri and California in 1940 combines appointment and election. *See also* JUDICIAL QUALIFICATIONS, 164; MISSOURI SYSTEM, 171.

Significance   Judicial selection is relatively simple at the federal level but quite complicated in the states. Supporters of an elective system maintain that, to bring government closer to the people, judges should be elected, and their terms should be short—two or four years. Opponents argue that when skill is desired, the appointment method should be used; voters are ill-equipped to select judges because they cannot evaluate the qualifications of the candidates. In the states the overwhelmingly popular method is that of election. If impartial and nonpartisan behavior of judges is essential to maintain credibility of the judicial system, election of judges weakens the realization of this goal. To become elected, it may be necessary for the candidate to return favors to the voters, thus encouraging corruption in the judiciary. Whatever method of selecting judges is used—nonpartisan election, partisan election, executive appointment, or the Missouri plan—there is little or no difference in results. Most judges remain in office until death or until poor health forces them to retire.

Where judges are elected, they seldom face opposition when running for reelection and are rarely defeated.

Judicial Tenure   (168)

The length of the term of office of judges or justices. Judicial tenure varies among states, within the states, and at the national level. In the highest state courts the longest terms for judges are life in Massachusetts and Rhode Island; age 70 in New Hampshire; 21 years in Pennsylvania; 15 years in Maryland; 14 years in Louisiana and New York; and 6 years in most other states. Judges in the lower state courts serve from 4 to 6 years. At the national level judges hold life tenure. Article III, Section 1 of the United States Constitution guarantees judicial tenure, stating "The Judges, both of the supreme and inferior Courts, shall hold their Offices during good Behaviour." Once appointed, a federal judge who sits on a constitutional court (a federal court established under the provision of the United States Constitution) serves for life unless removed by impeachment. *See also* JUDICIAL REMOVAL, 165.

Significance   Judicial tenure sometimes benefits the incompetent as well as the competent. Some experts argue that keeping the judges in office long is less dangerous than making the judiciary subservient to the whims of the legislative branches of government by giving the judges limited or no tenure. The independence of the judiciary must be protected so that justice can be dispensed fairly. If judges are afraid of losing their jobs, frequently they will be too dependent on the other two branches of government. This will jeopardize the coequality of the three branches of government, which is essential for the smooth functioning of democratic government, such as in the United States. At the national level judges are more independent, while at the state level they must maintain the support of the voters. The life tenure of federal judges is considered by legal scholars a major reason for their sound reputation. However, concern has been expressed because of the role of partisan politics in selecting judges and the difficulty of dealing with those incompetent due to advanced years. In this respect fixed tenure of judges, as in the case of states, works to the satisfaction of all.

Judiciary   (169)

The branch of the government charged with the authoritative interpretation of the constitution and the application of laws. The judiciary encompasses both the court system as well as all judges collectively. In the United States the judiciary is divided into national and state courts. The federal judiciary consists of a Supreme Court, 13 appellate courts, 94 district courts, and several special courts. Each state has a single supreme court (New York, Maryland, Kentucky, and West Virginia call it the court of appeals), circuit courts with varying titles, and several minor ones like justices of the peace. Many states have intermediate courts—county courts, probate courts, and juvenile courts. The national and state judiciary is independent except in cases involving interpretation of the Constitution and federal matters, the United States Supreme Court may review a state court's decision. Jurisdiction is determined by the federal and state constitutions and laws of the country. All federal judges are appointed by the president with Senate approval. In the state system judges are either appointed by the governor or elected by the people. *See also* COURT SYSTEM, 144.

Significance   The judiciary is the branch of government charged with the enforcement of law and settlement of disputes. It defends the rights of individuals as guaranteed by law, and prevents the other two branches of government—legislative and executive—from overstepping their spheres of authority. By guaranteeing coequality of the three branches of government, the judiciary acts as the keel of the ship of state. In addition, the courts may reject legislative and executive decisions and thereby participate in the policy making process of government. The last word in government comes from the judiciary, the ultimate authority in a democracy. The courts resolve problems of public policy differently from the other branches of government; they refrain from addressing policy issues and deal with them only in particular situations and when asked. The judiciary is considered impartial and independent of the legislative and executive branches, so its decisions appear objective and are respected by the people. This gives the judiciary a legitimizing influence in the sociopolitical arena.

Jury   (170)

A body of citizens randomly summoned to sit in judgment on charges brought in either civil or criminal cases. A jury is also called a *petit* or trial jury, which under common law must consist of 12 persons. Juries are of two principal types: grand and *petit* (a grand jury is traditionally composed of 23 persons). Neither the United States Constitution nor the state constitutions require as many persons; it is uncommon for state and federal courts to consist of less than 12 and to decide by less than a unanimous vote. In ordinary usage, the term *jury* signifies those who try issues of fact in civil and criminal cases. The work of the jury is to study evidence presented to them and to decide the innocence or guilt of the accused. The jury does not fix the sentence; the judge does. The jury deliberates in private. In criminal cases the state must prove that the defendant is guilty beyond a reasonable doubt. In some states a criminal defendant may waive a jury trial, and is not in all cases entitled to a jury trial. *See also* GRAND JURY, 161.

Significance   The jury performs a fact-finding as well as a rule-interpreting function. The chief value of a jury is its capacity to temper legal rules with equity by defining what constitutes justice in a particular case. It is a safeguard against bias and corruption. The jury provides civil participation by citizens. There has been much praise and dissatisfaction with juries in civil cases in recent years. Critics have proposed a variety of reforms to improve the calibre of juries. Sometimes the facts are technical and complicated by legal problems. Sometimes expert testimony is presented that members of the jury cannot evaluate. In such cases verdicts are reached by chance. Another criticism is that jurors are prejudiced by race, sex, and vocation. For these reasons, jury use is declining in the United States and is seldom used in Europe, where it originated. Despite these weaknesses, the jury system brings the common sense of the common man of the community to bear upon the judicial process. Jury selection is a time-consuming process, and prospective jurors can be challenged by the prosecutors or the defense for prejudice or incompetence.

Missouri System   (171)

An elaborate plan for selecting state judges that combines both election and appointment. The Missouri system has been in practice in the state of Missouri since 1940, and has been adopted since then in a few other states. Under this system, a commission of lawyers and laymen compiles a list of three persons suitable for judgeships from which the governor makes the final selection. These judges serve until the next election, when the voters have the option of retaining or rejecting them. In Missouri, judges of the supreme court, court of appeals, and certain other courts are appointed by the governor; they serve one year and then seek election on the basis of their record. The judges are the only candidates, and if approved by a majority of the voters serve for six to twelve years, depending on the court. If rejected, the process starts anew. Alabama, Alaska, Kansas, Illinois,

Iowa, and Nebraska have adopted the Missouri system. California has also adopted it, with some variations. The California governor, for example, is not restricted to a list of nominees, but his appointments must be reviewed by a judicial commission consisting of two judges and the attorney general. *See also* JUDICIAL SELECTION, 167.

Significance   The Missouri system is not a panacea for judicial problems, but it is considered an improvement over selecting judges on a partisan basis. It corrects some of the evils of both the election and appointment methods. The Missouri plan is unique in several respects: all vacancies are filled by the governor, who is required to select one of three candidates nominated by a judicial commission consisting of seven members. This nonpartisan commission includes three lawyers chosen by the bar association, three laypersons appointed by the governor, and the chief justice of the state supreme court, who presides. One of the main drawbacks of the Missouri system is that the election process is not competitive. There is no contest, and voters are merely asked to vote yes or no on the question, Shall the judge continue in office? No system of choosing judges is perfect, but to many observers the Missouri system seems best. It retains power in the electorate while freeing judges from campaigning and electioneering. The system has been hailed as a satisfactory compromise by the American Judicature Society.

Plea Bargaining   (172)

The process whereby the prosecutor and the defendant in a criminal case work out a mutually satisfactory disposition subject to court approval. Plea bargaining allows the accused to plead guilty in exchange for the prosecutor's willingness to accept a plea to a less serious charge. The objective of plea bargaining is to bring a recommendation to the judge for a reduced or favorable sentence. It is economic and expedient, saving money and time. Most criminal cases are disposed of by plea bargaining. Defendants prefer the certainty of a shorter sentence through plea bargaining to the risk of an uncertain outcome after trial on a more serious charge. Sometimes the accused plead guilty to win release from jail and probation. Those who receive maximum prison terms may be eligible for parole. Plea bargaining can also be used to induce a suspect to testify against another suspect. *See also* CRIMINAL PROCEDURES, 159.

Significance   Plea bargaining is a trade-off arrangement that is the result of negotiations between the prosecutor and the defense attorney. The process relies upon cooperation among the prosecutor, defense attorney, and judge in summarily disposing of the case. In plea bargaining, the role of the defense attorney is to convince the prosecutor and judge that his or her client deserves a lesser penalty, or that it will be difficult or impossible to gain a conviction for the more serious charge. The procedure is criticized because it places so much discretion in the hands of the prosecutor, who may use the process mainly to build his or her conviction record. The constitutionality of plea bargaining has been upheld by the United States Supreme Court, provided that the accused understands the meaning and consequences of the guilty plea (*Brady v. United States*, 397 U.S. 742: 1970). Opponents of plea bargaining feel that considerable pressure is placed on defendants to plead guilty and that the compromises made are contrary to the principles of fairness and justice. Plea bargaining leads to different punishments for different people for the same crime, providing a challenge to the impartial nature of the judicial system.

Stare Decisis (173)

A judicial term meaning "let the decision stand." *Stare decisis* means that judges' decisions in similar cases in the past will be used to resolve current cases. This Latin term signifies a legal principle in Britain and the United States that courts should apply the precedents established to all later cases with similar facts, unless there is a strong reason not to do so. The doctrine holds that when a court has laid down a principle of law, it will adhere in the future to that principle, regardless of whether the parties and properties are exactly the same. Under *stare decisis* the court's decision forms a binding precedent in the same court or in courts of equal or lower rank in future cases that are of a similar nature. The most important *stare decisis* cases occur at the federal and state supreme court levels. Cases decided by these two courts constitute precedents that override the decisions of lower courts. Cases decided ultimately by the United States Supreme Court take precedence over all other courts. Often the courts refuse to follow an earlier decision because conditions have changed markedly since the earlier case was decided. *See also* COMMON LAW, 143; STATUTE, 112.

Significance   *Stare decisis* is considered an objective technique that helps the courts to achieve credibility and the popular acceptance of decisions. Judicial decisions, in spite of politics and compromise, have occupied a unique position in the U.S. system. They have been generally admired and respected. Court decisions are not general declarations of law; each decision is based on specific facts. If an identical case were to reappear in the court, the same result would likely follow. However, identical cases do not occur that frequently. *Stare decisis* is only applicable in a limited number of cases. The question is, How do judges make law? The simple answer is that they do it by following their own decisions made in previous cases. Previous legal decisions influence present decisions. It should come as no surprise that liberal court majorities tend to render liberal decisions, while conservative majorities establish conservative precedents.

7. Bureaucracy and Civil Service

Administrative Discretion (174)

The ability of an administrator to choose among alternatives and make a decision based upon personal preference. Administrative discretion is a critical source of bureaucratic power. Most administrative decisions permit discretion, slight or major, with profound consequences for individuals, groups, and society. According to classical administrative theory, as propounded by Frank J. Goodnow and Woodrow Wilson, administrative discretion was conceived to extend to questions of means—actual administrative goals were to be determined by political officials. This approach sought to insulate administrative agencies from political pressure. Since these agencies had no policy-making function, they could be left free to render decisions on matters involving organization, personnel, procedures, and evaluation. This view predominated through the late nineteenth and early twentieth centuries, when government bureaucracy was in its infancy. Now, this view no longer holds, as public policy making has, to a large extent, shifted from the legislative to the executive branch, and bureaucratic decisions have become increasingly important, particularly in terms of their policy implications. *See also* ADMINISTRATIVE LAW, 176; BUREAUCRACY, 180; BUREAUCRATIC ORGANIZATION, 183; HIERARCHY, 190.

Significance Administrative discretion permits administrators to shape both decisions and key policy questions. Even routine decisions, which may seem unimportant, have profound consequences for the affected parties (e.g., an adverse finding by a licensing board or the awarding of a government contract). These decisions can and do shape the futures of individuals, private organizations, and local communities. In most cases, administrative decisions are subject to review and are governed by constitutional and statutory requirements. In the case of major policy-making decisions, administrative discretion can pose important social, political, and economic consequences, both national and international. Clearly, administrative discretion is not limitless; agency actions are influenced and controlled by sundry political actors (e.g., elected officials, judges, interest groups). Still, agencies possess vast discretionary authority. In exercising their authority, they may either extend or withhold benefits, exact or refrain from imposing penalties. However, administrative discretion is not altogether negative. If that were the case, it would either be eliminated or severely curtailed. When exercised responsibly, it can promote the general welfare and safeguard the public interest (e.g., public health inspections, safety regulations, consumer protection). Modern-day government could not function without the flexibility and choice that are inherent in administrative discretion.

Administrative Hearing   (175)

Adjudication by an administrative or regulatory agency of possible legal violations or of rules or regulations within its jurisdiction. Administrative hearings are also convened to allow interested parties to express their views on proposed rules and regulations prior to their adoption. These proceedings may be called by the agency itself or by the injured party. Ideally, administrative hearings closely resemble court proceedings, although they are less formal. Administrative hearings were established by the Administrative Procedure Act of 1946, which defines and delineates their authority. These hearings result in the issuance of administrative orders, which possess the force of law. Aggrieved parties may, if they wish, appeal these directives to the courts. In such cases, the courts will ostensibly limit themselves to reviewing the conduct of the hearings and the degree to which the order conforms to the agency's finding. In the case of proposed rules, administrative hearings permit interested parties to express their opinions and play a salient role in shaping the content and character of the rule. *See also* ADMINISTRATIVE DISCRETION, 174; ADMINISTRATIVE LAW, 176; ADMINISTRATIVE LAW JUDGE, 177.

Significance   Administrative hearings are an expression of the democratic process. If conducted fairly, they serve an important public good. For example, they may enable the hearing officer to arrive at a conclusion more expeditiously and inexpensively than would be possible in a court of law. This is due to the fact that cross-examination and formal rules of evidence are not required. Thus, the administrative hearing may, in certain cases, be preferable to an actual court trial. On the other hand, these hearings pose several disadvantages, chief of which is the lack of formal legal safeguards for the person under investigation. There have been cases, for instance, where the accused's attorney was denied access to pertinent records and/or was physically prevented from pleading his or her client's case. Moreover, these proceedings permit wide administrative discretion. Obviously, the system is not well served when the agency functions as both prosecutor and judge. Safeguards must be built into it to prevent the abuse of law and irresponsible administrative action. The integrity of the process depends upon principled individuals, codified rules and procedures, the protection of procedural rights, and a commitment to fairness and truth.

Administrative Law (176)

That branch of law that establishes government agencies, delineates their procedural methods, and defines their powers of judicial review. Administrative law also describes administrative rules and regulations, encompassing such areas as operating rules, rate making, individual and business rights, and the relevant powers of the courts. Administrative law is closely related to constitutional law, which concerns the powers and functioning of the government, as well as the protection of citizen and private rights as expressed in state constitutions and in the United States Constitution. Administrative law has steadily increased in influence, as administrative agencies have come to play a larger role in the decision-making process. Increasingly, administrators have wielded more and more power, owing to their broad discretion. With this discretion has come the need to establish legal guidelines and to operate within their parameters. *See also* ADMINISTRATIVE HEARING, 175; ADMINISTRATIVE LAW JUDGE, 177.

Significance Administrative law is widely used to regulate vital areas of economic and social life. Administrative agencies render countless decisions that have a major impact upon individual and group conduct. This has necessitated the creation of a body of law to oversee the actions and decisions of government agencies, so as to safeguard the rights of persons affected by their rules and regulations. Many individuals fail to appreciate the importance and implications of administrative decision making. For example, administrative agencies make many more substantive decisions than do the courts. Moreover, a single agency may have as many employees as an entire judicial establishment. Finally, promulgating rules and formulating decisions is central to an agency's mission and cannot be delegated to other institutions without inviting severe repercussions. In most cases, an agency is in the best position to determine its operating procedure. Still, the public must be protected from administrative policies that threaten their basic constitutional rights. Administrative law seeks to protect the public interest when it cannot be reasonably protected by other institutions of government. The system, however, is far from perfect. For example, many administrative judges are former administrators, which poses a potential conflict of interest. In addition, it is difficult for the average citizen to secure relief from an unfair administrative act. It is also difficult to win a judgment against an administrator, particularly when an action does not cause economic or personal injury (e.g., delay or rudeness). Finally, administrative law represents a negative check on the bureaucracy. It occurs after the fact, not before. As a result, it can only remedy injustices or squelch actions; only rarely can it compel administrative action.

Administrative Law Judge   (177)

An individual assigned to hear and decide cases concerning ordinary administration, as well as important regulatory matters. Administrative law judges (called "hearing examiners" until 1978) were a creation of the Administrative Procedure Act of 1946. They are part of a central pool, assigned specific cases, and are not associated with the programs they serve. They are independently supervised and may take as long as they wish to decide a case. Administrative law judges are burdened by a steep work load, long hours, insufficient staff, and escalating demands. Originally, they heard cases only in areas that were mired in appeals (e.g., public utility regulation). However, this changed with the passage of the Administrative Procedure Act. Those charged with implementing the act concluded that administrative law judges should be made available to virtually every government agency, which expanded the legal establishment and raised a plethora of new administrative concerns. See also ADMINISTRATIVE DISCRETION, 174; ADMINISTRATIVE HEARING, 175; ADMINISTRATIVE LAW, 176.

Significance   Administrative law judges were created to blunt the pre-1946 concern that the regulatory agencies were improperly serving as both the accuser and judge of those charged with rule violations. By creating judges with increased independence, Congress attempted to remedy the major shortcomings of the administrative adjudication of private rights. The contention was that such independence would strengthen the integrity of the process and protect individuals and groups from unwarranted discretion and possible conflicts of interest. According to the act, judges' decisions are presented to agency heads who have 30 days to reverse or alter the recommendations. If no appeal is made, the decision stands. In practice, this poses numerous problems for administrators, who, in many cases, are simply too busy to study the judges' opinions. Other administrators fear antagonizing the judges by challenging their decisions. Still other administrators believe that they will invite attention and criticism if they oppose the judges' rulings, knowing that these judges enjoy widespread institutional and political support, and that there is little if anything that can be done to remove them. In recent years, many experts have advocated full independence for administrative law judges, much to the consternation of administrators, who resent their intrusion into the administrative process.

Administrative Reorganization (178)

Agency reforms calculated to promote accountability, responsibility, productivity, and economy. Administrative reorganization is a broadly based concept. Attempts to reform government agencies have numerous implications—personal, political, institutional, and societal. Typically, administrative reorganization is proposed to (1) address substantive changes in an agency's mission or function; (2) reflect major technological developments, both within and outside the agency; (3) reflect changing needs in personnel; and (4) embody salient political and social changes in an agency's importance. In some cases, administrative reorganization is profound; that is, it dramatically alters the nature and structure of the agency. In other cases, it simply involves a cosmetic change, namely, the reassignment of personnel and/or the alteration of job titles. *See also* BUREAUCRACY, 180; BUREAUCRATIC INERTIA, 182; BUREAUCRATIC ORGANIZATIONS, 183.

Significance Administrative reorganization is, in its most serious application, pivotal to the future of an agency. Despite its apparent justification, administrators are likely to face a difficult battle, as reorganization involves sundry human considerations, chief of which are anxiety, insecurity, and distrust. Instinctively, most people fear the unknown—particularly when change threatens to alter a system that they both know and accept. In addition, many reorganization plans are poorly conceived and improperly communicated to agency personnel. This, in turn, triggers numerous problems: anger, frustration, defensiveness, and antagonism. In such cases, organizational warfare often ensues, with disastrous personal and institutional consequences. Moreover, administrative reorganization is, by definition, a political decision, one that involves bargaining, negotiation, and compromise. Reorganization plans rarely, if ever, survive in their natal form; they are subject to review, reappraisal, and redefinition. Clearly, the political system rewards incremental change—as opposed to major systemic change—and this results in the alteration of many reorganization plans. Finally, administrative reorganization, in and of itself, is rarely, if ever, a panacea. In most cases, it promises far more than it delivers. In the end, the chief beneficiaries are, with few exceptions, top-level administrators, who succeed in reshaping the agency to reflect their own personal and political agendas. Therefore, it should be no surprise that most reorganization plans are instituted by administrators themselves. These plans serve to centralize decision making in their offices, reinforce their power and authority, and project the impression that they are in command, even though reorganization itself may do little, if anything, to influence major policy outcomes.

Affirmative Action   **(179)**
The principle that preferential treatment should be granted to racial minorities and women in public employment to remedy the effects of past discrimination. Affirmative action has also been interpreted to apply to religious minorities and, in certain cases, to the elderly and handicapped. According to this principle, state and local governments that receive federal funds must initiate specific programs to increase the number of minorities and women in government positions. Studies reveal that blacks are generally well represented in state and local government, although they are clearly underrepresented at the higher levels. On the other hand, women are underrepresented throughout state and local government, particularly at the highest echelons. In addition to concern over past discrimination, many in the United States believe that bureaucracy should accurately reflect the diverse makeup of the population. *See also* CIVIL SERVICE, 184; MERIT SYSTEM, 193; PATRONAGE, 194.

Significance   Affirmative action embodies the belief that government should do more than simply eliminate discrimination—that it must initiate measures that recognize the importance of preferential or compensatory treatment for those who have historically been the victims of unequal treatment. Affirmative action programs originated with the federal government and date back to 1967, when the U.S. Office of Federal Contract Compliance required contractors bidding on federal projects to submit affirmative action plans. Federal policy has dictated the response of state and local governments, which depend, to a large extent, on federal funds. Affirmative action raises many unanswered questions—political, ethical, and legal. Some critics argue, for example, that quotas that grant preference to blacks violate the equal protection clause of the Fourteenth Amendment. In practice, the federal government eschews quotas as a means of measuring progress in this area, preferring instead to focus on the number of minorities hired, promoted, or admitted. Moreover, opponents argue that affirmative action favors minorities at the expense of better-qualified majority applicants, and that many state and local agencies have deemphasized traditional qualifications (e.g., test scores, grades, experience) to hire minorities, for fear that to do otherwise could jeopardize continued federal assistance. Advocates of affirmative action dismiss the argument of "reverse discrimination," insisting that the nation must make tangible sacrifices in order to realize a color-blind society. It is vital, they contend, that blacks and other minorities be granted a proportional share of government jobs; to do otherwise, they maintain, would be to reinforce the inequalities that presently exist. In the now-famous case of *Regents of the University of California v. Bakke* (438 U.S. 265: 1978), the United States Supreme Court held that race and ethnic factors may be considered in selecting applicants, but that specified quotas violate the equal protection clause. In its decision, the Court struck down racial "quotas," but approved the permissibility of racial "goals." Clearly, the issue remains unsettled, and litigation is likely to proceed unabated.

Bureaucracy (180)

An administrative system, charged with program development, implementation, and enforcement, that is characterized by specialization of functions, adherence to rules, and hierarchy of authority. *Bureaucracy* is a vague term, one with both positive and negative connotations. It is frequently employed to describe organizations plagued by runaway staff growth, unnecessary red tape, purposelesss routine, and resistance to change. In most cases, however, "the bureaucracy" is used to describe the administrative or executive branch of government. Bureaucracies are the means by which state and local governments translate government policy into concrete programs and services by performing the day-to-day operations of government. In the process, they develop a detailed knowledge of programs and delivery systems. For a bureaucracy to function properly, it must be able to take a complex task and break it down into manageable units. To achieve this objective, it must develop a means to organize and coordinate the various subunits. This necessitates the establishment of a pyramidal organizational structure—one that provides clear lines of authority and responsibility. *See also* BUREAUCRAT, 181; BUREAUCRATIC ORGANIZATIONS, 183; CIVIL SERVICE, 184.

Significance   The bureaucracy enjoys substantial political clout, and is often referred to as the fourth branch of government. Through their daily contact with lay citizens and organizations, agency bureaucrats develop a clientele—individuals and groups who interact with and are served by the agency. This relationship is mutually beneficial; individuals and groups derive tangible benefits from the agency, while the agency derives political influence and support from its clientele. Still, bureaucracies are not immune to criticisms or attack. Regardless of their standing with their clientele, they must actively court the backing of the governor and the state legislature. Indeed, their very existence is dependent upon legislative funding, and since the governor plays a pivotal role in the budgetary process, his or her support is also critical. Although bureaucracies enjoy considerable latitude, their discretion is limited. To survive, they must function without political incident, evidence expertise, employ sound management, and maintain the support of their clientele. On the other hand, they possess considerable political and personnel resources, owing to bureaucratic inertia and control of information. State and local bureaucracies have grown at a rapid rate since World War II. The complexity of life, increased demands on government, competition for scarce dollars, the technological revolution, and rising expectations have all contributed to the power and influence of the bureaucracy.

Bureaucrat   (181)

An individual who staffs a government agency, promulgates policy, executes assignments, and implements programs. Bureaucrats vary in background and attributes, skills and talents, attitudes and values, and influence and authority. The term *bureaucrat* is neither positive nor negative; it simply describes those who occupy agency posts. Research reveals that top-level bureaucrats represent diverse geographical backgrounds, possess considerable formal education, and are well trained in their formal specialties. Many bureaucrats enter government service upon completion of their education and develop subject expertise once employed. A large number who enter the top rungs are recruited from business, while a smaller number hail from academia. Most bureaucrats—particularly those at the higher echelons—are white males, typically in their late forties. *See also* BUREAUCRACY, 180; BUREAUCRATIC ORGANIZATIONS, 183.

Significance   Bureaucrats, argue political scientists Randall B. Ripley and Grace A. Franklin, share certain common beliefs and values.[1] They tend to (1) accept the ideological orientation of their agency; (2) embrace the philosophy of the free enterprise system; (3) support open access to bureaucratic decision making; (4) hold liberal beliefs about democracy and public policy; (5) endorse slightly more liberal stands on issues than the average U.S. citizen; and (6) oppose sweeping changes in the bureaucratic system. Despite these similarities, bureaucrats differ in terms of behavior. They also possess different values, motives, and goals. According to Ripley and Franklin, bureaucrats fall into four major categories: careerists, politicians, professionals, and missionaries.[2] Careerists identify their careers and benefits with the agency that employs them, do not envisage intraagency moves, and support their agency and its institutional role. Politicians expect to move up the career ladder—to elective or appointive office—and cultivate sundry sources outside the agency. Professionals seek job satisfaction, peer approval, appropriate responsibilities, and career development. Missionaries support social change, advance specific policies, and work for favored policy outcomes. The bureaucracy is composed, in large part, of careerists, while missionaries are extremely rare. Politicians and professionals come and go, depending upon conditions and circumstances within the government and agency, and exert only short-term influence.

Bureaucratic Inertia   (182)

The tendency of administrative agencies to resist change and reinforce the status quo. Bureaucratic inertia is a relatively new phenomenon. Beginning in the 1930s, with President Franklin D. Roosevelt's New Deal, bureaucracy played a major role in implementing social programs and served as an instrument of radical social change. At the time, bureaucracy was viewed as a friend of the poor and powerless and an enemy of big business and special interests. This, in turn, led conservatives to attack bureaucracy as a symbol of U.S. liberalism. In recent years, however, public perceptions have changed markedly. Today, liberal reformers question bureaucracy's capacity to address key social problems in an imaginative and creative manner. In their view, these agencies have failed to develop and implement policy in such vital areas as health care, education, and social welfare. Instead, they argue, bureaucracy has joined forces with powerful vested interests to prevent social change. *See also* BUREAUCRACY, 180; BUREAUCRAT, 181; BUREAUCRATIC ORGANIZATIONS, 183.

Significance   Bureaucratic inertia predominates at the federal as well as state and local levels. In many cases, agencies serve as an anchor, and not as a forward force, in terms of policy innovation. To be fair, bureaucracy has been attacked by conservatives as well as liberals. Conservatives argue that agencies often exceed their authority, while liberals charge that they have failed to live up to their responsibilities. However, both sides agree that bureaucracy is often unimaginative, reluctant to adopt new ideas, and slow to reject policies that have clearly failed. Many proposals have been advanced to combat the ills of bureaucratic inertia. Some experts contend that this is best accomplished by assigning innovative programs to new agencies, which are less tied to the past and are more willing to experiment with new approaches. Others contend that the answer lies in instituting a major change in the jurisdiction or resources of existing agencies. Still others maintain that the key is to encourage agencies to contract with organizations outside of government to initiate studies and propose policy alternatives. Bureaucratic inertia is particularly visible when agencies fail to cope imaginatively and aggressively with problems high on the list of public priorities. This is caused, in part, by bureaucracy's tendency to ignore problems, owing to a seemingly limitless capacity for nondecision. Moreover, agencies are prone to shift their attention when past policies have outlived their usefulness and bear little relationship to current realities. Bureaucracy also experiences difficulty in recognizing and correcting past mistakes, for fear that public admission may be institutionally dangerous. Finally, bureaucratic inertia may simply reflect the slowness inherent in most large organizations and the inability to marshal a new consensus.

Bureaucratic Organizations   (183)

The arrangement and assignment of persons to perform tasks, provide services, and solve problems in the most effective and efficient manner possible. Bureaucratic organizations achieve these objectives by developing structures, rules, procedures, and policies based upon the purpose(s) for which they are established. According to public administrator Phillip E. Present, organizations are created

(1) to execute a specific task; (2) to service certain societal groups; (3) to serve a particular geographic location; (4) to reward an individual or promote his or her objectives; (5) to implement requested policies or programs; (6) to create organizational spin-offs; and (7) to consolidate existing agencies into a single new one.[3] For an organization to function effectively, its members must have a clear understanding and appreciation of the organization's mission. If this is lacking, the organization will find it difficult to maintain its independence, secure adequate funding, implement program objectives, and assess its performance. *See also* ADMINISTRATIVE REORGANIZATION, 178; BUREAUCRACY, 180; CIVIL SERVICE, 184.

Significance   Bureaucratic organizations face numerous internal and external problems. "The organization exists, thrives, and survives," notes Saul Gellerman, in his book *The Management of Human Resources*, "by harnessing the talents of individuals. Its internal problem is to do so without hobbling those talents or turning them against itself."[4] An organization's success ultimately depends upon individuals; without them, it could not exist. On the other hand, organizations provide employment and rewards, both psychological and material, which are dependent upon the organization. Thus, the relationship is a reciprocal one. The administrator must recognize and foster this relationship. To do so, he or she must encourage and reward excellence—must identify and develop subordinates who possess talent, ingenuity, drive, and dedication. In addition to internal challenges, bureaucratic organizations face countless external challenges. To survive and prosper, the administrator must recognize that the organization is, in a real sense, a political animal. It must operate in a political world, composed of political actors, whose goals, motivations, and actions may, at times, conflict with those of the organization. It must seek to accommodate those actors, and their wishes, or face numerous assaults upon its independence, authority, and resources. Moreover, it must implement public policy, even when it may question the validity of that policy. In the end, its future is dependent upon pleasing those individuals and groups who are in a position to reward or punish its actions. This requires understanding, sensitivity, imagination, and cooperation. A bureaucratic organization is, in short, a political institution.

Civil Service   (184)
A system of government hiring in which individuals are selected on the basis of objective qualifications and performance, and enjoy

protection from political interference. Civil service was introduced in New York in 1883 and Massachusetts in 1884. By 1920, similar legislation was approved in eight other states (Illinois, Colorado, Ohio, California, Maryland, Connecticut, Wisconsin, and New Jersey). Eventually, all states and many local units enacted some form of civil service system. Civil service was instituted to eliminate such practices as nepotism and patronage, which award government jobs on the basis of family connections and political loyalty. Under the patronage system, individual qualifications played little, if any, role in government hiring practices, and those appointed to bureaucratic posts were required to perform a variety of favors (e.g., campaign contributions, electioneering, political activity) to maintain their positions. Civil service seeks to ensure that government employees possess superior qualifications and that, once hired, they are immune to political pressure. Under civil service, all government positions are classified on the basis of the kinds and difficulty of skills required. Once the job is classified, the successful applicant must demonstrate competence for the position. In most states, hiring officers are presented with the names of the top three candidates, from which they are free to select any one of the individuals (sometimes referred to as the "rule of three"). After holding the position for a specified period—usually three to five years—the civil servant is granted tenure (a form of government job protection). Thereafter, the person cannot be fired unless the state can prove "cause" (justifiable reason, in a hearing before the civil service commission). Hiring and firing rules are prescribed by the state, and vary from state to state. There are marked differences in these laws, both in terms of coverage and protection. *See also* AFFIRMATIVE ACTION, 179; MERIT SYSTEM, 193; PATRONAGE, 194.

Significance   Civil service has had a major impact on state government. In one study, George J. Gordon concludes that civil service has (1) created an experienced managerial class in policy positions; (2) protected individuals from unjust firings; (3) strengthened bureaucratic knowledge and experience in technical and program areas; and (4) provided continuity in state government.[5] More specifically, civil service has reduced executive control over agency personnel, safeguarded employees from capricious administrators, encouraged loyalty to the state (as opposed to agency heads or politicians), professionalized the bureaucracy, and protected the rights of employees. On the other hand, civil service has created its own set of problems. Its rigidity in terms of recruitment, qualifications, and remuneration often prevents administrators from attracting highly competent people to government. Moreover, civil service rules make it difficult for administrators to remove incompetent individuals or to reward truly outstanding ones. It also limits their ability to compel cooperation and maximum performance from agency personnel. As a result, many reformers have lobbied state legislatures to return power over personnel administration to the governor.

Clientele Agency (185)

A governmental unit established to assist or regulate an interest group. Clientele agencies seek to promote their client's interest, be it economic or social. Political scientist Joseph LaPalombara argues that a clientele relationship is said to exist when "an interest group, for whatever reasons, succeeds in becoming in the eyes of a given administrative agency, the natural expression and representative of a given social sector which, in turn, constitutes the natural target or reference point for the activity of the administrative agency."[6] In a clientele relationship, the administrative agency accepts the legitimacy of one interest group to the exclusion of others. Relationships of this kind are extremely common in bureaucratic organizations. Clientele agencies tend to accept a single interest group as the legitimate representative in a given area and often give little attention to other groups that may wish to present pertinent information. Although an agency may be required to consider the views of a wide range of interest groups, a clientele relationship makes it unlikely that it will give serious attention to other competing interest groups. *See also* ADMINISTRATIVE DISCRETION, 174; INTEREST GROUP LIBERALISM, 191; WHISTLE BLOWING, 197.

Significance   A clientele agency may, if it is not careful, make decisions that reflect a biased view of the issue in question. Clearly, a clientele relationship tends to slant the sources of information in a way that supports the initial policy biases of the agency. Although such a relationship may enhance the influence of a particular interest group, it is likely to reduce the overall influence of interest groups on key issues. The agency's lack of legitimacy will, in the end, prejudice the recommendations of the organization and reduce their chances of adoption. Moreover, other interest groups will be forced to devote a larger percentage of their resources to gaining access, instead of providing needed information. Most important, clientele relationships threaten the public interest and encourage apathy and alienation. At its worst, this relationship will lead the agency to become dependent upon the interest group for information, advice, and support; in some cases, it will even clear major decisions with the interest group prior to their adoption. On the other hand, the favored interest group will, because of its dependence, support agency decisions even when they are unwise, for fear that it will lose access. In the end, argues B. Guy Peters, the clientele relationship may subvert the public interest; instead of regulating the activities of these interest groups, the agency may actually promote the interests of the regulated.[7]

Collective Bargaining   (186)

Negotiations between the state and government personnel, usually represented by a union, concerning the terms and conditions of employment. Collective bargaining differs markedly from negotiation between an employer and an individual employee. Under collective bargaining, employers and workers are required to confer in "good faith" and to mutually approve a written contract that specifies the agreed-upon terms. Collective bargaining presupposes, in most cases, that government employees belong to labor unions (organizations of workers that endeavor to improve salary and working conditions through collective bargaining and political action). The right of U.S. workers to unionize and bargain collectively through their representatives dates back to 1935, and has since been official union policy. Union membership has steadily escalated at the state and local levels over the last two decades. Today, 38 percent of state personnel and 52 percent of local government employees belong to unions. Unions are particularly favored by teachers, police, clerical workers, and hospital staff. Most states that boast large union membership have enacted collective bargaining laws. States with the highest percentage of union membership include New York, Rhode Island, Connecticut, Massachusetts, and Hawaii. The largest public employee union is the American Federation of State, County, and Municipal Employees (AFSCME). *See also* CIVIL SERVICE, 184; MERIT SYSTEM, 193; PATRONAGE, 194.

Significance   Collective bargaining is a direct outgrowth of the movement toward public-sector unionization. Presently, state and local governments are more unionized than the private sector. This movement has gained momentum as government workers have fallen behind in salary and fringe benefits. Central to the collective bargaining process is the use of the strike. Since 1970, the number of strikes and work stoppages has increased dramatically at the state and local levels. Today, the right of at least some public-sector employees to strike is recognized in ten states (Alaska, California, Hawaii, Minnesota, Montana, Ohio, Oregon, Pennsylvania, Vermont, and Wisconsin). Collective bargaining typically includes mediation and fact finding, and occasionally, arbitration. Mediation involves a third party who attempts to settle the disagreement by reaching a mutually acceptable compromise. Fact finding ensues when mediation fails. Here, a neutral fact finder convenes quasi-judicial hearings and proposes recommendations to the two parties. When the two sides agree to arbitration, a third party is empowered to render a binding decision, in which both sides may be forced to accept concessions. A variation of arbitration called final arbitration permits the arbiter to choose the final offer of one of the two sides. The availability of this process usually encourages both sides to reach agreement out of fear that the arbitrator may select the other's final offer. Unionists insist that collective bargaining is necessary to protect their interests; without it, they argue, they would be unable to negotiate equally and effectively with state and local governments. On the other hand, public employers contend that collective bargaining and, for that matter, unions, are unnecessary. They insist that unions frequently ignore the public interest and that politicians often pander to the unions to court their support. This has encouraged some unions, they maintain, to make unreasonable demands and/or to strike when their demands are not met, often with disastrous consequences.

Decentralization (187)

An administrative concept applied by large agencies in which authority is assigned to lower levels of the organization. Decentralization came into prominence in the mid-1960s, in response to the excesses of centralization (the concentration of decision-making authority at the highest levels of administration). It reflected public dissatisfaction with the central agencies' lack of ability to resolve management, supervisory, and policy dilemmas. Moreover, centralization appeared to embody the indifference of the modern technological world and its de-emphasis of basic human values. Finally, the social eruptions of the 1960s (e.g., the race riots) seemed to underscore the inability of the system to effect social change. In practice, decentralization is most often accomplished through field-service operation or the delegation of tasks through specialization. *See also* ADMINISTRATIVE REORGANIZATION, 178; DELEGATION OF AUTHORITY, 188; HIERARCHY, 190; LINE AND STAFF, 192.

Significance   Decentralization allows meaningful participation by subordinates in the decision-making process and permits local units to shape public policy to reflect their unique circumstances. Clearly, no one administrator can make all decisions that affect his or her agency, although most major decisions are and probably should be made by high-level officials. Agencies differ markedly in the extent to which authority is centralized or decentralized. Furthermore, decentralization may take many different forms, among them: (1) the subordinate may be able to make a decision without securing supervisorial approval; (2) the subordinate may be required to inform the supervisor of the specific action; (3) the subordinate may be forced to notify the supervisor and delay action until approval is granted; (4) the subordinate may list various alternatives and propose one or more to the supervisor; and (5) the subordinate may provide all of the pertinent information to the supervisor, while the latter will make the final decision. In sum, decentralization varies from agency to agency, situation to situation, person to person. The issue is not whether centralization or decentralization is good or bad, but which of the two approaches will work best in a specific setting, under specific conditions, and for a specific goal. Both centralization and decentralization possess strengths and weaknesses; centralization promotes control and uniformity at the expense of time and flexibility, while decentralization's strengths and weaknesses are exactly the opposite. In selecting the correct approach, the administrator must ask which tasks must be performed and what specific benefits and costs will result from either centralization and decentralization.

Delegation of Authority   (188)

The assignment of decision-making responsibility and operating work to subordinates. Delegation of authority is a mark of an effective administrator. A manager who squanders precious time by performing nonessential tasks better left to underlings projects a lack of trust in their abilities to perform agency tasks—a move certain to undermine morale. Delegation of authority promotes organizational accountability, responsibility, and coordination. In assigning operating work, the administrator must attempt to balance authority and responsibility. Obviously, if a subordinate is granted an additional responsibility, he or she must also be granted the authority necessary to its accomplishment. In reality, many managers fail to delegate sufficient authority to execute the additional responsibilities. This produces an authority gap, which can be attributed, in large part, to (1) constraints on managerial control and coordination; (2) a lack of administrative influence over underlings; and (3) excessive centralization of staff functions. *See also* DEPARTMENT HEAD, 189; HIERARCHY, 190; LINE AND STAFF, 192; SPAN OF CONTROL, 195.

Significance   Delegation of authority depends, in large measure, on administrative self-confidence. The confident manager will willingly cede some of his or her authority to trusted subordinates. The effective administrator understands both the risks and benefits of delegation of authority. When both the manager and subordinate share such confidence, the agency will, in most cases, experience increased productivity, efficiency, and morale—which is clearly in the best interest of all concerned. In the process, delegation of authority will foster heightened initiative, respect, and loyalty to superiors. In addition, an administrator is less likely to be surrounded by overly obedient subordinates who blindly endorse his or her every action. An overbearing manager will encourage underlings who seek approval and recognition, while discouraging those who possess creativity and independence. Sadly, some administrators eschew delegation of authority, for fear that their subordinates will garner approval and praise. Unfortunately, these managers fail to appreciate that their success is determined, in large measure, by their skill at identifying and cultivating talent. In the end, these administrators deny themselves the assistance they so earnestly require, so that they can better focus their energies on more important tasks.

Department Head   (189)

Executes gubernatorial orders, implements legislative mandates, and oversees agency operations. Department heads are directly assisted by a team of non–civil service administrators, appointed by the department head or the governor. Together, they administer the affairs of the department, a pivotal administrative unit with broad responsibilities, which is subdivided into bureaus, divisions, sections, and other units. Department heads tend to be male, white, Protestant, and relatively young, typically under 50. They belong to the upper middle class and hold a college degree or have attended college. Over one-half are appointed by the governor, with the remainder being civil service employees. Generally, their salaries lag behind those in comparable positions in the private sector. *See also* ADMINISTRATIVE DISCRETION, 174; DELEGATION OF AUTHORITY, 188; LINE AND STAFF, 192; SPAN OF CONTROL, 195.

Significance   Department heads play a central role in shaping the character and direction of the agencies they administer. Despite their influence, department heads face numerous problems. Since a majority are appointed by the governor, they often find it difficult to supervise middle-level managers, who are career civil servants, possess considerable technical expertise, know far more about the department, and are likely to maintain their positions after the department head has left the agency (since the latter's tenure is tied to the governor's term in office). Moreover, department heads have few formal powers with which to exact cooperation and compliance. Since they lack authority and autonomy, department heads must lead by example. To do so, they must demonstrate subject-matter competence, management abilities, interpersonal skills, fairness and objectivity, political prowess, and dedication and drive. In addition, the department head must cultivate a close relationship with the governor, who can solidify the administrator's position. In this regard, the appearance of gubernatorial support can strengthen the department head's hand in managing the agency and supervising personnel. The department head must also address several major institutional obstacles, among them, (1) limited influence in the budget process; (2) inadequate resources and staff; (3) minimal power and discretion; (4) an unmanageable work load; (5) ongoing political pressure; (6) interest group opposition; (7) intraagency rivalry; and (8) media hostility. Ultimately, success depends upon myriad factors, chief of which is the recognition that the position itself is laden with contradictions. Although the job promises influence and authority, it is bounded by numerous limits and constraints. To succeed, department heads must exercise their prerogatives with intelligence and sensitivity, so as to improve performance, increase morale, prevent stagnation, and avoid reprisals.

Hierarchy   (190)

A principle of administrative organization in which each office and officeholder possess authority over those directly below them, and so on down to the lowest echelons of the structure. Hierarchies derive from the inability of administrators to supervise effectively the large number of subordinates for whom they are personally responsible. Hierarchy is a salient characteristic of bureaucratic organizations. However, the tendency to distribute authority on the basis of hierarchical rank has become less pronounced in recent years, as many organizations have permitted subordinates to make important administrative decisions—even when they are opposed by agency heads. In some cases, this can be attributed to their political influence; that is, subordinates are frequently able to garner sufficient support to override the decisions of their superiors. Still, hierarchy plays a prominent role in government agencies, owing to the complexity of decision making and the need for coordination of effort. Goals cannot be achieved, in most cases, unless decision-making authority is delegated to the top bureaucratic ranks. *See also* BUREAUCRATIC ORGANIZATIONS, 183; DECENTRALIZATIONS, 187; DELEGATION OF AUTHORITY, 188; LINE AND STAFF, 192.

Significance   Hierarchy serves sundry organizational purposes, including (1) it precludes contradictory objectives; (2) it minimizes duplication of effort; (3) it conserves personnel; (4) it promotes economy; (5) it spurs unity; (6) it stimulates communication; and (7) it fosters consensus. Hierarchy is supported by classical administrative theory, as well as modern political realities. Indeed, most reform proposals call for an increase in hierarchical authority and the elimination of multiple units with jurisdiction in overlapping areas. Hierarchy poses major implications for the policy process. It increases the likelihood that key policy decisions will be developed in a consistent and rational manner. In addition, hierarchy decreases the possibility of policy stalemate. It serves to eliminate logjams and prevent policy clashes at all levels of decision making. Thus, the need for negotiating and bargaining is greatly reduced. On the other hand, hierarchy poses several major problems. First, it does not necessarily guarantee rational calculation of policy alternatives. In some cases, the inequality of power gives added weight to the recommendations of top administrators—not because they are correct, but because of their advocates' status and position. Second, many experts question whether hierarchy is consistent with democratic theory—whether it permits full and candid discussion of policy options. Regardless of its defects, hierarchy predominates in most organizations. The challenge is to evolve ways of dealing with the lack of innovation and freedom of debate hierarchy may impose.

Interest Group Liberalism   (191)

A popularly accepted view of U.S. government in which rival interest groups compete for power and access. Interest group liberalism is predicated on the assumption that the policy agenda should be accessible to all organized interest groups, without judgment of their respective positions and claims. Interest group liberalism is based on the propositions that (1) organized interest groups are homogeneous and easy to define; (2) organized interests develop from every sector of society and accurately represent most of those sectors; and (3) government's responsibility is to promote interest group access and acknowledge the validity of the agreements they reach. Interest group liberalism embodies the competitive nature of the United States, as exemplified by its frontier spirit, Protestant ethic, and capitalistic philosophy. *See also* ADMINISTRATIVE DISCRETION, 174; CLIENTELE AGENCY, 185; WHISTLE BLOWING, 197.

Significance   Interest group liberalism is viewed by some scholars as the nation's official, reigning philosophy. As such, it exerts enormous influence and provides the standard by which most policy proposals are judged. Despite its acceptance, many respected authorities—most notably, Theodore J. Lowi, William L. Morrow, Grant McConnell, and Henry Kariel—believe that interest group liberalism is severely flawed. It has led, in the words of Morrow, "to the marriage of agency and group policy missions."[8] Interest group liberalism has fostered increased administrative discretion, which has, in turn, dramatically increased the power of government agencies. In the process, they have become ever more susceptible to interest group pressure. This, contend its detractors, has made it difficult, if not impossible, to effect change. According to Morrow, "Instead of counterbalancing the biases of the pressure system, groups are nourished by agencies that naturally reflect the values of such forces in any policy recommendations made to the legislature."[9] In short, interest group liberalism has, its critics maintain, encouraged corruption, alienation, and stagnation. Interest group liberalism, they argue, abets administrative discretion, as well as the tendency of agencies to delegate power and responsibility to major interest groups (e.g., the Alabama State Legislature granted the Alabama Medical Association the right to license doctors in that state). Given this situation, it is highly unlikely, insist opponents of interest group liberalism, that these agencies will give serious consideration to proposals that challenge the interests of these groups.

Line and Staff   **(192)**
An administrative concept that distinguishes agency work on the basis of whether it performs an operating or a supportive mission. Line agencies administer the implementation of policy and advise their political superiors on major policies. These agencies reflect the political biases of the administration and support the policy goals of their political superiors. This is particularly true at the state and local level, where line agencies typically adopt the policy missions of the chief executive and develop powerful constituencies to enhance their influence and effectiveness. Line agencies often view their roles

differently and define the public interest in different terms. At times, their goals and objectives run at cross-purposes and produce intraagency rivalries. Staff agencies are nonhierarchical structures established to assist the chief executive in implementation of policy and in formulating policy alternatives that may differ from those of the executive departments. Their chief goal is policy planning, which involves the long-term, systematic, and rational distribution of existing and future rewards. As such, staff agencies are political, particularly when they engage in policy planning. Political consider-ations are also involved in policy implementation, which may involve a multitude of competing political actors. Many staff personnel are well versed in various techniques that complement line functions. Common staff functions include legal advice, finance, person-nel assistance, organization, public relations, and management. *See also* BUREAUCRAT, 181; BUREAUCRATIC ORGANIZATIONS, 183; HIERARCHY, 190.

Significance   Line and staff operations are often difficult to distin-guish, as the classical differences have become less pronounced. In theory, line and staff functions are vastly different. However, the complexity that surrounds the public policy process and the need for specialized knowledge and technical assistance have served to blur these distinctions. In many agencies, line officials are intimately in-volved in staff functions, while staff personnel often accept assign-ments that were once exclusively performed by line officials. The term *facilitative staff* is commonly employed to describe administrative per-sonnel whose responsibilities cut across line and staff functions and who are deeply involved in virtually all aspects of the policy process. Still, disputes frequently arise between line and staff agencies, which often reflect conflicting biases and definitions of the public interest. This is inevitable, given their different missions and constituencies.

Merit System   (193)

A process by which individuals are hired, fired, and promoted on the basis of their experience, qualifications, and expertise in a specific job area. The merit system was initiated in response to widespread abuses in the patronage system, in which government positions were awarded on the basis of political loyalty instead of professional merit. Although this term is often used interchangeably with civil service, the latter is a specific personnel system, whereas the merit system advocates the ideal of positive initiatives in sound personnel manage-ment rather than simply eliminating the pitfalls of the patronage system. Under a true merit system, government jobs are awarded free of arbitrary factors unrelated to job performance. In reality, few civil service systems are pure merit systems, be it at the federal or state and local levels. Clearly, government employment is affected by various human and technical considerations. These include, among others, accepting applications only from personnel already within an agency, raising examination scores through veterans' preference points, employing oral as opposed to written examinations, and relying on the "rule of three," in which the highest-rated candidate does not necessarily have to be selected. These and other exceptions strengthen the argument that merit alone does not necessarily dictate government hiring practices. *See also* AFFIRMATIVE ACTION, 179; CIVIL SERVICE, 184; PATRONAGE, 194.

Significance   The merit system was initially viewed by government reformers as a corrective to the blatant abuses of the patronage system. In theory, government employees were to be judged by job performance, free of political considerations and the personal caprice of employers. However, the merit system engendered a host of new problems, many of which persist today. According to Phillip E. Present, an expert in public administration, the merit system's major flaws include (1) it is difficult to define merit, and even when it can be measured, it is only one of several criteria that should be considered in personnel decisions; (2) it overprotects the incompetent worker, while underrewarding the exceptional worker; (3) it plays a minimal role in yearly salary determinations, as most government agencies employ a step-increase method, whereby each employee is raised a step with an automatic commensurate increase in pay; and (4) it encourages unresponsiveness and unaccountability in employees, as they feel confident that severe disciplinary action against them is unlikely or will prove unsuccessful.[10] Myriad proposals have been advanced to reform the merit system, although each poses its own special problems. Many experts believe that true reform is impossible unless major changes are instituted in the way government employees are hired, fired, and promoted, In the end, the process must permit employers to fire or demote incompetent employees in a more rapid manner, while more quickly rewarding excellent employees, so as to encourage increased performance. Other experts have called for an end to automatic salary increases, special pay bonuses, and modifications in the veterans' preference system. Despite the problems of the merit system, these and other reforms have met with strong opposition, most notably from labor unions, veterans' groups, and some elected officials.

Patronage **(194)**

Awarding government offices or conferring franchises, licenses, contracts, or other favors on the basis of political loyalty as opposed to professional merit. Patronage is a coveted political perquisite of many state and local officials, in both the legislative and executive branches. It can be distinguished from the merit system, in which individuals are hired, fired, and promoted on the basis of their experience, qualifications, and expertise in a specific area. In 1829, President Andrew Jackson greatly expanded the number of government patronage jobs, which reached their zenith during President Abraham Lincoln's first term (1861–1864). This trend was sharply reversed in 1883, with the passage of the Civil Service Act (Pendleton Act). From that point on, patronage was supplanted by "civil service" (a system of job "classification," in which government jobs are awarded on the basis of "merit," as measured by an objective written examination) and the merit system, which was initiated at the federal level and has since spread to state and local governments.*See also* AFFIRMATIVE ACTION, 179; CIVIL SERVICE, 184; MERIT SYSTEM, 193.

Significance   Patronage has long been defended by party loyalists, who view it as an important recruitment device. In addition, its proponents contend that patronage permits the chief executive and various legislative leaders to appoint political stalwarts who share their philosophy and will help them to fulfill their campaign promises. Finally, its defenders argue that, at its best, patronage promotes competence, loyalty, and responsiveness—these appointees know that their careers depend upon pleasing a public official, who must be reelected, and this, in turn, can foster a more accountable and responsible bureaucracy. Critics contend that patronage frequently rewards individuals who have few if any qualifications and little if any interest in the job in question. They maintain that patronage promotes both incompetence and corruption and, in the process, undermines government efficiency. Although patronage may enhance the power and influence of various elected officials, it undermines their agendas by encouraging blind obedience and partisan wrangling. Despite these concerns, patronage is a political reality. The number of available patronage jobs varies from state to state; it is a powerful political tool in Indiana and Illinois, but is relatively unimportant in such states as California and Wisconsin, which have strong civil service systems. The last major strong-hold of the patronage system is county government. Also, there are myriad ways to circumvent the civil service system. For example, individuals may be appointed as "temporary" employees or may be hired in an exempt category, thereby bypassing the system.

Span of Control   (195)

An administrative concept refers to the number of agencies or subordinates an administrator can supervise effectively. Span of control has long been a subject of debate among public administrators. Although no clear consensus exists, most experts believe that no one administrator can supervise more than 20 agencies or persons. In most cases, it is relatively easy to calculate an administrator's span of control. For example, if an office manager oversees 18 administrative and clerical personnel, his or her span of control is 18. It is more difficult, however, to calculate the spans of the director of social welfare or the chief of police, since this depends upon how one defines the term *supervision*. It is extremely difficult to determine the ideal span of control, as conditions and circumstances vary among government agencies. Span of control is a fluid concept; it must constantly be redefined to reflect changing conditions, the skills of subordinates, and the goals and objectives of the agency. *See also* BUREAUCRATIC ORGANIZATIONS, 183; DECENTRALIZATION, 187; DELEGATION OF AUTHORITY, 188.

Significance   Span of control is a valuable concept for analyzing administrative performance. Generally, agencies with sizable spans of control possess fewer levels than those with a similar number of personnel with smaller spans of control. Organizations that have fewer levels are commonly referred to as "flat" organizations, while those with more levels are known as "tall" organizations. The mathematics are quite simple. With a similar number of employees, smaller spans of control encourage more levels; fewer levels produce a larger span of control. Tall organizations face several problems, one of which is time. Where there are more levels, it takes longer to communicate a policy from top to bottom. For example, if 16 subordinates must approve a decision, which must be implemented in two days, the process may be complicated by numerous factors. Communication can be expedited in flat organizations, where there are fewer persons involved in the process. Still, flatness, in and of itself, is not the objective. The key is whether the span of control is appropriate and functional at all levels of the agency. According to former federal administrator Rufus E. Miles, Jr., "Wide span of control satisfies many constituencies; narrow span of control satisfies few. If the chief executive wishes to fend off . . . special pleaders, he is likely to prefer a small number of officials directly answerable to him; if he can take the time and wants to hear what they have to say, he will enlarge the range of important membership in his immediate family."[11]

Sunset Laws (196)

Statutes that apply life spans to agencies at the time of their establishment. Sunset laws reflect the conviction that state agencies and programs should not be considered permanent—that they should be reviewed periodically and assessed in terms of their efficiency and effectiveness. Sunset laws were inaugurated in Colorado in 1976 and have since spread to 34 other states. Under these statutes, new agencies are created for fixed periods, for example, six years, and are then dismantled unless the state legislature votes to extend their life for an additional six-year period. This approach requires the legislature to scrutinize an agency's performance at specific intervals, as opposed to granting it permanent status. *See also* ADMINISTRATIVE REORGANIZATION, 178; BUREAUCRATIC INERTIA, 182; BUREAUCRATIC ORGANIZATIONS, 183.

Significance Sunset laws place the burden upon agencies to justify their existence, instead of requiring agency critics to prove that an agency has failed to achieve its stated objectives. These statutes enjoy widespread support. Conservatives support sunset laws, arguing that they serve to reduce the size of government, while liberals maintain that they require agencies to reassess their missions, as they embark upon new responsibilities in times of fiscal crisis. On the other hand, critics contend that sunset laws frequently apply only to regulatory boards and occupational licensing agencies, and not to major departments of state government. In addition, they insist that such statutes are not cost-effective—that they involve the expenditure of vast sums of money to eliminate agencies and boards. They further maintain that the evaluation process is often haphazard, particularly when a large number of agencies and boards are under review. For example, in Alabama, 100 hours were expended to review 200 agencies, or 30 minutes per agency. Moreover, all agencies and programs boast a clientele, large or small, strong or weak. Clearly, special interests are likely to oppose any attempts to eliminate a desired program, even when it has failed to achieve its objectives. Sunset laws boast mixed results. If success is gauged by the elimination of agencies, then sunset laws have not been particularly effective, as few agencies have been permanently dismantled.

However, if their purpose is to promote legislative oversight—and in the process to improve agency performance—then the results in Colorado and other states attest to their usefulness. At the very least, sunset laws have served to strengthen the evaluative process and to require agencies to produce tangible results.

Whistle Blowing (197)

Publicly exposing administrative waste, mismanagement, and corruption by disclosing confidential information to the public. Whistle blowing emerged in the 1960s but reached new heights in the 1970s and 1980s. Whistle blowing runs directly contrary to the organizational ethic, namely, loyalty. The modern-day whistle blower is often compared to his or her biblical mentor, Judas Iscariot, and is referred to by Tacitus, who, in about A.D. 100, wrote that "traitors are disliked even by those they favor."[12] Still, whistle blowing has gained increased currency in recent years, so much so that consumer advocate Ralph Nader recently organized a conference to honor nine government whistle blowers. Whistle blowers face numerous obstacles, both personal and institutional. Agencies view them as scoundrels; the public as martyrs. Martyrdom, however, has few rewards. In most cases, the limited media attention they garner is scant recompense for their shattered careers. The whistle blower is destined to face many career problems, chief of which is job security. Once a person blows the whistle on agency misconduct, he or she is apt to be a marked individual, perhaps for years to come. Despite their laudable motives and sense of social responsibility, employers view whistle blowers as detrimental to the welfare of their agencies. Upper management resents their intrusion into agency matters, which they perceive as a threat to their ego and authority. In addition, they contend that whistle blowers threaten the image of the agency, future legislative funding, institutional harmony, agency cohesion, and, most of all, organizational effectiveness. *See also* BUREAUCRATIC INERTIA, 182; CLIENTELE AGENCY, 185; INTEREST GROUP LIBERALISM, 191.

Significance   Whistle blowing can be compared to the classic Catch-22 situation: If whistle blowers exercise their conscience and expose agency wrongdoing, they face obstracism and retribution. If they remain silent, they perpetuate the very practices that demand attention and correction. Clearly, the whistle blower faces a difficult dilemma. It is one thing to advocate personal principles and civic duty; it is quite another to have to cope with the pain and anguish that accompany such acts. Although society preaches the gospel of individual responsibility and public accountability, it does little to guarantee the futures of those who challenge the system. Whistle blowers must possess considerable courage and patience and must be willing to pay the price for their actions. As their numbers increase, society must be prepared to answer several key questions, among them: Do individuals have the right to reveal confidential information? Does the First Amendment protect public disclosure? If whistle blowers are sued, who should pay their legal expenses? If they win, are they entitled to damages? Until these questions are answered, whistle blowers will continue to walk a long and painful road.

8. Counties, Districts, and Towns and Townships

City-States (198)

An approach to municipal planning in which the city is viewed as an ecological nation, with the goal of local self-reliance. City-states are predicated on the assumption that future progress depends on systematic planning and development. To achieve this objective, the city-state cannot build its future on one or two large businesses or industries to sustain its growth. Rather, it must adopt a developmental strategy that embodies its innate resources (e.g., food, energy, raw materials), as well as stimulates the growth of hundreds or thousands of small businesses. To become self-reliant, the city-state must view itself as a nation; it must analyze the flow of capital and evaluate its balance of payments. A city-state eschews ideological definition; it is neither liberal nor conservative. In such cities, the citizen is both the producer of wealth and a major actor in the political process of resource management. Self-reliant cities prize effective governance but minimize government. Moreover, the city-state seeks to blur the distinction between the public and private sectors, recognizing the inherent importance of a partnership rooted in mutual survival. *See also* CITY GOVERNMENT: MUNICIPAL CORPORATION, 229.

Significance City-states are inward-looking; that is, they realize the necessity of fashioning urban solutions predicated on existing resources (both natural and human). Advocates of these new city-states point with pride to such communities as Seattle, Washington; Davis, California; Hartford, Connecticut; and Madison, Wisconsin; which, in their opinion, have redefined their purpose to reflect the ideals of self-sufficiency and self-reliance. Specifically, these city-states have endeavored to strengthen their local economies, develop increased self-confidence, and identify and cultivate local skills. These city-states, argue their admirers, have succeeded because they recognize that prevention rather than treatment, and integration rather than separation promote self-reliance and self-sufficiency. Key to this process is local power. For the city-state to flourish, the population must be cohesive, and local government must foster stability. Moreover, the city-state understands that there are costs associated with growth. Increasingly, city-states have moved cautiously in courting large corporations to locate branch plants in their communities. They understand that corporate relocation brings with it a loss of control over capital—over jobs and factories. Instead, the city-state places a high premium on local small business development. Historically, the urban community has conceived itself as a site of finance, commerce, and service industries. The city-state, however, defines itself differently. It is both a producer of basic wealth and a processor of raw materials, as well as a site of commerce and trade.

County   **(199)**
A principal local unit of government established to implement state policies, programs, and services. Counties exist in most states, with the exception of Connecticut and Rhode Island. Louisiana has county subdivisions, but calls them "parishes," while Alaska recently created a county-like unit known as a "borough." In most cases, counties play a relatively minor role in New England. There are 3,041 counties in the United States, ranging from 3 in Delaware to 254 in Texas. Counties vary in size, structure, population, and function. However, most counties perform certain basic functions. These include property tax collection, election administration, road construction and maintenance, police protection (in unincorporated areas), jail and court administration, record keeping, hospital and recreational operations, welfare, and public education. Originally, the county served as the primary vehicle of rural governance, whereas today it provides a wide variety of urban services, among them; managing parking facilities, enforcing building code regulations, and supervising stadium operations. Approximately two-thirds of the U.S. population resides in counties with a population of over 100,000 people. Interestingly, nearly two-thirds of all counties have less than 25,000 people. *See also* COUNTY COURTHOUSE GANG, 204.

Significance   Counties were established to function as the administrative arms of the state and to exercise local governmental responsibilities. Despite myriad societal changes, counties have remained relatively unchanged, either in structure or function. Some counties are rural, while others are urban; some have gained, while others have lost population; some have increased in influence, while others have declined; some have expanded their resources, while others have depleted their resources. Herbert S. Duncombe, an authority on counties, has divided counties into six main types: (1) metropolitan core counties encompass most of the nations's largest cities; (2) metropolitan fringe counties completely or partially surround metropolitan core counties; (3) single-county metropolitan areas lack large numbers of commuters, but frequently serve as trade and shopping centers for wide areas; (4) urbanized metropolitan areas boast a growing commercial center surrounding a farm area, and a county seat of 20,000 to 40,000 people; (5) less urbanized counties include one city that supports the shopping needs of the area's population and contains from 2,500 to 20,000 people; and (6) thinly populated counties are devoid of an urban area in excess of 2,500 people.[1] Regardless of type, counties face countless problems, compounded by archaic administrative structures, the absence of a chief executive, the long ballot, and the patronage system. Even so, many counties are changing, although hundreds are still controlled by what one author calls a "patronage-dispensing county courthouse gang."[2] Progressive counties have inaugurated a plethora of new services, including job training, drug information programs, energy conservation, and consumer protection. Many counties have approved county charters, county home rule, and county managers. Intergovernmental relations have steadily improved, and fewer counties are dependent on the property tax as a major source of revenue.

County Agent   (200)

The individual who informs the farm community of recent innovations in agriculture by demonstrating new techniques on the farmer's own land. The county agent promotes agriculture under the federal, state, and county cooperative extension program, which was established by the Smith-Lever Act of 1914. This act created the modern extension service, which gave rise to the county agent program. Actually, the county agent concept originated in 1906, when Texas inaugurated the first such program. It has since been extended to every state. The county agent is nominally appointed by the county board (the principal governing body of the county) and serves at its pleasure. The functions of the county agent vary from county to county, and state to state. However, in general, county agents assist and encourage farmers in developing and marketing their agricultural products. They also instruct farmers in approved agricultural methods and recruit outside experts, where necessary. Moreover, county agents foster balanced production and formulate marketing strategies. They have also supported the creation of farmers' cooperative associations, both for production and marketing purposes. Finally, county agents play a role in organizing and directing agricultural clubs for young farmers (e.g., calf clubs, swine clubs, corn clubs). *See also* COUNTY BOARD, 201.

Significance   The county agent has, in many instances, improved the quality and quantity of livestock in the counties, and is primarily responsible for furthering the dairy and poultry industries. To achieve these objectives, the county agent attempts to reach the farmer through advice, demonstrations, conferences, and exhibits. He or she is assisted by a representative group of local farmers, who also sponsor meetings in their communities. Specifically, the county agent provides information in such disparate areas as cultivation methods, soil conservation, new breeds of poultry and livestock, and cooperative marketing. Despite these services, only a small percentage of county farmers avail themselves of the county agent or are guided by his or her advice, but the number is steadily increasing. Although the county agent is, at times, the object of criticism, or receives scant appreciation, he or she is one of the few officials who makes a tangible contribution to increasing the county's tax base and its overall prosperity. In many cases, the county agent's efforts have markedly increased the wealth of a county, as well as increased the incomes of hundreds of thousands of farmers.

County Board   (201)

The principal governing body of the county. The county board is called by over 30 different names, including county commission, board of supervisors, common freeholders, board of revenue, county court, and fiscal court. County boards vary in size, term of office, and method of election. There is no single pattern of organization. There are, however, several common characteristics. The typical board has four members, is elected at large, and serves for staggered four-year terms. The county board is headed by a chairperson, either selected by the board or elected by the voters. In most instances, the structure of the county board is dictated by one or more state statutes. If a county wishes to change its board's structure, it must secure formal approval from the state legislature. In essence, the county board is an administrative body; it performs few legislative functions and is limited in its ability to tax and appropriate funds. The county board possesses three main functions: (1) determination of fiscal policy through its budgetary powers; (2) regulation of personal conduct through its ordinance-making powers; and (3) general administration of county affairs. *See also* COUNTY MANAGER, 207; COUNTY SINGLE-EXECUTIVE PLAN, 211; URBAN COUNTY PLAN, 220.

Significance   The county board plays a pivotal role in local gover-nance. This is attributable, in part, to the increased importance of urban counties, which now wield substantial power and influence. Despite its position, the county board has received considerable criticism. Indeed, political scientist Joseph F. Zimmerman contends (1) There are too many counties, some of which are too small and densely populated, to permit effective implementation of their func-tions; (2) They lack a single chief executive, which often results in the fragmentation of authority; (3) Their organizational structure under-mines accountability and responsibility; (4) The long ballot encour-ages the election of myriad officials, many of whom have purely administrative functions; and (5) Many counties are controlled through special legislation by the state legislature, which makes it difficult to initiate action and implement programs.[3] Many authorities argue that counties must assume a more aggressive, innovative role. If county boards are to plan and control suburban growth, as well as improve and enhance services to expanding populations in unincorporated areas, board members must lobby for several major reforms, among them, (1) improved coordination and integration of administrative leadership; (2) increased professionalism in county government; and (3) expanded powers and greater flexibility. Clearly, county boards face many institutional obstacles in achieving these objectives, not the least of which are state domination and governmental tradition.

County Clerk   (202)
Serves as secretary to the county board and exercises sundry admin-istrative duties. The county clerk performs many functions, among them, supervision of election laws, issuance of business licenses and certificates, operation of amusement establishments (outside city limits), and maintenance of vital statistics (e.g., birth, marriage, and death records). In addition, the county clerk may handle deeds, mortgages, and plats. The county clerk, who is elected in over one-half the states, works closely with the county board (the principal governing body of the county), and is responsible for safeguarding the minute book and ordinance book. The county clerk also carries

out any additional tasks assigned to his or her office by the county board. In past years, the register of deeds—the official who maintains records of real estate ownership and transfers and keeps various other county records—often served as clerk to the board. However, this practice has declined in recent years. Some county boards have clerks who have no additional responsibilities, while others assign a county official or employee to function as clerk to the board. *See also* COUNTY BOARD, 201.

Significance   The county clerk's office has, in recent decades, become a general clearinghouse for county affairs, and the clerk is, in many counties, an influential political figure. Although county governments differ markedly in their organization, the county clerk stands at the heart of the political process. The clerk wields considerable influence, owing to his or her experience, training, and personality. The county clerk attends board meetings, knows the commissioners, understands the process, boasts numerous contacts, and implements board policy. This places the county clerk in a unique position. Although the county clerk enjoys scant policy-making authority, he or she is perceived as a valuable source to cultivate. Frequently, private individuals and special interest groups attempt to make end runs around the county board by soliciting the support of the county clerk, who they hope will use this position to influence board policy. For these reasons, many students of government believe that the county clerk should be an appointive rather than an elective position, and that the clerk's office should be regularly monitored to preserve the integrity of county government.

County Coroner   (203)

The official responsible for determining the cause of death when an unattended or questionable death occurs within the county. County coroners exercise several quasi-judicial functions. When a death is reported, it is their responsibility to conduct a preliminary investigation to ascertain whether the death resulted from a criminal act or failure to act on the part of another person. In the case of the former, the county coroner must decide whether a criminal homicide may have occurred. If the county coroner concludes that it did not, then the case is closed without further inquiry. However, if the county coroner decides that an act of homicide may have been committed, then he or she is charged with conducting an investigation, called an *inquest*, to resolve the matter or to identify the person(s) responsible for the crime. Generally, a jury of six individuals will hear the evidence presented by the county prosecutor. If the verdict is death by criminal homicide, then the county coroner may order the arrest of, establish bail for, or commit to jail any person(s) who may be criminally liable. In most cases, the county coroner is elected, although several states permit an appointed medical examiner (a physician, serving in a medical capacity, who investigates the cause of death when it appears to be unusual, unnatural, or suspicious) to conduct the duties of the county coroner, and have assigned the inquest function to the county prosecutor. *See also* COUNTY MEDICAL EXAMINER, 208.

Significance   County coroners possess broad legal powers, in that they must decide how, when, and by what means an individual died. However, their powers are not unlimited. For example, county coroners (and juries) may not order an autopsy (the examination of a body to determine the cause of death); only the medical examiner may do so. Moreover, the county coroner may not lawfully sign the death certificate unless that person is a licensed physician or has been delegated that power by the chief medical examiner. In actuality, the county coroner is an investigative officer, authorized to conduct inquests and preliminary hearings. The county coroner cannot, however, issue a search warrant or warrants generally. The power to issue arrest warrants is limited to the person(s) appearing before the county coroner or jury when the former concludes that the individual(s) may be culpable (blameworthy) in the death under investigation. Unlike law enforcement officers, the county coroner lacks specific authority to make arrests without a warrant. To serve as county coroner, a person is not required to have any special education or experience. However, the position does require extensive medical knowledge, as well as an understanding of criminal investigation and judicial proceedings. Nationwide, many counties have called for the appointment of physicians as medical examiners, the elimination of the county coroner's jury, and reliance on the county prosecutor to render legal decisions relating to the county coroner's office.

County Courthouse Gang (204)

A coterie of elective and appointive officials who, together with top business and community leaders, exercise inordinate influence on county government. The courthouse gang consists of the county's political establishment, as well as prominent business leaders whose economic interests bring them in close contact with key county officials. This group includes suppliers, road contractors, printers, attorneys (e.g., those involved in probate law), painters, and ex-politicians, among others. As the business community is dependent on the county officials, so, too, are the politicians reliant on the business establishment, which exercises considerable political clout. In addition to votes, the business leaders provide county officials with campaign contributions, workers, equipment, supplies, endorsements, media coverage, and political guidance. Together, the members of the courthouse gang cooperate in their mutual interest, often at the expense of the public interest. *See also* COUNTY BOARD, 201.

Significance   The county courthouse gang represent a potent political force. Typically, one person is accepted as the boss. This individual may be the president of the local bank, the head of the farm organization, the editor of the newspaper, the scion of the oldest and wealthiest family, or the leader of the party organization. In some locales, the role of the boss may be played by an elected county official who is assumed to enjoy substantial influence. The pattern varies markedly: in Ohio, South Carolina, and Indiana, it is the chairperson of the county board; in Missouri, it is the county court judge; and in Alabama, Tennessee, and Kentucky, it is the probate or county judge. In practice, the courthouse gang may rule several county governments, regardless of any formal institutional arrangements. This group exercises influence, in part, because of voter apathy, indifference, and alienation. Although the courthouse gang may differ on some issues, its members tend to share similar values and goals, namely, the pursuit of political and economic power. With a courthouse gang, county elections are a sham because the real power lies elsewhere. Together, the political officials and business leaders possess vast power and reap vast rewards. Still, studies reveal that the influence of the courthouse gang has declined nationally, in large part because of civil service reform, the loss of patronage, the demise of the political machine, and increased voter sophistication. In most counties, the courthouse gang no longer dominates the political process. Powerful as it may be, it has failed to prevent the passage of environmental, consumer, product safety, and zoning laws. Increasingly, the courthouse gang has been challenged by organized citizen groups, which have concentrated on many access points. Clearly, multiple power centers are available for groups that wish to use them.

County District Attorney   (205)

Chief official who represents the county in all criminal prosecutions. The county district attorney (often called the prosecuting attorney, state's attorney, or county solicitor) is elected in 45 states, for a term of two to four years. Generally, the county district attorney performs four main duties: (1) prosecuting criminal cases; (2) dispensing legal advice to county officials; (3) preparing contracts for the county; and (4) serving as defense counsel for the county when it is used. Many county district attorneys devote as much as three-fourths of their time to the preparation of criminal cases. In one study, Robert B. Morgan and C. Edward Alexander found that most county district attorneys view their prosecutorial role in one of four ways: (1) trial lawyers for the police; (2) advisors to the police on legal questions; (3) court representatives, whose purpose it is to foster justice (even if it means losing a case); and (4) representatives of the public, who would, under certain circumstances, weigh public opinion when deciding whether to prosecute a particular case.[4] *See also* COUNTY BOARD, 201.

Significance   The county district attorney possesses vast influence. As chief prosecutor, the county district attorney must decide whom to prosecute and on what charges; assist judges in deciding such issues as bail, probation, and sentences; and accept or reject a plea bargain (where the prosecutor agrees to reduce the charges in exchange for a guilty plea). In addition, the county district attorney enjoys considerable discretion. For example, the county district attorney, who is largely independent, cannot be compelled to bring charges against a person. Once charges have been filed, the county district attorney is free to drop them without explanation. The county district attorney can also decide whether or not to plea bargain. Despite the latitude of county district attorneys, both the state legislatures and courts have been reluctant to impose constraints on this official's powers. Still, there are some notable exceptions. For instance, in 1971, the United States Supreme Court held in *Santobello v. New York* (404 U.S. 257) that, "When a plea rests in any significant degree on a promise or agreement of the prosecutor, so that it can be said to be a part of the inducement or consideration, such promise must be fulfilled." If the prosecutor fails to keep that promise, the defendant is legally entitled to withdraw the guilty plea. The office of the county district attorney is extremely political. Frequently, ambitious young county district attorneys will use the position as a springboard for higher office. A county district attorney may make a decision not based on the legal facts of a case, but on its potential political repercussions. This is particularly true in deciding which cases to prosecute. County district attorneys sometimes choose not to prosecute certain cases for fear of angering the community or the local political establishment.

County Health Director (206)

The official who serves as the administrative head of the county health department. The county health director possesses several statutory powers, including authority to impose a general quarantine and to oversee the sanitation function in the county. In addition, the county health director disseminates public health information and implements policies aimed at promoting public health. In many cases, the county health director works closely with local school officials to protect the health and safety of young people. As chief administrator, the county health director's main functions include (1) the selection of department personnel; (2) program development; (3) budget preparation; (4) in-service training; (5) department relations; (6) public information; (7) enforcing health laws and regulations; (8) proposing new health regulations; and (9) purchasing equipment and supplies. These functions vary from county to county and may be performed by either the county health director or a subordinate. *See also* COUNTY BOARD, 201; COUNTY MEDICAL EXAMINER, 208.

Significance   The county health director administers a wide variety of programs and services. These include sanitation and environmental health, rodent and fly control, laboratory services, health education, clinic services, cancer screening, vaccinations, communicable diseases, public health nursing, school health, and nutrition, among others. The county health director and department possess several major powers. For example, they may promulgate rules and regulations necessary to maintain public health. These rules, however, must be both reasonable and consistent with court-imposed guidelines. If a health emergency should ensue, the county health director may be granted additional authority to protect the public health. In most cases, however, the county health director is bound by state regulations. County health directors and departments may, if they choose, adopt national or state codes and standards as part of their local requirements. This may be accomplished by *reference*, that is, by citation only. It is unnecessary to define such requirements in full. Moreover, the county health director and department are required to enforce statewide public health nuisance laws, as well as state health service regulations (e.g., nursing home licensing, sanitation control of restaurants and lodging establishments, meat market and processing plant standards).

County Manager (207)

A professional administrator, appointed by the county board, who implements board policies and directs and supervises the administrative apparatus of county government. The county manager's role varies, based on the ability, skill, training, experience, personality, and interests of the manager, the county board, and other county officials. In addition, the county manager's role depends on the economic and political goals of the populace, the political climate in the county, citizen support of or opposition to various issues, and many other factors. Professor Donald B. Hayman, an authority on county government, has described the county manager as "the eyes, ears, and legs of the county board."[5] The county manager accumulates facts, conducts research, gathers information, explains board policy, and performs sundry other assigned duties. Specifically, county managers (1) appoint, suspend, and remove county officials, employees, and agents with board approval; (2) direct and supervise all county offices, departments, boards, commissions, and agencies under the board's aegis; (3) attend meetings of the county board and present recommendations to the members; (4) execute board orders, ordinances, resolutions, and regulations; (5) submit the annual budget and capital program to the county board; (6) prepare an annual report on the finances and administrative activities of the county; (7) compile additional reports, as requested by the board, concerning the operation of county offices, departments, boards, commissions, and agencies; and (8) perform other assigned duties, as directed by the county board. *See also* COUNTY BOARD, 201; COUNTY SINGLE-EXECUTIVE PLAN, 211; URBAN COUNTY PLAN, 220.

Significance The county manager's position arose out of a desire to professionalize county government and make it more efficient. Many observers felt that county affairs had become so complex that they could no longer be effectively administered by citizen-amateurs. To achieve their objective, numerous counties sought to recruit an experienced administrator, one who was trained in such disparate areas as accounting, planning, zoning, personnel administration, and program evaluation. As of now, over 500 counties (of 3,041 in the United States) have chosen to appoint a county manager. The county manager's position is a difficult one. Because he or she serves at the pleasure of the county board, there is little or no job security. Moreover, the position is intensely political. To survive, the county manager must maintain the active support of a majority of the county board. Failing that, or when there is an ideological shift in the makeup of the board, the county manager could face immediate dismissal. Needless to say, the county manager must not only be a professional administrator, but must also be a skillful politician. The county manager's job is, in many respects, a thankless one. While often well paid—as high as $50,000 to $80,000, in a large county—the county manager is forced into the position of working long hours, making difficult decisions, mastering countless skills, and defending unpopular policies. As a result, county managers tend to serve short tenures, suffer from premature burnout, and experience a variety of personal and career problems.

County Medical Examiner   **(208)**
The official charged with investigating the cause of death when the circumstances surrounding a death are unusual, unnatural, or suspicious. The county medical examiner is, in most cases, a local physician selected by the state health commissioner from a list of names recommended by the county or district medical society. In cases where a local physician is unavailable, the coroner may be designated as acting medical examiner. Most county medical examiners serve on a part-time basis, for a fixed term of office. When a person dies by what appears to be a criminal act, by suicide, while an inmate at a penal or correctional institution, or by any questionable means, notification of the death must be made to the county medical examiner. The body of the deceased must not be disturbed without formal approval by the county medical examiner. Upon receipt of the body, the county medical examiner initiates an investigation, and submits a written report to the chief medical examiner, an experienced pathologist, who coordinates the statewide system of postmortem examinations. Copies are also given to the district attorney and to those parties in a court action who may request them. *See also* COUNTY CORONER, 203; COUNTY HEALTH DIRECTOR, 206.

Significance   The county medical examiner works in tandem with the coroner, and conducts an independent investigation whenever it appears that the deceased may have died due to a criminal act or neglect of an individual. In such cases, the county medical examiner is required to notify the coroner of deaths, so that the latter may schedule an *inquest* (investigation) and preliminary hearing when necessary. The county coroner is required to submit a formal report to the county medical examiner as well as to the county district attorney. Like the county coroner, the county medical examiner possesses the power of *subpoena* (a legal writ to appear to give testimony). The county medical examiner may conduct an autopsy when requested to do so by the chief medical examiner, by a superior court judge or district attorney, or whenever it is judicious and in the public interest. The law prohibits the burial, embalmment, or cremation (except of a stillborn delivered in a hospital) of a body without written permission of the county medical examiner.

County Ordinance (209)

A local legislative enactment that has the force of law. An ordinance may be distinguished from a statute, which is a law or act approved by Congress or a state legislature. An ordinance is adopted to implement a local policy initiative. Once established, it prescribes a permanent rule of conduct. County boards, the principal governing body of the county, may enact ordinances regulating such areas as subdivision control, zoning, domestic animals, and use of county property. Furthermore, all county fiscal decisions require a formal budget ordinance. There are two major types of ordinances: regulatory and special. Acting under its police power, the county board can regulate public health, safety, and welfare. To do so, it enacts ordinances ranging from noise abatement to zoning requirements to Sunday closing laws. A special ordinance is required in such matters as the budget, zoning, and franchises. To pass ordinances in these areas, the county board must generally first hold a public hearing. *See also* COUNTY BOARD, 201.

Significance   Ordinances underscore the subordinate position of the county to the state. Indeed, all ordinances must conform with state constitutions, general laws, and charters. Most counties mandate a specific procedure that must be adhered to in approving an ordinance. This process varies substantially throughout the country. However, the following steps are quite common. First, an ordinance may be proposed at a regular or special meeting. In the case of the latter, due notification must be given that the ordinance will be considered. Once the ordinance is introduced, the county board may act in one of four ways: (1) The ordinance may be approved by a unanimous vote of all board members, in which case it is considered enacted. (2) If a proposed ordinance receives a majority vote—but not a unanimous vote— it must then be reconsidered at the next regularly scheduled board meeting, and may be passed then by a majority vote. (3) If the ordinance fails to receive a majority vote when first introduced, it dies. It must then be reintroduced, at a later date, for future consideration. (4) An ordinance may be proposed and debated, but not voted upon when introduced. In this case, it is treated as though it had received a majority vote but not unanimous approval. It must then be reconsidered at the next regular meeting, and may be approved by a majority vote.

County Register of Deeds   **(210)**
Maintains records of real estate ownership and transfers and keeps various other county records. The county register of deeds is elected in approximately half the states. This official is charged with registering or filing documents concerning land transactions (e.g., deeds, mortgages, subdivision plats). In addition, the county register of deeds issues marriage licenses, files security agreements relating to commercial transactions, and compiles data on the county's real estate holdings. The functions of the county register of deeds' office are fixed by state statute. This official enjoys wide latitude, particularly in personnel matters. In many states, the county register of deeds possesses the exclusive right to hire, fire, and supervise the employees in his or her office. The county board exercises minimal authority with respect to the register of deeds' office, except in the area of finances. Generally, the fees levied by the county register of deeds are set by statute and conform to statewide standards. If the fees fail to offset the expenses of the office, the county will subsidize the difference. *See also* COUNTY CLERK, 202.

Significance   The county register of deeds is an important but unglamorous position. Although the county register of deeds boasts little policy-making authority, this official is a principal figure in the daily operations of the county. Practices of county registers of deeds vary considerably from county to county, and state to state, depending on size, mission, and resources. Many larger counties have adopted new technological innovations, including the recording of legal documents through microfilm or other technical means. In other cases, counties continue to maintain records in longhand in bound volumes. The latter counties face several major problems, owing to the loss and/or destruction of official records. Many old documents are illegible, faded, damaged, or misfiled. Others have been destroyed by fire and other natural disasters, water leakage, improper storage conditions, public misuse, and general neglect. Although the register of deeds is an elected position in many states, few authorities believe this is wise. The office requires specific job-related skills, few of which lend themselves to public debate. Moreover, many experts fear the politicization of the office and the potential for abuse.

County Single-Executive Plan   **(211)**
A form of county government that provides for the election of a single executive who is charged with the administration of county

services and programs. The county single-executive plan was inaugurated in 1938 in the suburban counties of New York City (Westchester and Nassau counties). By 1984, New York state included 16 elected county executives. Today, the National Association of Counties reports over 150 counties with a single elected executive, among them, Baltimore, Maryland; Baton Rouge, Louisiana; and Milwaukee County, Wisconsin. This represents approximately 6 percent of the total. The county single-executive plan closely resembles the strong-mayor form of city government (a form of municipal government in which the mayor appoints the department heads with city council approval, plays a major role relative to the council, and serves as chief executive officer of the city). Under this system, the elected single executive possesses the influence necessary to administer the executive agencies and influence the county board. *See also* COUNTY BOARD, 201; COUNTY MANAGER, 207; URBAN COUNTY PLAN, 220.

Significance The county single-executive plan is particularly well suited to highly urbanized counties. In this sense, it boasts considerable advantages over the typical county government, which provides for a large number of elected officials, none of whom have sole responsibility for developing, implementing, and overseeing county policies and programs. Like the county-manager plan, the county single-executive plan seeks to integrate executive authority and reduce the impact of political patronage. Despite its apparent advantages, this plan has engendered substantial criticism, owing, in part, to strong opposition from incumbents slated for reorganization. Clearly, many county officials view the single-executive plan as a threat to their existing power base and political prerogatives. This resistance, combined with widespread voter apathy, has prevented broader acceptance. Nevertheless, an increasing number of counties have adopted the county single-executive plan. Former Vice-President Spiro T. Agnew served as county executive of Baltimore County prior to his election as governor of Maryland.

District: School District   (212)
A governmental unit that administers the school system in nearly half the states. School districts are autonomous entities and do not conform to county, city, or town or township lines. In New England, the town or township plan prevails, whereas the county plan predominates in the South. In Delaware and Hawaii, the entire state is considered one school district. School districts are created by the state. However, until the 1960s, they were controlled primarily by locally

elected boards of education. Since that time, the federal government has played an increasingly larger role in school policy, particularly as it relates to such explosive national issues as racial integration and school busing. Today, most school districts are governed by elective boards, which, in turn, appoint a superintendent to administer the system. In certain areas, the school district is part of city government, and the school board is appointed or selected by the city council. Nearly one-fifth of all local governmental units are school districts. Together, they account for about one-half of all expenditures by local governments.

Significance   School districts are vitally dependent on federal, state, and local assistance. This has occasioned several major problems. Frederick M. Wirt, in a seminal work on educational politics and policies, discovered that states that appropriate large funds to local school districts often attach strings to the expenditure of this money.[6] This, of course, gives those states substantial control over school district, policies and programs. On the other hand, states that contribute relatively small sums of money to local school districts lose such control, as local governments are then forced to seek the needed revenue from other sources. Although control over the classroom remains with the local school district, there is widespread evidence that both the federal and state governments have attempted to shape educational policy through the use of financial incentives and public opinion. Although each school district is free to levy taxes at a rate acceptable to fund the district's school system, usually through the use of the property tax, it is clear that citizen support for public education has declined. This is due, in part, to escalating costs, declining test scores, and soaring social problems (e.g., violence, drugs, sexual freedom). Moreover, state assistance for public education has decreased in many parts of the country, occasioned by cutbacks in state and federal aid, dwindling enrollments, and taxpayer opposition to new school bond referenda. Clearly, school districts face an enormous challenge—one that will require an increased commitment to excellence, a willingness to experiment with new ideas and approaches, and heightened awareness of the importance of public education and its role in U.S. society.

District: Service District   (213)

A geographically defined part of the county in which the county board levies additional taxes and provides additional services. A service district differs from a special district, in that the former is not a separate governmental unit. Under many state constitutions, the state legislatures are empowered to authorize counties to assess extra taxes in order to finance, extend, or maintain services, functions, or facilities equal to or greater than those provided in the entire county. Thus, counties may impose upon special districts a property tax that is higher than the rest of the county. However, it must expend this additional revenue on the designated service(s). The county board may establish a service district to provide any of the following functions: fire protection, solid waste collection and disposal, water supply and distribution, sewage collection and disposal, beach erosion control and flood and hurricane protection, recreation, and rescue squad or ambulance services. *See also* DISTRICT: SPECIAL DISTRICT, 214.

Significance　　　A service district may be created if either the service is not presently provided countywide, or, if it is provided, to expand the function beyond the countywide level to serve a special need or problem. A county may, if it chooses, establish a service district to provide a combination of services. Moreover, the law permits different service districts to provide overlapping services. Generally, a service district may be created by a simple action of the county board. This action does not require citizen initiation or approval. In fact, most counties do not provide a mechanism for the voters to express themselves on the establishment of special districts. Thus, the county board is solely empowered to make such a decision—hopefully, after collecting and analyzing the pertinent facts. In reaching its decision, the county board is usually governed by two factors: first, whether the district requires the additional service(s), and whether the residents support this action; and second, whether the district can fund the extra service(s). Because a service district is not a separate governmental unit, it does not require an independent governing board. Indeed, all service units are administered by the county board. In most cases, service districts are financed by the property tax, user charges, and, occasionally, special assessments. In addition, the county board may, if it wishes, issue general obligation bonds to finance construction within a district.

District: Special District　　　　　　　　　　　　　(214)

Separate governmental unit that performs one or more specific services. Special districts have tripled since 1942 (from 8,000 to 28,700), so that they now comprise 35 percent of all local units. Almost two-thirds of these are concentrated in eleven states. A special district provides such services as soil conservation, water and irrigation, mosquito control, sewage disposal, mass transit, libraries, and airports, among others. These functions are administered on a metropolitan-wide or intermunicipal level. The popularity of special districts reflects the logic behind their creation, namely, to provide a desired service in a businesslike manner. Generally, a special district is established to address problems that transcend local boundaries or to circumvent debt restrictions and taxation imposed upon local governments by state law. Special districts are created under state law, and usually require district voter approval. They are governed by an elected or appointed board or commission, which is granted taxing and bonding powers, and, in some cases, the power of *eminent domain* (the power of the state to take private property for public use upon compensation of the owner). A special district provides for large-scale or technical services (e.g., a public water system or a local airport), as well as for low-priority services (e.g., cemetaries or mosquito abatement). The largest special districts, in terms of revenue and expenditures, concern transportation. These include transit authorities in large cities, as well as The Port Authority of New York and New Jersey, which operates ports, bridges, tunnels, airports, railroads, and terminal facilities in the New York metropolitan area. *See also* DISTRICT: SCHOOL DISTRICT, 212; DISTRICT: SERVICE DISTRICT, 213.

Significance   Special districts enjoy widespread support for several reasons: (1) they provide efficient and specialized information; (2) existing governments often lack the resources required to provide the special service; or (3) they may serve a specific political purpose (e.g., they may include or exclude desirable or undesirable groups from the district). Their appeal is greatest in homogeneous suburban communities. To prevent annexation (a process whereby adjoining areas are incorporated into existing cities) by older, more established cities, many of these communities incorporated, often with insufficient planning and resources. In many cases, they proved unable to provide the full gamut of public services. Thus, several of these areas joined together—in a special district—to deliver a particular service. Special districts are popular, in large measure, because they support the status quo; that is, they do not threaten existing political loyalties, political jobs, or the tax structure. Despite their popularity, however, special districts can pose several problems, including: (1) they lack accountability; (2) they suffer from administrative duplication; (3) they promote premature incorporation, racial segregation, and inferior services; and (4) they frequently become outmoded, but resist reorganization. Although most citizens view special districts as nonpolitical, the reality is quite different. Still, there is little evidence that special districts are likely to diminish in popularity or number.

New Class (215)

Young, rich, single, or new families that are transforming old, mixed neighborhoods to reflect their own upwardly mobile personal and financial objectives. The new class has, in many areas, displaced many old, poor, and middle-class city dwellers who historically populated major U.S. urban centers. Members of this new class have achieved their goals, in part, because they have been able to take advantage of skyrocketing rents and the dislocation of scores of urban merchants. Increasingly, the nation's affluent are quietly purchasing vast numbers of inner-city housing units, many of which have been bought by attorneys and investment bankers for over $100,000 per apartment. Clearly, this is a long-term investment, one the new class hopes will pay off in huge financial dividends. Although these transitional communities lack many amenities, the new class looks to the future potential of these neighborhoods. Indeed, this is the case with New York's Upper West Side, which has become known as "Yuppie Country." *See also* CENTRAL CITY, 222.

Significance The new class believe that these transitional communities will attract large numbers of young, upwardly mobile singles and married couples, who will be drawn by the unique features these neighborhoods boast, chief of which is their ethnic diversity. For many large investors, these transitional communities offer numerous advantages, including excitement, challenge, opportunity, and variety. Generally, the new class is socially and politically liberal, adventurous and hardworking, ambitious and well educated, and eager to transform these neighborhoods into prosperous urban communities. On the other hand, the new class brings with it sundry problems, particularly for the existing population, which has become increasingly fearful of displacement. The influx of new residents has clearly squeezed out many long-time dwellers, who are unable to afford steep rent hikes or to purchase expensive new homes. This has resulted in a sharp increase in eviction notices, even in neighborhoods with rent-stabilized tenants. The new landlords, in many cases, possess the economic and political muscle necessary to enforce their position. Their goal is to rebuild and modernize, in spite of the wishes of their tenants, and owners often view tenants as impediments to their plans. Absentee landlords are especially eager to eliminate low-rent tenants. Still, there is scant evidence of outward hostility or violence between the two groups; goon squads and arson are extremely uncommon. Tenants have become increasingly sophisticated at fighting back, and are supported by many elected officials and tenant-advocacy groups who argue their case. As a result, both groups—landlords and tenants—have adopted new strategies. For instance, New York's landlords succeeded in winning an Appellate Term Court decision in which the court ruled there is no limit on the amount of space an individual landlord can claim for "personal use." This had led many landlords to employ personal-use evictions to accomplish their purposes. On the other hand, tenants have succeeded in garnering favorable press attention and mobilizing public support for what many believe will be a long and painful struggle.

Privatization   (216)

Heavy reliance by municipalities on the private sector to both formulate and implement major urban decisions. Privatization is an old idea that acquired modern currency in the late 1980s, fueled, in part, by citizen tax revolts and government-imposed spending limitations. Increasingly, state and local governments are hiring private contractors (e.g., investors, speculators, businesspersons, and other entrepreneurs) to provide such basic services as street cleaning, staffing air control towers, and supervising golf courses. Over the years, private industry has performed such essential functions as garbage collection, road repairs, and mass transportation. Currently, governments are not only contracting more of these services, but they are contracting additional functions to private industries. For example, Parsons Corporation, a Pasadena, California–based international engineering company, is financing and building the $20 million first phase of a wastewater treatment plant it will operate for Chandler, Arizona. Another private contractor, Browning-Ferris Industries, a prominent industrial waste-removal company, contracts to collect city garbage in over 340 municipalities. Indeed, the enormous increase in private contracting has given rise to an entire new industry, and several well-known accounting firms, including Arthur Young and Touche Ross, presently advise scores of cities on what services to contract to the private sector. *See also* CITY-COUNTY CONSOLIDATION, 223.

Significance   Privatization is not a panacea for what ails the nation's cities. Indeed, the long and checkered history of government contracting—from Revolutionary War times to today's inflated defense contracts—provides ample proof that private contractors are no less susceptible to waste, mismanagement, and corruption. Moreover, the prospect of employing private contractors to provide government services raises, in and of itself, several worrisome questions, among them: Will private entrepreneurs put profit ahead of service? Will they submit a low bid to obtain the contract, only to inflate the costs— or even worse, abandon the service once it becomes unprofitable? Still, past results suggest that the taxpayers can save 20 percent or more by assigning some services to private contractors. It remains to be seen how many functions state and local government can contract to such private concerns. For example, many officials would balk at privatizing police and fire protection, but Scottsdale, Arizona, boasts a superior for-profit fire department that evolved from the private protection service that existed prior to incorporation. Despite its successes, private contracting has encountered strong opposition, most notably, from the American Federation of State, County, and Municipal Employees. Political and labor opposition has prevented the spread of privatization in the East and Midwest, whereas it has won favor in the less-unionized Southwest and West.

Rust Belt   (217)

Refers to the nation's aging and deteriorating industrial cities of the Midwest and Northeast. The rust belt describes scores of cities that once represented the economic, political, and social hub of the industrial United States. Today, many of these cities face a seemingly unsolvable crisis—one that must be resolved if they are to stave off further decline. The rust belt describes such cities as Detroit, Cleveland, St. Louis, Newark, and Chicago. In each case, these cities have experienced a major population exodus, deriving, in part, from a steady decrease in jobs. For example, in the last 20 years, Chicago has lost over 100,000 jobs, while its neighboring suburbs have witnessed a sixfold increase. St. Louis, for instance, has lost nearly one-half of its residents over the last four decades. Moreover, the rust belt has shifted from a manufacturing base to a service-oriented economy, heavily populated by the poor, minorities, and uneducated. Since the mid-1960s, many rust belt cities have become increasingly distressed. Today, they are characterized by hopelessness, bitterness, alienation, and dependence. *See also* CENTRAL CITY, 222.

Significance   The rust belt faces an uncertain future. Experts are divided as to what lies ahead. Some critics contend that the forces of urban decay now at work in many cities are both uncontrollable and irreversible. They point to the continuing loss of jobs and middle-class residents, the failure to attract new industry, and the inability to entice suburbanites back into the cities. Several studies suggest that in spite of positive initiatives to rebuild these older industrial cities, it is unlikely that the decay and stagnation that make genuine progress impossible can be reversed in the near future. Still, many observers such as Cleveland Mayor George V. Voinovich contend that current trends portend a more optimistic future. They insist that urban dwellers will return to the rust belt in search of excitement, camaraderie, culture, recreation, and diversity. The keys, they maintain, are imagination and support. Although many rust belt cities have faced severe financial difficulties, some critics argue that there are clear signs of recovery. For example, Detroit, which only six years ago faced a major crisis in the automobile industry, is today the beneficiary of an increasingly healthy economy. Although few forecasters predict that industrial production and employment will once again reach their record-high 1979 levels, it appears to some observers, at least, that manufacturing will continue to hold the key to the future. As a result, many rust belt cities are attempting to rebuild their industrial infrastructure while recognizing that, in order to survive, they must become more competitive. On the other hand, some experts predict that the current short-term increase in service jobs will not keep pace with the long-term decline in manufacturing jobs. Ultimately, the future of the rust belt will depend upon its own initiative as well as on forces beyond its control.

Town or Township   (218)

A unit of local government. A town includes an urban hub as well as its surrounding rural area, whereas a township is usually a subdivision of a county covering an area of 36 square miles as a result of the congressional township system of identifying land. Towns and townships exist in 20 states (there are over 17,000 towns and townships) and represent nearly 50 million people. These units are particularly common in New England, New York, Pennsylvania, New Jersey, Michigan, and Wisconsin, and possess considerable administrative and financial influence. In many cases, they perform functions similar to those of cities and counties in other states and regions, as well as possess geographic borders that reflect legitimate community ties. Sometimes, both also include smaller municipalities, such as villages. Of the 20 states with town or township governments that permit voters to directly make policy by participating in local meetings, 11 can be described as strong town or township states. This is especially true in New England, where towns predominate. The 10,000 township units located in 9 states perform few formal functions, and most lack any full-time employees. At their inception, they were fashioned after the New England towns of Colonial times, but they failed to achieve the same measure of success. Like those in New England, the rural townships were conceived as an experiment in direct democracy. However, in recent decades, these Midwest townships have lost much of their authority, particularly in such fields as law enforcement and highways, and exist today as modified versions of the town so prevalent in New England. *See also* TOWN OR TOWNSHIP MEETING, 219.

Significance Towns and townships symbolize a long and rich tradition. Although they possess many of the same functions as counties (the largest administrative division of a state), they usually govern a far smaller geographic area (usually 20 to 40 square miles). Town government includes many special features, one of which is the well-known annual town meeting, in which the voters assemble, approve the town budget, pass ordinances, and establish town policies and programs. In addition, the voters typically elect a board of selectmen—usually three to five members—who administer the town between meetings and oversee the daily operations of government (e.g., grant licenses, manage town property, monitor other town officials, and summon special meetings). The town's voters and selectmen also elect or appoint numerous other officials, including a town clerk, treasurer, assessor, constable, and school board. These individuals supervise such activities as health, roads, schools, and welfare. The future of towns and townships remains uncertain. Presently, urban towns face fewer problems than their rural counterparts, particularly in the suburban areas of larger cities, where town government has been eclipsed by metropolitan growth. For example, in states such as Pennsylvania, town governments exercise powers and implement programs once thought to be the exclusive province of city governments. In addition, the school consolidation movement has eroded the powers of town government, to the advantage of county government, which enjoys greater influence in these areas.

Town or Township Meeting (219)

The governing authority of a town or township, in which all eligible voters gather, usually annually, to elect town officials, pass taxes, and enact laws. The town meeting derives from the Colonial era, and is most prevalent in New England towns and many midwestern townships. An experiment in direct democracy, it represents one of the oldest and most prized forms of self-government. Initially, the town meeting was conceived to provide local rule and public services to small and isolated rural settlements. The rules were simple: an annual town meeting was called, to which all qualified adult males were invited (this has since been changed to include women), to decide key policy questions. The voters passed a town budget, approved ordinances, established policies, and elected officials. Between meetings, an elected board of selectmen—typically, three to five members—was empowered to oversee the activities of the town. In addition, the voters elected a town clerk, tax assessors and collectors, constables, justices of the peace, numerous commissioners, and school board members. These officials served on a part-time basis, and received little if any remuneration. *See also* TOWN OR TOWNSHIP, 218.

Significance   The town meeting has long embodied the spirit of U.S. democracy. However, its value has been the subject of persistent debate. For example, President James Madison attacked the town meeting as divisive and dangerous: "A pure democracy, by which I mean a society consisting of a small number of citizens who assemble and administer the government in person, can admit of no cure from the mischiefs of faction."[7] Furthermore, argues Madison, "Such democracies have ever been spectacles of turbulence and contention, have ever been found incompatible with personal security and the rights of property, and have in general been as short in their lives as they have been violent in their deaths."[8] Still, proponents of the town meeting maintain that this forum promises the potential for public debate and discussion, as well as decision making. Moreover, they contend that the town meeting stimulates political education, fosters citizen participation, and encourages consensus and unified action. In theory, the town meeting can and, at times, does represent the public will. However, the reality, in many cases, falls far short of the stated ideal. Typically, attendance ranges from 10 to 40 percent. For example, in Massachusetts, in 1970, attendance averaged from 20 to 25 percent. Although some smaller towns boast greater participation, the overall trend suggests dwindling interest. Clearly, this is the result of a loss of discretionary power, which has been absorbed by other governmental bodies. In addition, it results from a growing population, annexation, and the complexity of urban problems. Despite its claim to represent the ideal of participatory democracy, the town meeting has, like many other governmental bodies, been dominated by the local elite and sundry activist groups. Even so, the town meeting still thrives in many communities, especially in New England, where there is widespread support for the institution. Many towns have modified the traditional annual meeting to reflect changing conditions and circumstances. For instance, some towns elect representatives from precincts to attend town meetings. Others have sought to professionalize town government by delegating management responsibility to a town manager who reports directly to the elected board of selectmen.

Urban County Plan (220)

An attempt to promote metropolitan coordination and reduce fragmentation by transferring to county governments various functions exercised by multiple government units within the county. The urban county plan has won favor in many states, including California and Florida. In California, several counties have assumed responsibility for such functions as law enforcement, prison administration, health services, and tax assessment and administration. Dade County, Florida, for example, is organized as a metropolitan or urban county. In Dade County, cities within that jurisdiction, including Miami, have delegated many municipal functions to the county, including water supply, sewage disposal, traffic problems, and physical and economic planning. The urban county plan differs markedly from city-county consolidation, which requires the complete merger of a county government with all other bodies within the county. *See also* COUNTY BOARD, 201; COUNTY MANAGER, 207; COUNTY SINGLE-EXECUTIVE PLAN, 211.

Significance The urban county plan is relatively easy to implement, as most metropolitan areas exist within a single county. This encourages the transfer of functions, as the county already exists as an established government unit. As a result, no new government must be created nor must any unit(s) be abolished. Increasingly, urban counties are providing traditional city functions to unincorporated county areas and, on occasion, to cities as well. Unfortunately, many county governments are ill equipped to provide such services, as they are poorly organized and have failed to adopt many techniques of modern administration, including the merit system. Advocates of this approach contend that the urban county plan will (1) ensure improved public services; (2) provide more effective coordination; (3) eliminate discrepancies in financial burdens; and (4) establish clear lines of responsibility. This argument has been challenged by many authorities, who argue that (1) the transfer of functions is often uneconomic; (2) counties have not fared particularly well in solving municipal problems; (3) financial inequalities continue to exist, and demand not only reorganization, but also the political will necessary to eliminate them; and (4) counties, like cities, may refuse to act, even where a popular consensus exists.

9. Cities and Metropolitan Areas

Annexation (221)
The process by which a city expands its boundaries by absorbing outlying areas. Annexation is a widely used practice, particularly among large cities, which have reached their present size through incorporation of adjacent political units (e.g., Los Angeles, Oklahoma City, Houston, Kansas City, Phoenix, and Dallas). Annexation reached its zenith during the early 1900s, at which point many states enacted laws requiring a voter *referendum* (the practice of referring legislative measures to the electorate for approval or rejection) in the affected areas. In many cases, annexation was met with strong voter opposition. Moreover, in recent years, legal obstacles to annexation have been relaxed, with the result that many suburban communities have chosen *incorporation* (the process by which a local governmental unit, such as a city, village, and, in some states, a town or borough, acquires formal legal status) in preference to annexation. Because of the legal difficulties attendant to annexing incorporated areas, many cities, such as Chicago, Milwaukee, and Minneapolis, have become completely surrounded by other cities, with no prospect of annexation. Research reveals that annexation is most popular in the West and South, and least popular in the Northeast and Midwest. Annexation by a central city is more likely, argues political scientist Thomas R. Dye, in smaller metropolitan areas, if the central city has a city manager, in more recently urbanized areas, and if the population of the central city is of higher socioeconomic status than people in outlying areas.[1] *See also* CITY-COUNTY CONSOLIDATION, 223; COUNCILS OF GOVERNMENTS, 233.

Significance   Annexation has served to promote governmental consolidation and integration. In addition, it has enabled larger cities

227

to expand their tax bases and improve municipal services. Still, annexation has met stiff resistance in many cities, particularly in established suburban communities, whose efforts are buoyed by state laws that make it difficult for central cities to annex such areas without their consent. Annexation procedures are defined by state law and usually require voter approval in both the central city and the affected area. In some states, such as Texas and Virginia, annexation may be accomplished by action of the central city alone or through judicial procedures. Many suburban opponents of annexation fear the loss of community identity, increased taxation, the extension of zoning and subdivision regulations, and political control by lower socioeconomic groups. Critics in the central city frequently oppose annexation because of class differences and the need to raise taxes in order to extend services to the newly annexed area. In many cases, however, annexation serves an important public purpose. It enables central cities to expand their tax base, prevents residents of outlying communities from receiving city services without contributing to their cost, and discourages the creation of rival city governments. The annexed area also benefits, by gaining improved facilities, better services, greater efficiency, less duplication, and coordinated authority.

Central City   (222)
The largest and most densely populated city in a metropolitan area. The central city is, in most cases, surrounded by numerous suburbs (residential communities bordering a larger city). During the late 1800s, the central city represented the core attraction of urban life. However, as property costs escalated and big-city problems multiplied, large numbers of middle-class urban dwellers migrated to the suburbs. As the exodus continued, many central cities simply *annexed* (a process whereby adjoining areas are incorporated into existing cities) these new communities to prevent the loss of people and resources. This trend persisted until the early twentieth century, and resulted in a significant increase in incorporated cities. This was made possible by several developments, chief of which was the popularization of the automobile. Increasingly, residents of the central city migrated to the suburbs in search of affordable housing, better job opportunities, and a more relaxed lifestyle. As their numbers multiplied, they became a significant force in state politics and marshaled their influence to prevent further annexation. To stem this migration, the central cities incorporated many smaller cities in the surrounding areas. This resulted in a marked change in metropolitan

government, in which the ever-expanding central city gave way to a dramatic increase in adjoining city governments. The results are clearly evident in the demographics: In 1940, 60 percent of all metropolitan residents lived in central cities, while 40 percent resided in suburbs. By 1975, the figures were completely reversed. *See also* CITY-STATES, 198; NEW CLASS, 215; PRIVATIZATION, 216; RUST BELT, 217; SUBURB, 236.

Significance   Central cities face myriad problems, among them, pollution, crime, congestion, unemployment, and racial strife. This has sparked a spirited debate about the future of the central city. Some scholars, such as Eugene Raskin, argue that U.S. cities are no longer capable of servicing such needs as defense, commerce, and excitement.[2] Others, such as Edward C. Banfield, appear more sanguine, noting, "The plain fact is that the overwhelming majority of city dwellers live more comfortably and conveniently than ever before."[3] In short, contends Banfield, the basic problem surrounds the poor, the uneducated, and the hopeless. These individuals, notes Banfield, "are cut off from the rest of the city, feel little attachment to society at large, and lack the ability to imagine a future or sacrifice for future rewards."[4] The statistics paint a grim picture. According to a recent study by Richard P. Nathan and Charles Adams, three-fourths of the central cities studied experienced worse problems than their adjoining suburbs.[5] These problems were most pronounced in the East and Midwest, while conditions were better in the South and West. In addition to the abovementioned woes, the central city faces numerous other problems, including the loss of population, high-income taxpayers, and industry and jobs. Most central cities are plagued by serious economic difficulties, exacerbated by a dwindling tax base. Furthermore, they have proven incapable of stemming the rising tide of such ills as crime, drugs, and racial tension. Hopefully, the experts are wrong when they predict that the problems of the central city of today may well signal the future of U.S. suburbs tomorrow.

City-County Consolidation   (223)

The merger of a county government with one or more cities to form a single unit of government. City-county consolidation seeks to reduce metropolitan fragmentation by combining separate governments and/or the services they perform. Specifically, it attempts to (1) provide services in a logical manner; (2) eliminate duplication of functions; (3) end inequalities in taxation; and (4) create governments that can solve their own problems without national and state assistance. Despite its presumed advantages, city-county consolidation is likely to face numerous obstacles. Typically, it requires the approval of the electorate. In most instances, voter *referenda* (the practice of referring legislative measures to the electorate for approval or rejection) have been soundly rejected. However, there are several noteworthly exceptions: Nashville–Davidson County, Tennessee (1962); Jacksonville–Duval County, Florida (1967); Indianapolis–Marion County, Indiana (1969); Columbus–Muscogee County, Georgia (1970); and Lexington–Fayette County, Kentucky (1972). Usually, city-county consolidation is more likely to succeed where it involves the efficient delivery of services (e.g., street lighting, garbage collection, health care, and record keeping), as opposed to the elimination of an existing government. City-county consolidation may take various forms. For instance, a county may merge with one or more of its cities, usually the largest one (e.g., Nashville–Davidson County). This results in an entirely new government. In other cases, established governments may remain intact, but may combine services (e.g., Miami–Dade County). Between 1945 and 1984, approximately 25 consolidations were approved in the United States. *See also* ANNEXATION, 221; COUNCILS OF GOVERNMENTS, 233.

Significance   City-county consolidation referenda have met with mixed results. In his study of metropolitan reorganization, political scientist Brett W. Hawkins found that consolidation is more likely to be opposed by (1) suburbanites (individuals who live in primarily residential communities adjacent to large cities) than central city (the largest and most densely populated city in a metropolitan area) dwellers; (2) blacks than whites; (3) those who are content with the present level of services; (4) those who believe that consolidation will require additional taxation; (5) those with minimal formal education; and (6) those who are less politically informed.[6] Overall, consolidation referenda are more likely to be approved when they involve service rather than governmental mergers. Indeed, rarely are city-county boundaries redrawn to become coterminous. Nationally, most successful referenda have occurred in the South. This may be explained by two facts. First, southern metropolitan areas have fewer cities than their nonsouthern counterparts. Second, the socioeconomic gulf between central cities and suburbs is frequently less in the South, where per capita income tends to be as great in central cities as in the suburbs. Many political scientists advocate total consolidation of all small governmental units into one large, regional (usually county) system. However, such mergers rarely if ever occur. As a result, compromises must be struck; this is, after all, the essence of politics.

City Government: City Councilperson   (224)

A member of a legislative body of a city. City councilpersons represent all sectors of community life: lawyers, small businesspersons, realtors, school teachers, engineers, sales clerks, and local activists. Typically, the aspiring council member is likely to be a local merchant, with extensive contacts in the community. It is rare for corporate executives to run for a city council seat, owing to their extensive business commitments. As a result, most council members belong to the middle class rather than the city's financial elite. Unlike most candidates for higher office, both federal and state, city councilpersons are neither particularly well educated nor white-collar professionals. While they may be more affluent than the average voter, and perhaps a bit older, they tend to mirror the background characteristics of the communities they represent. Individuals run for the city council for a variety of reasons, among them, influence, status, business contacts, and service. In most cases, council members serve on a part-time basis and receive little or no remuneration. Most council candidates run on long ballots in nonpartisan elections in citywide, rather than district elections. On average, most councilpersons serve four-year terms, and members run on a staggered basis. City councils average from five to nine members, although large councils may exceed twenty members (this is particularly true in the older cities of the Midwest and Northeast). Many councilpersons are initially appointed to office, to fill an unexpired term. These individuals boast political contacts among council members or hold other city offices at the time of appointment. Nearly 80 percent of incumbent councilpersons win reelection. Indeed, voluntary retirement is the principal reason for council vacancies. *See also* CITY GOVERNMENT: CITY MANAGER, 225; CITY GOVERNMENT: COUNCIL-MANAGER PLAN, 227; CITY GOVERNMENT: MAYOR, 228.

Significance   City councilpersons are most often part-time generalists, who depend upon the mayor and/or city administrators for information, assistance, and advice. In addition to formal council meetings, members attend study sessions, conference sessions, committee sessions, and emergency sessions. Usually, council members are briefed on city business by administrators in advance of council meetings, and receive reports and recommendations concerning the various items on the agenda. City councilpersons perform sundry functions. They review the administration of city programs and services, analyze zoning and planning issues, prepare the annual budget, debate proposals initiated by fellow councilpersons, hear individual constituent requests, approve appointments and/or personnel decisions, and recognize local and visiting dignitaries. These activities vary widely, depending on the size of the city. Councils in large cities expend more time on zoning, planning, and executive proposals than do small city councils. Small city councils devote more time to reviewing administrative functions, constituent requests, appointments, and personnel matters, and to recognizing local and visiting dignitaries than do those in large cities. Raymond L. Bancroft, a well-known political scientist, conducted a comprehensive study of city councilpersons in the United States, in which he surveyed over 500 council members from various regions and different-sized cities concerning which functions were most difficult to perform.[7] Council members rated zoning and land-use decisions most difficult and budgeting and finance decisions the second most difficult. Other difficult decisions included establishing growth policies, designing new city programs, and assessing city services. Less difficult decisions involved handling citizen complaints, determining administrative policy, and enacting legislation. Like many mayors, city council members experience countless frustrations. This can be attributed to heavy constituent demands, time away from family, minimal pay, extensive homework, and loss of income resulting from conflict of interest legislation. Despite the myriad problems and frustrations, city councilpersons perform an invaluable service. The constraints notwithstanding, council members attempt to balance resources and needs in the context of their individual values, citizen demands, interest group pressures, and political obligations.

City Government: City Manager   (225)

The chief administrative officer of a city. The city manager is a professional administrator, selected by the city council (the legislative body of a city) and serves at its pleasure. Typically, city managers are predominately male (women represent only 3 percent of the total), white (blacks and Hispanics represent about 1 percent of the total), native born, and Protestant. Unlike some municipal officials, city managers are generally well educated. Most hold advanced degrees in public administration and possess a broad understanding of fiscal administration, municipal law, personnel management, and city planning. The average city manager earns $40,000, although big-city managers earn as much as $60,000 to $80,000 a year. Many city managers start out as a staff assistant for a local official, move to assistant city manager, then manager of a small town, and still later to a large city. Unlike most city councilpersons (a member of a legislative body of a city), city managers are usually born outside the communities they serve. However, approximately 90 percent of all city managers reside in the communities in which they work and belong to an average of five or more local groups and organizations—professional, business, service, and church. The turnover rate for city managers averages approximately 7.5 percent per year, and the average tenure of those who resign or are dismissed from office is about five years. City managers may serve on a full-time or part-time basis. The latter is especially prevalent in smaller cities. In this case, the city manager may have a single secretary, whereas in larger cities the manager may have a sizable personal and professional staff. The functions of the city manager vary with the size of the city and the political climate. In larger cities, city managers are less likely to be involved in the day-to-day affairs of city departments. Overall, the city manager's role is to implement the policies and programs of the city council. In addition, he or she assists the council in making decisions about city matters. Most city managers eschew partisan politics and electioneering, and this contributes to the manager's ability to persuade the city council to follow his or her recommendations. Since the council is the policy maker, the city manager is expected to support council decisions and defend them in the community. City managers perform numerous functions, among them, supervising their staff; developing and controlling the city budget; hiring and firing department heads; meeting with the city council, individual councilpersons, and heads of departments; developing and preparing agency reports; and serving as a liaison with state and federal agencies. *See also* CITY GOVERNMENT: CITY COUNCILPERSON, 224; CITY GOVERNMENT: COUNCIL-MANAGER PLAN, 227; CITY GOVERNMENT: MAYOR, 228.

Significance   City managers vary markedly in terms of personal influence, based, in large part, on their relations with the mayor, city council, executive departments, other governments, and the public. In a major study of city managers, Jeptha J. Carrell found that effective city managers are well versed in conflict control.[8] When conflicts do erupt, they do so for one or more reasons: (1) differences over the distribution of power between the council and the manager; (2) personality schisms; (3) the political environment; (4) the rupture of communication between the manager and the council; and (5) the tendency of councilpersons to bend city policies to serve their political objectives. Moreover, city managers differ as to how they perceive their policy role. Some managers promote bold, often controversial policies. They lobby for support and approval of their policy preferences. Others tend to be reluctant policy participants who avoid taking strong stands on public issues. Some are content to be professional administrators and are eager to avoid policy clashes. Others are pragmatic public servants who recognize the importance of negotiation and compromise. However, regardless of their orientations, city managers are expected to separate politics from administration. For instance, the first code of ethics of the International City Managers Association states unequivocally that "no manager should take an active part in politics."[9] While most city managers agree that they should forsake partisan wrangling and election politics, they are sharply divided as to the proper role of managers in the policy-making process. Some view themselves as policy managers and seek to provide civic leadership; others see themselves as administrative managers, limiting their activity to the supervision of municipal functions; and still others perceive themselves as policy leaders. While most city managers accept this last view, many council members view them as administrators, which is why, in most cases, successful city managers do not wish to appear to be policy makers even when they are. Like other city officials, managers experience countless frustrations. Usually, these concern job insecurity, excessive hours, political pressures, and lack of privacy. Approximately 10 percent of all city managers have been fired at least once, citing such reasons as poor working conditions, relationships with the city council, and political disputes. The greatest challenge to an incumbent city manager occurs when the city council is split over a critical issue and the manager is pressured into supporting the majority's position. If the minority on the council becomes the majority after the next election, the manager's position as an objective administrator may become untenable. Still, city managers serve as a major policy force in most cities, helping to shape the agenda for city council meetings. This enables them to select the issues to be raised, as well as the policy alternatives to be considered. Although the city council will not accede to all of their recommendations, it will give them thoughtful consideration. This, in itself, is an important source of power and influence.

City Government: Commission Plan   (226)

A form of city government in which a group of commissioners (usually three to nine) serve as the city council and oversee the city's executive departments. Commission plans vary widely across the country, but share several common characteristics: (1) all legislative and executive powers are exercised by a small board elected at large on a nonpartisan ballot; (2) the city council possesses the authority to enact ordinances and establish spending priorities; (3) a commissioner is empowered to supervise an administrative department (e.g., public safety, finance, public works); and (4) the mayor is elected from the ranks of the city council but has few if any formal powers. The commission plan, which originated in 1900 in Galveston, Texas, was the outgrowth of a devastating flood that claimed the lives of over 5,000 people and resulted in millions of dollars worth of property damage. The then-mayor and aldermen proved incapable of governing the city, which encouraged a small group of local businesspersons to assume leadership. Shortly thereafter, they proposed a new form of local rule, namely, commission government, in which legislative and administrative powers would be vested in five commissioners. The state legislature agreed. At the time, this was viewed as a bold departure in municipal governance, as it violated the traditional doctrine of separation of powers by placing legislative and executive authority in a single body. Not long after, an attorney for Des Moines, Iowa—after visiting and studying the Galveston model—proposed a similar system for his own city, but also advocated the *initiative* (a process by which a specified number of voters may propose legislation), the *referendum* (the practice of referring legislative measures to the electorate for approval or rejection), and the *recall* (whereby a public official may be removed from office by a vote of the people upon petition). This became known as the Des Moines plan, and by 1917, nearly 500 cities had adopted the Des Moines model. *See also* CITY GOVERNMENT: COUNCIL-MANAGER PLAN, 227; CITY GOVERNMENT: STRONG-MAYOR PLAN, 230; CITY GOVERNMENT: WEAK-MAYOR PLAN, 231.

Significance　　The commission plan was greeted with widespread approval, until many of its defects became apparent. For example, in Galveston, commissioners became advocates of the departments they headed and often engaged in lengthy logrolling contests in city council meetings, in which deals were struck and alliances established that threatened effective governance. Departments that lacked political clout on the city council were relegated to the back burner and often received inadequate funding. Moreover, since the executive departments were administered by the commissioners themselves, members tended to be disinterested in city programs and spending policies that transcended their individual responsibilities. As long as the commissioners could reach agreement on city matters, the system worked reasonably well. However, when that consensus disintegrated, city government became fragmented and disorganized, to the point that the proceedings were threatened by conflict and stalemate. The commission plan disappointed both reformers and party bosses, both of whom opposed the system for different reasons. The reformers saw the plan as an attempt to reduce the influence of the less affluent and powerful, while party bosses were suspicious of its antipolitical orientation. In the end, the commission plan fell out of favor. By 1982, only two cities of over 250,000 people were governed this way (Tulsa, Oklahoma and Portland, Oregon). Ultimately, the reformers withdrew their support and endorsed the council-manager plan (in which policy-making responsibility is lodged in an elected council, and administrative functions are delegated to a professional administrator known as a manager).

City Government: Council-Manager Plan   (227)

A form of city government that employs a professional administrator, selected by the council, to act as the chief executive. The council-manager plan separates the legislative and executive functions in city government, vesting policy-making responsibility in a small council or commission composed of five to seven members elected at large on a nonpartisan ballot. Administrative authority is delegated to a professionally trained city manager, who is chosen by the city council, with the power to hire and fire government personnel within the limits of the merit system, and who reports to the council, which possesses the power of removal. The mayor may be elected separately or selected from within the city council, but has few executive responsibilities. Overall, the task of the city manager is to ensure the efficient operation of city government. The council-manager plan seeks to separate politics from administration. Ideally, the city council engages in political campaigning, legislative lobbying, citizen mobilization, and policy development, while the city manager implements council initiatives, supervises personnel, prepares the budget, and attends to various administrative details. *See also* CITY GOVERNMENT: CITY MANAGER, 225; CITY GOVERNMENT: COMMISSION PLAN, 226; CITY GOVERNMENT: STRONG-MAYOR PLAN, 230; CITY GOVERNMENT: WEAK-MAYOR PLAN, 231.

Significance   The council-manager plan, which was first adopted in 1912 in Sumpter, South Carolina, constitutes the most popular form of municipal government, particularly in cities with populations between 25,000 and 250,000. It exists in over one-third of cities whose population is above 5,000 and about one-half of those over 25,000. However, only five cities over 500,000 (Dallas, Phoenix, San Antonio,

San Diego, and San Jose) have adopted the council-manager plan. This system is especially popular in suburban cities—most notably, in New England, the southern Atlantic coast states, and Pacific coast states—where it appears best suited. These suburban cities are more likely to boast homogeneous populations, and generally prefer to delegate administrative responsibility to trained professionals. The council-manager plan offers several advantages, including (1) functional simplicity; (2) clear lines of authority; and (3) reliance on experts. It is popular with the council, which prizes the assistance rendered by the city manager, as well as with the voters, who laud the city manager's success in raising policy alternatives. Still, the question remains, Does the council-manager plan remove politics from administration? The answer depends on one's definition of *politics*. City managers generally escape campaign pressures, political patronage, and partisan wrangling. On the other hand, city managers are, by definition, political; that is, they propose policy measures that are inherently political. Moreover, both the city council and the voters view them as political actors, which forces the successful city manager to support the majority coalition on the council. This is especially true when the existing majority shifts, at which point the city manager must alter his or her allegiance or face dismissal. In addition, critics of the council-manager plan contend that it fails to promote a strong leader (particularly in large cities) and is, by nature, undemocratic, in that the city manager is an appointed official, even though the individual is accountable to an elected city council.

City Government: Mayor   (228)
The chief executive and/or titular leader of a city. Mayors vary widely in background, training, experience, power, role, and leadership. The typical mayor is 40 to 50 years old, holds a college degree, hails from law or business, and has prior grassroots or political experience. While most mayors are males, many large cities have elected women mayors, including San Francisco, Houston, Phoenix, and Honolulu. Of the over 19,000 municipal governments in the United States, over 1,000 cities are led by women. In addition, an increasingly large number of major cities have black mayors (now over 230), among them, Los Angeles, Atlanta, Chicago, Philadelphia, New Orleans, Newark, and Washington, D.C. Hispanics have occupied the mayor's office in Miami, San Antonio, Denver, and Tampa. Big-city mayors earn between $40,000 and $80,000, while mayors of middle-sized cities earn between $25,000 and $45,000. Some mayors are appointed, while others are elected. Mayoral terms range from one to

six years, although two-year and four-year terms are most common. Mayoral powers also vary widely, and to a large extent, this determines their influence and role in municipal affairs. Where mayors are selected by their city councils or commissions, they generally wield less authority. Frequently, their job is ceremonial—they dedicate shopping centers, preside over pageants, ride in parades, and perform other mundane functions. In other cases, mayors possess considerable legislative, administrative, and political powers, which include the right to submit budget messages, to make policy recommendations, to appoint city officials, to mediate disputes, to reconcile competing interests, and to provide strong leadership. Mayors are expected to be quintessential problem solvers, even when the problems transcend the limits of their office. They must have ready answers to such problems as dog and pet control, traffic management, rezoning, potholes, tax rates, sewer service, crime, water service, sanitation, crime, health care, housing, drugs, and fire protection. While some of these problems may appear to be pedestrian, a mayor can ill afford to ignore them. *See also* CITY GOVERNMENT: CITY MANAGER, 225; CITY GOVERNMENT: STRONG-MAYOR PLAN, 230; CITY GOVERNMENT: WEAK-MAYOR PLAN, 231.

Significance   Mayors have a wide range of formal and informal powers. Some mayors have more, others less. Still, they are expected to wield influence over the city council, oversee executive agencies and departments, process citizen complaints, enforce the law, appear at ceremonial functions, and resolve crises. Inevitably, most mayors come to the realization that they possess few formal powers. To exercise leadership, they must master such skills as persuasion, bargaining, compromise, and public relations. Many mayors face enormous frustrations, including job demands, lack of privacy, low pay, long hours, minimal security, family pressures, political conflicts, and budget dilemmas. In a major study, political scientists John P. Kotter and Paul R. Lawrence attempted to analyze the phenomenon of mayoral leadership.[10] In their study, they identified four main types of mayors: the ceremonial mayor, the caretaker mayor, the crusader mayor, and the program enterpreneur. The ceremonial mayor possesses little subjective vision, few broad goals, a limited staff, tenuous political alliances, and attempts to handle tasks personally (e.g., Walton H. Bachrach of Cincinnati, 1963–1967). The caretaker mayor has slightly more subjective vision, fails to establish a policy agenda, deals with problems individually, surrounds himself with loyal staff, delegates authority to others, and attempts to forge political alliances (e.g., Ralph S. Locher of Cleveland, 1962–1967).

The crusader mayor has a strong subjective vision, but serves in an office that lacks the basic preconditions for effective leadership. Typically, this style predominates when the mayor is an ambitious, creative, and energetic individual who possesses a weak power base (e.g., John V. Lindsey of New York, 1965–1973). Finally, the program entrepreneur has great ambition, possesses the institutional prerequisites for success, develops clear objectives and priorities, focuses on short- and long-range goals, forges political alliances, and hires competent staff (e.g., Richard C. Lee of New Haven, 1954–1969). While most scholars extol the virtues of the program entrepreneur, current trends predict many obstacles to such leadership in the future, most notably, the lack of resources and money. As political scientists John F. Sacco and William M. Parle observe, "In the retrenchment environment of the early 1980s, many mayors have had to function as brokers balancing off the various political pressure groups in the city, or as caretakers aiming at efficient management of the city's scarce resources."[11] Even so, there is recognition of the need for strong mayoral leadership. This is reflected in recent efforts to increase mayoral powers, augment existing resources, hire additional staff, raise salaries, and expand city jurisdiction in vital policy areas.

City Government: Municipal Corporation (229)

A multipurpose form of local government established at the behest of its citizens. Municipal corporations are referred to by a variety of names, among them, cities, towns (except in states with organized towns and townships), villages, and boroughs (except in Alaska). There exist over 19,000 municipalities, with nearly 140 million residents. The creation of a municipal corporation closely parallels that of a private corporation, in that it is initiated by a desirous population, which seeks various powers, benefits, and services. Municipal corporations are required to secure charters from state governments, in which they identify their geographic boundaries, governmental functions and powers, organization and structure, means of finance, and powers to elect and appoint officials and employees. Municipal corporations, like other governmental bodies, may only exercise those powers delegated to them by state constitutions and laws. Once established, they continue to remain subdivisions of the states. Indeed, state laws take procedence over any and all laws passed by municipal corporations. Moreover, they are required to implement and enforce all state laws within their perimeters. They may enact local laws (ordinances), but these are only applicable within their geographic limits. Throughout most of U.S. history, the powers of municipal corporations have been narrowly defined by the courts, which have strictly interpreted their charters. Municipal corporations exist in every state, although they vary dramatically in terms of size, institutions, governance, and resources. Thus, it is extremely difficult to define or describe a typical municipal corporation. *See also* CENTRAL CITY, 222; COUNCILS OF GOVERNMENTS, 233; DILLON'S RULE, 234; METROPOLITAN STATISTICAL AREA, 235.

Significance   Municipal corporations have, since their inception, been heavily dependent on the decisions and actions of state legislatures, although this is less true today. Until the early twentieth century, municipal corporations were usually established and governed by special acts approved by state legislatures. If a community wished to apply for a charter as a municipal corporation, it would petition the state legislature for formal approval, which then decided whether to grant the charter and what powers the municipal corporation should properly exercise. Generally, these charters were so restrictive in their delegation of powers that municipal corporations were obligated to secure state legislative approval for such mundane matters as road repairs, installation of fire hydrants, and salary increases for elected officials. Frequently, the state legislature would approve legislation bearing upon a specific municipal corporation without weighing the views and opinions of the citizens involved. Reformers argued that the fortunes of a municipal corporation were almost totally dependent upon the personal whims and political motives of state legislators, who, in their view, were unqualified to make such decisions. Ultimately, the reformers prevailed, and state legislatures enacted constitutional protections against special legislation. In most states, laws require that issues relating to municipal corporations be addressed through general rather than specific legislation. Today, municipal corporations are classified on the basis of sundry factors, including size or the value of property. Thus, a municipality may be classified as a first-class city, a second-class city, or a town instead of a city. These classifications dictate the governmental form and powers of a municipal corporation. Once a community is classified, it is subject to all laws governing that classification. As a result, state legislatures routinely enact laws for all first-class cities or towns as a group, rather than for specific municipalities. This practice reflects existing prohibitions against special legislation (an act applicable to one unit of local government). In recent years there has been a marked decline in direct state legislative control over local governments, coupled with the realization that most state legislators have neither the time nor the expertise to resolve complex local problems outside their own districts.

City Government: Strong-Mayor Plan (230)

A form of city government in which the mayor appoints the department heads with city council approval, plays a major role relative to the council, and serves as chief executive officer of the city. Under the strong-mayor plan, the mayor has wide appointive powers, conducts city council meetings, establishes their agendas, enjoys strong budget-setting powers, and commands a veto. In large cities, such as Los Angeles, New York, Chicago, and Washington, D.C., the mayor is assisted by one or more deputy mayors, who supervise the routine operations of city government. This permits the mayor to focus on public policy questions, as well as to exercise political leadership. To be a strong mayor, the chief executive must possess the legal and political tools required to govern the city, as well as possess a clear vision of what needs to be done and how best to do it. The strong-mayor plan has an elected mayor who serves as chief executive and who has (1) control over the city's administrative aparatus, including the powers of appointment and dismissal; (2) veto power over city council actions; and (3) tight control over the budget. *See also* CITY GOVERNMENT: CITY MANAGER, 225; CITY GOVERNMENT: MAYOR, 228; CITY GOVERNMENT: WEAK-MAYOR PLAN, 231.

Significance The strong-mayor plan is employed in most cities and has been endorsed by many political scientists, who prefer it to the weak-mayor plan (a form of city government in which the mayor, who is primarily a figurehead, must share executive authority with other elected and appointed officials and the city council). Jeffrey L. Pressman, an authority on municipal governance, argues that strong mayoral leadership requires seven major preconditions: (1) sufficient financial resources with which a mayor can launch innovative social programs; (2) city jurisdiction in the vital program areas of education, housing, redevelopment, and job training; (3) mayoral jurisdiction within the city government in those policy areas; (4) a salary sufficiently high that the mayor can work full time at his or her office; (5) adequate staff support for the mayor, such as policy planning, speech writing, intergovernmental relations, and political work; (6) ready vehicles for publicity, such as friendly newspapers and television stations; and (7) politically oriented groups, including a political party, which the mayor can mobilize in support of administration initiatives.[12] The strong-mayor plan boasts several important advantages. It provides for the centralization of authority, clear lines of executive authority, strong political leadership, modern administrative procedures, and the appointment of competent staff. Are strong mayors more likely to be effective? Yes, contends political scientist John J. Harrigan, who opines, "Strong mayors are a prerequisite for executive leadership. . . . It takes a strong mayor to bend the city bureaucracies to overall policy guidelines. The strong mayor is more likely . . . to make the city responsive to its residents' demands and to make the city accountable to them. Some evidence suggests that strong mayors are able to deal more effectively with a city's interest groups than are weak mayors."[13] In addition, strong mayors are more likely to advocate expanded public programs to solve basic citizen problems and to be able to coordinate those programs more skillfully. Research also indicates that strong mayors are more likely to advocate tax reforms and municipal services that disproportionately benefit the less affluent and powerful.

City Government: Weak-Mayor Plan   (231)
A form of government in which the mayor, who is primarily a figurehead, must share executive authority with other elected and appointed officials and the city council. The weak-mayor plan developed in response to the public's innate distrust of strong chief executives, for fear that the concentration of power would lead to widespread abuses and the usurpation of power. In earlier times—and in some cities today—department heads were elected by the voters and empowered to dispense patronage jobs (to make political appointments to government posts). The weak-mayor plan is characterized by five main features: (1) the mayor is elected on a long ballot (the typical state and local ballot, which includes large numbers of offices, candidates, and issues to be decided), along with various department heads, boards, and commissions, to administer the affairs of the city; (2) the mayor has finite discretion in the appointment and dismissal of city officials; (3) the city council has the power to appoint numerous officials; (4) the mayor either lacks the veto power (the right of the chief executive to reject bills passed by the city council) or has limited prerogatives in exercising the veto; and (5) the city council plays a salient role in administrative functions, including the preparation of the budget. *See also* CITY GOVERNMENT: CITY MANAGER, 225; CITY GOVERNMENT: MAYOR, 228; CITY GOVERNMENT: STRONG-MAYOR PLAN, 230.

Significance   The weak-mayor plan was ideally suited to an earlier era, when cities were smaller and government less complex. It has since been supplanted in many U.S. cities, particularly in the larger municipalities, by the strong-mayor plan (a form of city government in which the mayor appoints the department heads with city council approval, plays a major role relative to the council, and serves as chief executive officer of the city), because today's problems demand strong leadership and effective coordination. Today, most cities recognize the problems of the weak-mayor plan, which encourages fragmented authority and bureaucratic independence. Rooted in the traditions of Jacksonian democracy (progressive reforms associated with the presidency of Andrew Jackson), the weak-mayor plan undermines official accountability, governmental coordination, administrative management, and program delivery. On the other hand, it prevents the concentration of power in any one individual and promotes a complex system of checks and balances to thwart unwarranted power. Still, most U.S. citizens fear "invisible government," which the weak-mayor plan fosters, and oppose any system that places inordinate power in the hands of scores of unelected officials. Today, U.S. cities require strong, creative, dynamic leadership if they are to solve the present urban crisis. Indeed, political scientist Thomas R. Dye contends that the mayors are in the hot seat of U.S. politics and must be able to address these and other problems in a forceful manner.[14] Few other elected officials face the burgeoning problems that confront U.S. cities, which is why, perhaps, former President Lyndon B. Johnson once observed, "Things could be worse; I could be a mayor."[15] Clearly, the weak-mayor plan understates the importance of the mayor as the kingpin of municipal government and the role this individual can and must play in shaping the future of U.S. cities. Still, most mayors have few formal powers to cope with the mounting problems facing local government, apart from their own qualities of leadership. The weak-mayor plan further complicates their task and makes effective governance difficult if not impossible.

Community Power (232)

Describes the power structure within a municipality and the individuals and processes that dictate government policy. Community power is a major concern at the local level, as it determines who exercises influence and to what end. Are community issues decided by democratically elected public officials, or is the government run by a small elite of power brokers who shape public policy in such vital areas as taxation, education, housing, redevelopment, zoning, and so on?

Among social scientists, there are sharp differences over the answer to this question. Those who subscribe to the "power elite" model (e.g., Floyd Hunter) believe that municipal power is concentrated in a small group of people—typically, the city's financial establishment—who decide government policy. Other social scientists, who view themselves as "pluralists" (e.g., Robert Dahl), argue that power is shared by many competing interests who represent, more or less, the wishes of the populace and who exert power as a result of the elections process and citizen participation. Despite their differences, elitists and pluralists agree that most important policy decisions are made by small minorities whose actions are often motivated by their own social, political, and economic interests. *See also* NEW CLASS, 215; PRIVATIZATION, 216.

Significance   Community power theorists recognize the difficulty inherent in identifying those actors and institutions that dictate local affairs. Apart from the elitists and pluralists, most social scientists believe that the truth lies somewhere between these two explanations. In his book *Politics in States and Communities,* political scientist Thomas R. Dye succinctly summarizes the major research findings on the subject.[16] According to Dye: (1) communities without substantial class or racial cleavages have more concentrated power structures; social differences and community conflicts tend to be associated with a pluralist political system; (2) an upswing in many different kinds of industrialization tends to increase political pluralism, whereas power structures tend to be found in communities with a single dominant industry; (3) metropolitan central cities tend to be pluralist in nature, while suburbs in those same metropolitan areas are usually more elitist; (4) the larger the city, the greater the likelihood of a pluralist structure; (5) the older a community, the greater the likelihood of an elitist structure; (6) southern cities tend to be more elitist than northern cities; (7) cities with nonpartisan elections, council-manager governments, and highly professional bureaucracies tend to be associated with elitist power structures, whereas cities with partisan elections, a mayor-council form of government, and relatively more patronage positions available in city government normally are associated with pluralism; and (8) community power tends to destabilize over time, so that communities with elitist power structures tend to evolve into pluralist systems. In addition, the research reveals several other noteworthy conclusions, among them (1) political scientists are less likely to subscribe to the elitist view than sociologists; (2) the business establishment is less influential than many proponents of elitism believe; (3) power is structured differently in different localities, and the structure of power changes over time; (4) the number of influential decision makers is very small; and (6) politically significant individuals derive their influence from holding positions of institutional leadership.[17] In the end, the major differences between the elitists and pluralists are partly explained by the different methodologies they employ to study political power. For example, the elitists focus on the total social structure of a community; they view power as a result of social and economic position. Those who are in a position to dictate the social and economic life of a community are said to possess political power whether they wield it or not. On the other hand, pluralists view power in terms of involvement in decision making. Individuals are said to have power only when they participate directly in a particular community decision.

Councils of Governments (COGs) (233)

Metropolitan associations of governments and government officials that coordinate intergovernmental planning and policy. Councils of governments came into prominence in the mid-1960s, with the passage of the Model Cities Act of 1966. This measure required that all grant applications for federal funds be reviewed by metropolitan planning agencies under a procedure that later became known as the A-95 review process. In addition, the 1965 Housing and Urban Development Act guaranteed federal funds for metropolitan planning. Thus, the availability of federal funds, combined with the A-95 review requirement, spawned the creation of COGs in virtually every major metropolitan area. Today, there are over 500 such councils, the vast majority of whose members are cities (although counties and general-purpose governments may also join). The councils range from 6 to 100 member governments. The smallest council encompasses an area of approximately 100,000 people, while the largest one exceeds 15 million. Councils of governments were established to serve as forums for analysis, discussion, and recommendations regarding common metropolitan problems. As voluntary advisory associations, they possess little if any formal authority. However, they have, in many instances, played an important coordinating role. In the past, COGs have dealt with such problems as community development, pollution abatement, regional planning, airport construction, and water systems. *See also* CITY GOVERNMENT: MUNICIPAL CORPORATION, 229; METROPOLITAN STATISTICAL AREA (MSA), 235.

Significance Although councils of governments lack formal power, this should not be interpreted to mean that they are ineffectual. For example, if COGs are able to reach consensus on an issue, they may well be able to persuade the member cities to adopt their recommendations. Indeed, many COGs can point to impressive records of achievement. The COG in Washington, D.C., for instance, drafted a model air pollution control ordinance that was subsequently endorsed by most member cities, and the Atlanta COG established an academy for training police personnel in that area. Councils of governments have proven popular for many reasons, owing, in large measure, to a major increase in suburbs and the widespread fragmentation that has plagued many metropolitan areas. These developments stimulated the desire for improved coordination of metropolitan areas. Unlike other alternatives (e.g., radical reorganization and government mergers), COGs enjoy considerable political support. According to Nelson Wikstrom, this is because membership is voluntary, COG recommendations are nonbinding, and the operation of a COG does not alter the existing structure of local government.[18] Moreover, preliminary research suggests that COGs are equally popular among the voters. In Oklahoma, for example, in three voter referenda (referrals of legislative measures to the electorate for approval or rejection), a majority of the voters approved their community's involvement in COGs. While councils of governments have succeeded in reducing metropolitan fragmentation, they have proven less effective in reducing tensions between the central city and its suburbs on extremely controversial social issues.

Dillon's Rule   (234)

A legal decision by Judge John F. Dillon, an expert on municipal corporations, which holds that local governments may exercise only those powers expressly delegated to them by state law. Dillon's rule (also known as "creatures of the state"), which was enunciated in an 1872 treatise entitled *Commentaries on the Law of Municipal Corporations*, served to restrict the independence of municipal governments.[19] The rule stated: "It is a general undisputed proposition of law that a municipal corporation possesses and can exercise the following powers, and not others: first, those granted in express words; second, those necessarily or fairly implied in or incident to the powers expressly granted; third, those essential to the accomplishment of the declared objects and purposes of the corporations—not simply convenient, but indispensable. Any fair, reasonable, substantial doubt concerning the existence of power is resolved by the courts against the corporation, and the power is denied."[20] *See also* CITY GOVERNMENT: MUNICIPAL CORPORATION, 229.

Significance   Dillon's rule was upheld by the United States Supreme Court in 1923 when it ruled, in *City of Trenton v. State of New Jersey*, (262 U.S. 182), that state governments possess the legal authority to define the administrative and political powers of their subunits of government. Moreover, a state government may eliminate previously delegated powers or abolish any or all local subunits if it wishes. Local governments are not protected against unilateral destruction. For example, the right of municipal governments to establish a government structure (if the option exists), impose taxes, appropriate monies, prescribe citizen conduct, or deliver public services requires formal state approval. A state may transfer power to its local subunits in one of two ways: either through broad general grants of power, or through narrow, specific grants, one power at a time. These transfers may be made constitutionally or by statute. Practically speaking, note political scientists Edward C. Banfield and James Q. Wilson, this means that "a city cannot operate a peanut stand at the city zoo without first getting the state legislature to pass an enabling law, unless, perchance, the city's charter or some previously enacted law unmistakably covers the sale of peanuts."[21] As interpreted by the courts, Dillon's rule severely limits the authority of municipal governments, as well as subjects them to close, unremitting scrutiny. Overall, it has created considerable uncertainty about local legal powers.

Metropolitan Statistical Area (MSA)   (235)

A central city (or twin cities) with a population of at least 50,000, combined with the adjacent territories that are economically and socially dependent on the city. A metropolitan statistical area must contain a minimum of 50,000 people and a total MSA population of at least 100,000 (75,000 in New England). Several metropolitan areas that exceed 1 million inhabitants have been designated as consolidated metropolitan statistical areas (CMSAs). These incorporate individual primary metropolitan statistical areas (PMSAs). The boundaries of an MSA or CSMA reflect municipal or county lines and may overlap state lines. As of 1983, there were 343 MSAs and 23 CMSAs in the United States. These encompassed three-fourths of the nation's population and were governed by over 26,000 local jurisdictions. Interestingly, several metropolitan areas include over 500 governments. For example, the Chicago area has over 1,000 government units, while the New York region exceeds 1,400. The four-county Pittsburgh metropolitan area numbers 704 local governments, 441 of which can levy property taxes. In Allegheny County alone, there are 84 municipalities, 42 townships, 62 school districts, and at least 129 school boards. Nationwide, each metropolitan area averages approximately 90 governments, with 50 per metropolitan county. *See also* CENTRAL CITY, 222; CITY GOVERNMENT: MUNICIPAL CORPORATION, 229; DILLON'S RULE, 234.

Significance   A metropolitan statistical area is typically created around a central city, branches out into two or more counties, and subsumes numerous municipalities, school districts, and special districts. These government bodies deal with such problems as discrimination, transportation, education, housing, pollution, and crime. The average metropolitan area includes a nexus of diverse communities and governing bodies. In no case does a single political authority speak and act for the entire area. For example, the governor speaks for the state; the mayor speaks for the city. However, no one highly visible spokesperson speaks for the metropolitan area. This makes it difficult, if not impossible, to create one large constituency with a knowledge of and interest in metropolitan concerns. In short, the metropolitan problem can be attributed, in part, to the existence of too many governments, as well as to the fact that the above-mentioned problems simply cannot be solved within the existing boundaries of these myriad local jurisdictions, even if they were significantly reduced in number. The metropolitan problem, maintains political scientist Robert L. Lineberry, involves four main aspects: (1) externalities or spillover effects (where one municipality's actions affect the other parts of the region, but where the latter has little or no involvement in the policy process); (2) political nonresponsibility; (3) a lack of coordination; and (4) fiscal and service inequalities.[22]

Suburb   **(236)**
A primarily residential community adjacent to a large city. Suburbs have dramatically changed the face of urban life. Not only have they limited geographic expansion of cities, but they drew from them a vast number of affluent people and the resources they represent. In their place, the city was bequeathed to the poor, the powerless, and the dispossessed. As the white middle class fled the central cities, they were replaced by millions of blacks, Hispanics, and poor whites, who migrated to the cities in vast numbers. Ultimately, this resulted in the creation of massive *ghettos* (a section of a city inhabited predominantly by minorities). By 1970, for the first time in U.S. history, a majority of urban dwellers resided outside the central cities, a development that had begun 50 years earlier. In the process, the central city took on a new character; eventually it bore little resemblance to the earlier city

it replaced. Experts prophesied an inevitable conflict between the central city and the suburbs. In many ways, their prediction proved true. For example, the Advisory Commission on Civil Disorders, in its report on the causes of the race riots of the 1960s, described the United States as "two nations, one black and one white."[23] However, the central city–suburb dichotomy proved to be far more complex than a simple contest between the cities and the suburbs. Nevertheless, a fundamental rift emerged between the central cities and the suburbs. This resulted in a number of problems: unemployment, crime, drugs, physical decay, and the loss of businesses and jobs. Many suburbanites were attracted by the mystique of these new communities—open space, a healthy environment, sundry amenities and services, an exhilarating social atmosphere, and instant happiness. Despite its questionable validity, the suburban myth served the economic objectives and ideological purposes of those who preached its gospel. This group included home builders and developers, entrepreneurs and speculators, and ideologues and politicos. *See also* ANNEXATION, 221; CENTRAL CITY, 222; CITY-COUNTY CONSOLIDATION, 223; PRIVATIZATION, 216.

Significance   Suburbs may invite racial and social class segregation. Indeed, they have sometimes separated black from white, rich from poor, and young from old. Suburban promoters marketed these new communities on the basis of traditional American values, as well as their intrinsic amenities and advantages. In some cases, however, their motives were less than pure. In the end, many suburban hawkers were motivated by personal profit and gain, as well as a desire to preserve the racial and social composition of what had once been the exclusive province of the affluent white middle class. Despite their promise of paradise, many suburbs face the same problems that beset the central cities. In recent years, fiscal and social problems have brought renewed attention to the suburbs, which today confront such serious issues as industrial pollution, racial discrimination, rampant violence, inadequate transportation, soaring housing costs, and an aging population. What will be the future of the suburb? Some urbanologists predict the polarization of owners and renters, increased urbanization, burgeoning isolation, the breakdown of family values, and social anomie. On the other hand, they also prophesize the upgrading of U.S. culture, new entrepreneurial opportunities, the proliferation of alternative life-styles, and boundless adventure. Suburbanization has resulted in increased costs to central cities, in addition to the above-mentioned problems. In many ways, the central city has become a receptacle for all those functions the suburbs do not wish to absorb, which range from social welfare to heavy industry. In addition, the central city is presently experiencing debilitating costs as a result of suburban exploitation of city services, in the form of increased congestion as well as increased need for police, fire, water, and other services. Unfortunately, many suburbanites do not pay for the benefits they receive, which puts an added strain on the limited resources of the central city. Ultimately, suburbanites must come to the realization that they enjoy a symbiotic relationship with the central cities. Indeed, the status of suburbs as viable communities depends, in large part, on the health of central cities and their economic markets. Neither can survive independently.

10. Financing State and Local Government

Assessment (237)

The process by which property valuation is determined for tax purposes. Assessment, assigning property values at regular or irregular intervals, was employed in Colonial times and in our early national period. In 24 states, counties handle assessment; in 17, towns, townships, or districts; in others, counties and towns assess separately. The property tax is usually levied on real estate and personal property. Real estate consists of land and buildings, whereas personal property applies to tangible (e.g., jewelry, machinery, automobiles) and intangible (e.g., stocks, bonds, bank accounts) property. The assessor is commonly an elected official who assigns the value of personal and real property for purposes of local taxation. In a number of states assessors are township or district officers whose duties are subject to review by county authority. The assessed valuation is usually 30 to 50 percent of the true market value of the prop- erty, although some local governments assess at 100 percent value. *See also* PROPERTY TAX, 255; PROPOSITION 13, 257.

Significance   Assessment to levy taxes is difficult, highly complicated, and extremely controversial. After the assessors have completed their work, an opportunity must be given for complaints. Many locally elected assessors are poorly qualified to perform the difficult task of property tax assessment, and assessed values vary because there are no absolute standards by which they can be determined. Among the methods used are estimating the replacement cost of the property, determining the selling price on the market, and comparing the price of similar properties in the same neighborhood or in the same type of locality. Another problem assessors face is the difficulty

251

associated with locating movable property. Despite these difficulties the property tax will remain and will probably increase in many states, as it is the major source of revenue for local government. Because the property tax is politically unpopular, many states and local communities have sought more acceptable alternatives to enhance revenue.

Auditing (238)
A way of assuring that all expenditures have been incurred in accordance with law and for authorized purposes. Auditing is an attempt to determine accurately whether money is spent for the appropriated purposes. It is conducted by an officer called an auditor, auditor general, comptroller, or examiner. The auditor is elected in all states except New Jersey, Tennessee, and Virginia, where election by a joint vote of the two houses of the state legislature is required. The auditor is responsible for a number of functions. He or she typically performs two main types of audit: first, the internal or preaudit and, second, the external or postaudit. The internal audit reviews the operating practices of employees to determine conformity with established policies and to see that expenses do not exceed the amount budgeted for the purpose. The external audit is made after the transactions have been completed and constitutes a review of what has been done. In a few states these different functions are divided between the auditor and a comptroller. All governments—federal, state, and local—have auditors, and auditing of accounts is legally required by all governments. *See also* COMPTROLLER, 120; LEGISLATIVE OVERSIGHT, 251.

Significance   Auditing must be done properly and frequently in order to control proper accounting of public (or private) funds. If audit reports and observations are not made expeditiously, they are of little value to a new administration, which is not responsible for the fiscal conduct of its predecessor. The auditor is charged with checking the administrative branch of government. A reluctant auditor or one who belongs to a different party from the executive can employ his or her preaudit powers to delay or cripple government programs, and thus embarrass the administration. Auditing has undergone radical changes in recent years, as government corruption and mismanagement have increased. One new approach is called performance auditing or operational auditing, which probes efficiency in the organization and management of a department or the entire government. Not all states encourage performance auditing because they do not want to venture beyond accuracy and legality in financial matters. Simply put, these states do not wish to open a can of worms. The importance of the auditing function today can be appreciated by observing the magnitude of federal and state spending, with the former over $1 trillion annually and the states reaching into the hundreds of billions of dollars each year.

Budget Process (239)

All stages of budget planning and analysis, as well as the rules and procedures by which revenues and expenditures are proposed, debated, approved, and executed. The budget process defines and mandates the government's taxing and spending policy. At the state and local level, there are three main types of budget processes: executive, committee or board, and legislative. The executive budget system is the most prevalent. It closely resembles the federal budget process. Under this system, the chief executive prepares the budget, which is then presented to the legislature for approval. This committee or board approach is employed by governments that are characterized by administrative decentralization. The committee includes the governor and the administrative heads of the various departments. Once the budget is prepared, it, too, is submitted for legislative approval. The legislative approach is practiced primarily by smaller units of local government, where a municipality is governed by a city council. The legislative agency is charged with both the preparation and adoption of the budget. Despite minor differences, most states follow similar procedures in formulating their annual or biennial budgets. At the beginning of the fiscal year (in many cases July 1), state agencies submit their requests for the following year's appropriations. These requests are scrutinized by a state budget agency, which works in consort with the governor. The executive budget is then prepared. In early January, this document is submitted to the state legislature which studies it until the beginning of the fiscal year. Once the budget is approved by the governor and enacted by legislature, it becomes law, at which point the process begins anew. The same process is generally followed by local governments. *See also* GOVERNOR'S BUDGET, 249; LEGISLATIVE OVERSIGHT, 251.

Significance The budget process at the state and local level differs markedly from the federal budgetary process. It is designed to control government expenditures and to ensure the success of the chief executive's policy initiatives. Government expenditures are contingent on revenues received from taxation, federal (state) grants, and bonds for capital projects. This last source is restricted by state and local debt limits. This is not true at the federal level, which permits deficit spending. At the state and local level, the trend is toward the executive approach to budgeting. This fact, when coupled with spending limitations, enhances the chief executive's efforts to implement public policy through program funding. Additionally, chief executives frequently possess the item veto, which enables them to disapprove those budget items to which they take exception. The governor's involvement in the formulation and adoption of the budget serves to increase his or her influence and authority in securing approval of a budget which reflects administration priorities. Still, the budget process involves the efficient allocation of scarce resources to meet soaring citizen demands. Despite the governor's authority, it is not unlimited, as agencies are exempt from executive control. Moreover, the governor's ability to shape the budget is reduced by the necessity of earmarking revenue from specific programs by statutory or constitutional requirements. In addition, traditional budgeting is, by definition, an incremental process—one that precludes major changes. In most cases, agencies receive small increases or decreases based on the previous year's allocations, a process that ensures stability and predictability. The budget process is structured so as to preclude a systematic analysis of state and local expenditures. Finally, the governor must recognize the political realities which attend the budget process, never forgetting that the budget is, after all, a political document. This necessitates cooperation, compromise, negotiation, and consensus.

Budget Process: Incremental Budgeting   (240)

The process of setting annual appropriations based on the previous year's budget as the base from which small additions or subtractions are made, usually to reflect the rate of inflation. Incremental budgeting seeks to reduce risk and to minimize error; thus it rejects extreme alternatives and untried methods. Unlike some budgeting techniques (e.g., zero-base budgeting), it favors piecemeal adjustments over exhaustive program-by-program scrutiny. These increments may either be positive or negative: positive, by the addition of new programs or increases in existing programs; negative, by cutbacks in other programs. Incremental budgeting is preferred by many state legislators, who view it as a safe and rational way to avoid poorly calculated decisions. According to Ann H. Elder and George C. Kiser, "Since the legislators already know the consequences of having adopted existing programs, they can anticipate a similar response if they enact essentially similar programs and policies."[1] *See also* BUDGET PROCESS, 239; BUDGET PROCESS: ZERO-BASE BUDGETING, 243.

Significance Incremental budgeting is the most often used method for determining agency appropriations. This is attributable, in part, to the conservative bias of the budgetary process, which seeks to preserve the status quo. Incremental budgeting, argues political scientist Thomas J. Anton, has produced several informal folkways. These include: (1) Spend all of your appropriation. Failure to do so indicates excess, which is likely to result in reduced funding the following year. (2) Never request less money than your current appropriation. It is far easier to justify increases than to explain reductions—not to mention the attendant embarrassment to agency officials. (3) Top-priority items should be built into the basic budget, which is within current appropriation levels. Programs that appear to be part of existing operations will rarely be challenged. (4) Proposed increases should appear to be small and reflect ongoing procedures. (5) Inflate your budget, so as to allow for cuts. It is wise to propose large increases in existing programs, as well as myriad new programs. This will afford the politicians and budget cutters an opportunity to "save" the public money and score political points with the voters.[2] Incremental budgeting boasts several advantages: it expedites the budgetary process, minimizes political confrontation, accommodates diverse interests, and embodies the prevailing political wisdom. On the other hand, it discourages program analysis, prefers existing programs to new ones, rewards piecemeal scrutiny over comprehensive examination, and fosters policy neutrality.

Budget Process: Line-Item Budgeting (241)

A format that lists annual agency expenditures for such items as salaries, equipment, supplies, maintenance, and contractual services. Line-item budgeting resembles the traditional budget, in the sense that each item and its cost appear in the budget. This approach has existed since the beginning of government, dating back to the ancient courts of Egypt, Babylon, and China. In the United States, the line-item budget was introduced by political reformers, who sought to promote honesty and efficiency in government. It reflects the view, perhaps best expressed by Charles G. Dawes, the first director of the Bureau of the Budget (predecessor to the Office of Management and Budget), who, in 1923, observed, "The Bureau of the Budget is concerned only with the humbler and routine business of government. It is concerned with no question of policy, save that of economy and efficiency."[3] In a line-item budget, the funding categories remain relatively constant from year to year. Budgetary calculations for specific items are not figured anew each year, but are reliant on the previous year's calculations or the initial funding level. For example, if you were the mayor of Notoville, California, and wished to discover how well the city park system was functioning, the line-item budget would provide scant information, other than to tell you whether city funds were overspent. It would tell you little about how the money was spent or whether it was spent wisely. In this regard, line-item budgeting fails to address such issues as efficiency and effectiveness. *See also* BUDGET PROCESS, 239; BUDGET PROCESS: INCREMENTAL BUDGETING, 240; BUDGET PROCESS: ZERO-BASE BUDGETING, 243; GOVERNOR'S BUDGET, 249.

Significance Line-item budgeting is employed by most state and local governments. It assumes the efficacy of individual entries based on their existence in the previous year's budget. As such, it embodies the principles of incremental budgeting—small additions or subtractions, usually based on the rate of inflation. Moreover, line-item budgeting poses little threat to the existence of any agency or program, as this is assured. Thus, its approach is politically expedient. On the other hand, it has several drawbacks. Accepting the validity of a program, simply because it appeared in the previous year's budget, ignores the question of whether or not the program is still necessary and/or effective. Historically, line-item budgeting looks backward, not forward to future policy goals. It represents a commitment to the status quo, with certain minor adjustments. It also poses other problems, including the fact that small errors are magnified over the course of many years. It also allows for possible program overlap. Two different programs may have similar objectives, which could be more effectively combined into one program. Efforts to resolve these shortcomings have inspired several alternative approaches, among them, zero-base budgeting (in which budget managers assume a zero-dollar base and must justify all expenditures based on need and performance), and the planning-programming-budgeting system (which requires agencies to define their goals precisely and measure the costs and benefits of alternative programs to achieve those goals). Still, line-item budgeting predominates among state and local governments, as these and other alternatives are often unwieldy, costly, and in many cases, ineffective.

Budget Process: Planning-Programming-Budgeting (242) System (PPBS)

A budgeting tool that requires agencies to identify program objectives and the most cost-efficient manner in which they could be realized. The planning-programming-budgeting system seeks to promote increased rationality in the budgetary process by defining program objectives, assessing future implications, ascertaining pertinent costs, and analyzing major alternatives. It is predicated on such concepts as cost-benefit analysis, program budgeting, systems analysis, and cost effectiveness. PPBS assumes that government decision making would be markedly improved if agency officials and budget managers would designate program objectives, which they could then quantify. By identifying all possible alternatives, administrators could then test their efficacy by applying cost-benefit analysis to each one. The alternative that promised the greatest benefits, for the least cost, would constitute the optimum choice. In many ways, PPBS closely resembles the underlying principles of the rational decision-making model. *See also* BUDGET PROCESS, 239; MANAGEMENT BY OBJECTIVE, 253.

Significance   The planning-programming-budgeting system was formally instituted by President Lyndon B. Johnson in 1965, although it was initially implemented in the Department of Defense in 1961. A highly regarded tool, its use quickly spread to state, county, and city governments. Interest in the system led to several intergovernmental pilot projects, one of which involved five cities, five counties, and five states. In his study of the project, six years later, investigator Allen Schick found "few stories to emulate, few examples of what works, and no solid evidence of the benefits to be derived from PPBS. The traditions established in earlier years continue to dominate the budget process, while PPBS stands on the outside, a fashionable but peripheral feature of state administration."[4] PPBS produced similar results at the federal level. In essence, many government programs defy quantification. For example, foreign policy goals preclude budgetary analysis. It is equally difficult to apply such methods to domestic programs, particularly weighing long-term benefits. Moreover, it is extremely difficult to calculate the financial costs of a program, as these frequently include numerous nonmonetary factors. After all, future costs and benefits are, at best, problematic, and depend, to a large extent, on the methods employed, which are often imprecise. PPBS critics argue, with some force, that the system sought to depoliticize the policy-making process, which, they insist, is both unrealistic and unwise. Although PPBS fell into disfavor at the federal level, it is still widely practiced by many state and local governments. Overall, it has demonstrated greater results in agencies that generate material benefits (e.g., highway construction) than in agencies that produce social benefits (e.g., health care).

Budget Process: Zero-Base Budgeting (243)

A technique that requires budget planners to start with a zero dollar base and to justify each budget item, thus necessitating a year-to-year reevaluation of each program. Zero-base budgeting seeks to eliminate superfluous and cost-inefficient programs. The technique consists of two stages: First, agency program managers begin at zero by identifying each program and then evaluate its costs and benefits at various levels of funding. Their objective is to determine the optimum level of funding. The result of this process is called the "decision package." Second, program managers send the decision package to their superiors, who then rank the packages according to their priority within the agency. These are called "budget choice units." Since a monetary value is attached to each package, a cutoff line can be drawn at a level marking the agency's funding for that year. Budget line flexibility permits program managers to shift up or down according to the actual funding. In the end, the decision makers are, theoretically speaking, in a better position to choose the appropriate level of spending for each program. Low priority items are eliminated. *See also* BUDGET PROCESS, 239; BUDGET PROCESS: INCREMENTAL BUDGETING, 240.

Significance   Zero-base budgeting was developed in 1969 by Peter A. Pyhrr for use in private industry. Pyhrr argued that the primary goal of zero-base budgeting is to "force us to identify and analyze what we are going to do in total, set goals and objectives, and make necessary operating decisions, and evaluate changing responsibilities and work loads as an integral part of the budget process."[5] In 1972, then-Governor Jimmy Carter implemented zero-base budgeting in the state of Georgia. Upon his election as president, he required all executive department and agency heads in 1979 to employ zero-base budgeting for the fiscal year. In practice, the experiment failed. The essential problem, concluded John D. La Faver, in his study of New Mexico's experience with zero-base budgeting in 1973, is: "It is not reasonable to expect an agency to routinely furnish information that might result in a lower appropriation—no matter what the justification might be."[6] Clearly, zero-base budgeting is not a cure-all. Its use involves enormous paperwork, as well as the development of thousands of decision packages, which require an inordinate amount of time and effort. In addition, it is politically unfeasible to assert that an agency's base is devoid of permanent or ongoing programs. Finally, the cost of implementing zero-base budgeting is extremely high. In states where this technique has proven successful, it has been modified to reflect local needs and circumstances.

Earmarked Revenues   **(244)**

Tax monies allocated for specific purposes by constitutional or statutory requirements. Approximately one-half of all state revenue is earmarked for specific purposes. For example, earmarked levies include gasoline taxes (e.g., for highway construction and maintenance) and the general sales tax (e.g., for education). Revenues from hunting and fishing licenses are frequently earmarked for conservation and natural resources, while state pension funds are earmarked for benefit payments. Earmarking limits the governor's and the state legislature's ability to control governmental programs and to effectively control agencies that receive earmarked revenues. These provisions were enacted during the late 1800s and reflected public concern over the lack of fiscal responsibility and accountability at the state level. Today, earmarking has stirred widespread debate and discussion, as it establishes state spending priorities that may fail to embody current policy objectives. Although these programs enjoy ongoing funding, they may do so at the expense of other programs that may prove more desirable or necessary at a given time. *See also* GOVERNOR'S BUDGET, 249; USER FEES, 264.

Significance   Earmarked revenues are used at all levels of government. For example, in 1984, federal insurance trust revenues topped the $220 billion figure. Earmarking is often based on the benefit theory of taxation, that is, taxing those who benefit from government services. For instance, gasoline taxes are paid by motorists who use roads and highways built and maintained by taxpayer dollars. Despite public criticism, earmarking enjoys wide support, particularly from interest groups that wish to see government funds routinely channeled into favored programs without having to travel the legislative obstacle course. These groups much prefer to avoid legislative scrutiny, evaluation, and the appropriations process, and earmarking provides such funds without the attendant political difficulties. The more popular the program, or the more influential the interest group, the more likely it will prevail in the state legislature. In addition, earmarked revenues are frequently tied to a widely supported expenditure with perhaps an unacceptable method of finance. Many states have sought to justify the adoption of a lottery by earmarking the anticipated revenue for education. Once the earmarked tax is instituted—buttressed by constitutional and statutory provisions—it becomes difficult, if not impossible, to discontinue future funding. Moreover, critics contend that earmarking undermines the budgetary process, makes administration intricate and cumbersome, and weakens representative government. The public interest would be better served, they argue, if the governor had increased authority over the allocation of tax dollars and if the state legislature were better able to determine the expenditure of tax revenues. Clearly, the absence of gubernatorial control and legislative review makes it exceedingly difficult to evaluate the effectiveness of governmental programs.

Excise Tax (245)

A tax on the manufacture, sale, transportation, or consumption of goods. An excise tax is an indirect duty extended to include various license fees and goods sold or transported within a country. The main excise taxes used by the states and federal government are sales and user taxes. Federal excise taxes must be uniform throughout the United States, giving no preference to one state over another. Excise taxes are imposed on gasoline, alcohol, radios, television sets, phonograph records, telephone services, travel, luggage, and amusements. Excise taxes take the form of sales taxes, but they are also consumption taxes. Some of the major excises are (1) an alcoholic beverage tax collected by states through wholesale distribution or through licensing; (2) a cigarette and tobacco tax levied on tobacco products as a group, and taxes applicable only to certain forms of manufactured tobacco such as cigarettes and cigars; and (3) a gasoline tax collected by dealers who sell gas to consumers. *See also* SALES TAX, 260; USER FEES, 264.

Significance   Excise taxes, like other taxes, receive much criticism. They affect the poor disproportionately since they represent a larger percentage of the poor's income. Although the purpose of taxation is to raise revenue, some excise taxes, such as the one on liquor, act to discourage consumption because their use is socially undesirable. Excises on tobacco products discourage their use because they are regarded as hazardous to health. The tax on gasoline is justified on the benefit theory of taxation since the taxpayers receive some benefit for this tax money in the form of road and highway construction and maintenance. Growing revenue requirements at all levels of government have led to overlapping, double taxation, and most excises fall into this category. While the federal government collects the lion's share of the taxes, the states need more funds to alleviate local problems. In many cases they have failed to receive the necessary revenue from the federal government, which has made problem solving difficult.

Fiscal Year (246)

A period of one year starting on the day that governments or business enterprises begin recording their annual financial activities. The fiscal year is not uniform for federal, state, and local governments. The federal government begins its fiscal year on October 1, while it is often on the first day of January, April, July, or September in the states. The term *fiscal* is derived from the Latin *fiscus*, meaning "purse." *Fiscal* or *financial* refers to anything relating to income or expenditure. In the past, the states' fiscal year was the same as that of the federal government—from July 1 to June 30—until the federal government changed its year to October 1 through September 30. During the fiscal year, annual appropriations are to be sent, taxes collected, and accounts maintained. Some state legislatures meet in January or February of the odd-numbered years and usually adjourn before summer. At that time they prepare a biennial or two-year budget. Many local governments use the calender year (January 1 to December 31) as the fiscal year. *See also* APPROPRIATION, 84; BUDGET PROCESS, 239.

Significance   The fiscal year is a cycle of 12 consecutive months used by governments as the period for adoption of budget and annual reports. The federal government changed its fiscal year to give Congress more time to enact appropriations, while states such as Alabama and Michigan followed suit. Texas adopted a fiscal year from September 1; New York from April 1. Traditionally, many state legislators were farmers, and they preferred legislative sessions in the winter. A fiscal year beginning in July was most suitable to the farmer-legislators as they could finish legislative business before the farming season. Although the makeup of legislature has changed to include more professionals, legislative sessions and fiscal years have remained the same in many states. At the end of the fiscal year all account books are closed, and the financial standing of the government or business concern is determined. Many departments rush to spend money in the final days of the financial year so they may claim an equal or greater amount in the next fiscal year, and fiscal irresponsibility is not uncommon at this time.

General Obligation Bonds (247)

Bonds backed by the "full faith and credit" of the issuing government. General obligation bonds are often referred to as "guaranteed bonds." In essence, they represent a charge against the holdings of all property owners in the city or state. In most cases, general obligation bonds are subject to a voter referendum, in which the electorate agrees to increase taxes to pay the interest and to eventually retire the bond. Like revenue bonds (nonguaranteed bonds, financed by income from self-liquidating projects), the interest on general obligation bonds is exempt from federal taxation. However, unlike revenue bonds, these bonds are backed by the issuing government, are less risky, and pay lower interest rates. General obligation bonds are the least costly method of borrowing. As a result, investors view them as safe and are willing to accept lower rates of interest. This view is supported by the very small number of defaults. The ability of state and local governments to issue general obligation bonds is prescribed by constitutional and statutory limitations. However, many issuing governments have fashioned inventive methods to circumvent these requirements (e.g., by issuing revenue or nonguaranteed bonds), which are not backed by the government's full faith and credit, are more risky, and pay higher interest rates. General obligation bonds comprise approximately one-third of state and one-half of local long-term borrowing. *See also* GENERAL REVENUE, 248; LOCAL DEBT LIMIT, 252; REVENUE BONDS, 259; STATE DEBT LIMIT, 262.

Significance   General obligation bonds have become less popular in recent years, owing to the increased importance of state and local borrowing. This trend emerged in the 1930s, when the Public Works Administration encouraged state and local governments to change their laws to allow the issuance of nonguaranteed bonds. Regardless of the type of bond, state and local governments view borrowing as a legitimate way to finance much-needed capital projects, such as highways, buildings, sewage facilities, schools, and other public enterprises. Although debt per capita doubled between 1973 and 1984, debt service payments as compared to general revenue declined. Nationwide, the debt picture appears healthy, despite several recent noteworthy exceptions (e.g., New York City and Cleveland). Still, current trends underscore the importance of prudent borrowing policies. Between 1941 and 1984, for example, state indebtedness increased sixfold. In addition, there were pronounced shifts in specific items, most notably, highway and water transportation debts, which have since been supplanted by education as the major source of state and local debt. Other items, such as hospitals, have also increased in importance. Furthermore, long-term borrowing—as opposed to short-term borrowing—has become increasingly common (as of 1984, it represented 64 percent of all state and local borrowing). To prevent possible problems associated with indebtedness, state governments have sought to limit the potential borrowing power of municipalities by imposing constitutional limitations, establishing debt ceilings, and requiring that new debts be approved by referenda.

General Revenue   (248)

A government's principal income. General revenue is collected mainly from taxation, income of businesses owned by government, payment made into government-run insurance plans by subscribers, and lotteries. Income tax, sales tax, property tax, and excise duties contribute most to general revenue. State and local governments spend over $300 billion a year, which they raise from various sources of revenue. State governments rely on sales taxes, income taxes, borrowing, and aid from the federal government. Local governments depend heavily on property taxes, state and federal aid, and user charges. All governments in the United States provide monetary assistance to each other, which is called revenue sharing. Under this system, the federal government funnels money to the state and local governments through its General Revenue Sharing (GRS) Act of 1972. The state governments may spend GRS money for any legal purposes, but the local units must spend these funds for environmental protection, health services, transportation, recreation, and public libraries. *See also* EXCISE TAX, 245; INCOME TAX, 250; PROPERTY TAX, 255; SALES TAX, 260.

Significance   General revenue sharing is needed by federal, state, and local governments to maintain public services, many of which have increased in the past half century. While not increasing as rapidly as the federal government's expenses, services provided by state and local governments have grown dramatically. Considering the present attitude of the federal government on revenue sharing, it has become increasingly necessary that state and local authorities recognize all potential sources of revenue. In 1986, 16 states raised taxes totaling $1.3 billion, with excise taxes on gasoline and cigarettes the most commonly raised levies. Some states raised general sales taxes. Federal, state, and local relationships are complex because of structural and legal complications. They are also problematic because the federal government collects most of the revenue and uses it for its own expenses, while most of the problems are centered in state and local communities, which are hampered by a serious lack of resources. Informed observers believe that federal, state, and local conflicts in almost all areas of revenue raising are likely to increase substantially.

Governor's Budget   (249)

The income and expenditure of public money proposed by the governor for the state government. The governor's budget requires the state legislature to appropriate funds to run the state government.

The governor's power in the budgeting process rests with his or her initiatory role, the ability to influence the legislature, and the threat to veto (except in North Carolina, where the governor has no veto power). Before the legislature convenes, the governor draws up a budget of recommended appropriations and anticipated revenues. This document is formally presented to the legislature by the governor. It includes reasons for increases and decreases in appropriations, based on proposals submitted by the various departments and agencies. The departments and agencies may request more than they spent previously, and sometimes the legislature is given the department's original requests along with the governor's recommendation. In most states the governor appoints a budget director who prepares the state budget on his or her behalf. *See also* BUDGET PROCESS, 239; GOVERNOR, 123; LEGISLATIVE OVERSIGHT, 251.

Significance　　The budget helps the governor to control the state administration much in the same way the president maintains control over the federal government. By controlling the budget the governor imposes his or her policy over the state administration and influences decision making. After the governor submits the budget proposal, the appropriations committees of the legislature may alter the amounts requested before sending the bill to floor debate and final passage. During the entire budgetary process, the governor's budget, like the United States' and the local government budgets, is incrementally developed on the previous year's budget, with special attention given to new items and unusually large requests, politically sensitive projects, and programs in which personal interests predominate. The governor oversees the lawful expenditure of appropriations by the various departments. Finally, the legislative branch, through its auditors, checks the budget's accuracy and compliance with law by the executive departments.

Income Tax (250)

A tax levied on salaries, rents, interests, dividends, commissions, royalties, business profits, and other income. Income taxes are imposed on personal and corporate income. The federal and most state governments impose individual and corporate income taxes, with different rates. State rates are lower than the federal rate. Wisconsin was the first state to legislate an income tax, in 1911. Many states and some of the major cities adopted an income tax shortly thereafter. A federal income tax based on income from "whatever source derived" was enacted by the Sixteenth Amendment to the

United States Constitution in 1913. The national government and most states assess income taxes on a progressive basis, with higher rates applied to higher incomes. The corporate income tax is levied on the net profits of private corporations, usually at a fixed rate. An income tax typically is levied on net income and, as such, it allows deductions for expenses incurred in producing that income. These deductions exist for business, nonbusiness, and, in some cases, for personal expenses. Most taxpayers pay through the payroll withholding system. At the federal level the income tax is administered by the Internal Revenue Service, and at the state level by the state's revenue department. All income tax returns may be subject to audit. *See also* GENERAL REVENUE, 248; PROGRESSIVE TAX, 254.

Significance   The income tax occupies a major role in the federal and state tax picture today. An income tax has several advantages and disadvantages. Some of the advantages are (1) it is easy to collect; (2) it is fairly predictable so that accurate governmental budgeting is possible; (3) it can be adjusted so as to increase or decrease revenue by the relatively simple device of changing the rate; and (4) it, unlike many other taxes, is direct and is presumed to make taxpayers conscious of the socioeconomic responsibility of living in a modern society. A major weakness is that the revenue derived from the income tax may vary substantially with prosperity or recession. Another weakness lies in the income tax's complicated filing system. Studies have shown that most taxpayers tend to underreport their income and claim more deductions than they are entitled to take. Yet, on balance, individual and corporate income taxes have made it possible, despite all their warts and blemishes, to provide financial support for broad-gauged federal and state economic and social programs.

Legislative Oversight   (251)

Monitoring of the executive branch to see that it carries out its legislative mandate. Legislative oversight seeks to ensure that the laws passed by the legislature are being administered effectively and according to legislative intent. Standing and special committees appointed by the legislature investigate executive departments concerning their overall performance or their administration of a program or policy. Legislatures, through their auditors, review government accounts and the management of financial affairs. Legislative committees may investigate suspected waste, bribery, and fraud. The committees may require periodic reports from the executive offices and can audit their expenditures. Oversight or watchdog functions may be conducted by both houses of the legislatures through their committee systems. The purposes behind oversight include (1) overseeing of executive offices; (2) uncovering questionable activities of public officials; (3) discovering public opinion; and (4) seeking partisan political gain. *See also* GOVERNOR'S BUDGET, 249; LEGISLATIVE BRANCH, 95.

Significance   Legislative oversight is a tool employed by the legislature to probe activities of the executive branch. A legislative investigation is considered valid so long as it does not encroach on executive and judicial powers, and if constitutional guarantees—especially those providing for a separation of powers—are not violated. The legislature may summon witnesses, books, and papers from the executive offices. This is an important nonlawmaking function of a legislature. In recent years the expanded use of investigations by the Congress and state legislatures underscore their power. There is always a chance the legislature may misuse its watchdog functions for political reasons. Legislative investigations can become publicity circuses, serving mainly to advance the investigators' political careers or to damage the credibility of those summoned to testify. Many legislators do not like oversight functions because they see themselves primarily as lawmakers.

Local Debt Limit   (252)

A restriction imposed by state constitutions or statutory law on the borrowing level of local governments. Local debt limits are usually set as a percentage of the total assessed valuation of taxable real estate in a particular locality. This ranges from 5 to 10 percent of the locality's assessed valuation. Debt limits were initially proposed in response to excessive spending by local governments in the last three decades of the nineteenth century and a 10 percent default rate on municipal bonds in the 1930s. In addition to limits on the size of the debt, some states also limit the purposes for which localities may borrow and the time span over which bonds may be retired. Only four states (Alaska, Florida, Colorado, and Nebraska) have no constitutional or statutory limits on the ability of local governments to incur long-term debts. The existence of local debt limits clearly implies that state governments have the legal authority to restrict local governments' powers to levy taxes and incur debts. *See also* GENERAL OBLIGATION BONDS, 247; REVENUE BONDS, 259; STATE DEBT LIMIT, 262.

Significance   Local debt limits, combined with local tax limits (the percentage of the assessed valuation at which property may be taxed), have been defended as protecting the taxpayer against excessive taxation to finance questionable capital projects. In sum, they exist to prevent short-sighted and imprudent spending. Opponents of local debt limits argue that local officials possess the requisite skills to evaluate the needs of the citizens, and should thus be permitted greater discretion in the development and implementation of local fiscal policy. Moreover, local debt limits are thought to restrict the ability of local officials to provide public services required by the people. The demand for public services, coupled with the lack of fiscal resources, has forced local officials to turn to the federal government for assistance, specifically, in the form of grants. Despite state efforts to curb local debt, debt limits can be circumvented in several ways. First, debt limits only apply to guaranteed bonds or general obligation bonds, which are charged against general revenues. By issuing nonguaranteed revenue bonds (where buyers of bonds rely on the ability of the enterprise to repay them), a city can finance specific projects, such as public transit and sewage treatment facilities. Second, debt limits usually apply to each unit of government. By establishing a special unit (e.g., a water district) within a city's boundaries, the debt limit may be doubled. Third, a city may lease a building or facility, only later to assume ownership upon termination of the lease. (Leasing is not covered under debt limits.) Efforts to evade the New York state debt limits by New York City contributed to the city's financial crisis in the 1970s.

Management By Objective (MBO) (253)

A process by which managers and supervisors establish annual objectives—both for their agencies and for personnel—and develop measures by which their performance can be evaluated. The term *management by objective* was coined by Peter F. Drucker in a 1954 book entitled *The Practice of Management* (New York: Harper and Row, 1954). The system was designed to aid administrators in the development of improved management skills. It was first employed in the private sector, but has since been adopted at the federal, state, and local levels. MBO seeks to enhance program performance, as well as augment basic management skills. It works as follows: Administrators identify program objectives, and then develop a decentralized structure to achieve them. Specific goal strategies are determined by middle- and lower-level personnel. MBO places strong emphasis on program monitoring, so that agency personnel who are involved are aware of problems as they arise. When a problem does occur, the areas affected are encouraged to solve the problem rather than turn to top management for assistance or authority. MBO has enjoyed widespread acceptance, due, in part, to its many applications: budgeting operations, program assessment, policy development, personnel training, and decision analysis. In addition, MBO has several other advantages, including: (1) it aids in goal selection; (2) it distinguishes conflicting goals; (3) it promotes shared decision making; and (4) it possesses built-in control and evaluation procedures. *See also* BUDGET PROCESS, 239; BUDGET PROCESS: PLANNING-PROGRAMMING-BUDGETING SYSTEM, 242.

Significance   Management by objective was initiated by President Richard M. Nixon in 1970 as an alternative to the planning-programming-budgeting system (PPBS, a management tool that requires agencies to define their objectives, develop means to evaluate their cost-effectiveness, and then choose the optimum alternative) inaugurated by President Lyndon B. Johnson. Unlike PPBS, which sought to alter policy priorities, MBO seeks to stimulate management efficiency. PPBS failed for several reasons, one of which was its inattention to political considerations, which served to create unease among administrators. In contrast, MBO does not challenge the validity of agency programs, nor does it alter the internal decision-making apparatus within agencies. Instead, it encourages administrators to clarify their objectives and to develop means to achieve them in the most cost-efficient manner possible. When applied to the budgetary process, however, MBO raises several practical problems. For example, agencies have historically resisted attempts to measure program effectiveness. Moreover, if not limited, doing so may result in increased paperwork and red tape. The standardization of measurement criteria also poses several difficulties, as agencies differ in many important ways (e.g., mission, environment, methods). MBO requires the collection and application of vast amounts of data, which are beyond the capacity of many agencies. Finally, MBO's implementation raises numerous statutory questions that Congress will have to resolve. Still, MBO has scored a number of successes. It has stimulated administrative awareness of the relationship between budgeting effectiveness and organizational structure and has helped high-level officials to better manage their agencies, given the recent explosion in the size and scope of their activities. In the process, it has underscored the importance of information, communication, coordination, performance, and evaluation.

Progressive Tax   (254)
A levy in which the affluent pay a larger percentage of their earnings

in taxes than lower-income groups. This can be compared to a regressive tax, where the tax burden falls more heavily on low-income groups. Progressive taxes are more prevalent at the federal level, owing to the existence of the income tax, than at the state and local levels, which rely extensively on the sales and property taxes. In the latter case, tax rates are fixed and are applied to goods and property irrespective of income. The income tax is the best example of a progressive tax (with certain limitations). Under this tax, individuals might pay 10 percent on their first $5,000 of income, 15 percent on the next $5,000, and so forth, with a maximum rate for all income above a specified amount. In other words, the tax rate increases as income rises. Still, the income tax is not wholly progressive, as it permits numerous exemptions and allows corporations to shift their tax burden onto consumers. Other examples of progressive taxes levied by the federal and state governments include estate and gift taxes. *See also* INCOME TAX, 250; REGRESSIVE TAX, 258.

Significance   Progressive taxes are less common among state and local governments, which are forced, by and large, to adopt tax measures different from those of the federal government. Generally, the higher-tax states tend to exhibit greater progressivity than the lower-tax states. In the former, the upper and middle classes bear the largest percentage of the tax burden. Typically, the most progressive states are located in the West and Midwest, while the most regressive are concentrated in the South. Despite these regional differences, state and local tax policies are, to a large extent, regressive, particularly when compared to federal taxes. Moreover, they are regressive for virtually all income groups. For example, Donald Phares, in his book *Who Pays State and Local Taxes?*, found that "considered nationwide, state and local taxes are highly inequitable in terms of any correlation with the wealth of the taxpayer."[7] In another study, Joseph A. Pechman and Benjamin A. Okner concluded that "state and local tax rates decline by one-third to one-half from the bottom of the income ladder to the top."[8] Still, it is important to note, as Pechman argued in a companion work, that the overall progressivity of the tax system should not be overstated. According to Pechman, "The tax system in 1980 was only mildly progressive or slightly regressive, depending on the incidence assumptions."[9] These and other studies raise the question, What, if anything, can be done to create a more progressive tax system? Public opinion reveals few if any answers. Despite popular lore, most U.S. citizens do not favor imposing steep taxes on the wealthy. In this regard, in 1976, Massachusetts voters rejected a proposal to institute a graduated income tax. Similarly, a progressive "fair tax" was defeated in Ohio in 1980. The progressive tax is not without its critics, who contend that such taxes penalize talent and ingenuity, thereby undermining the free market system. In their view, progressive taxes retard growth and development. Instead, they favor regressive taxes, based on consumption and investment, which should stimulate savings and investment. Opponents of regressive taxes take strong exception, insisting that such taxes are discriminatory and unjust—that they penalize those least able to pay. Moreover, opponents maintain that regressive taxes contribute to other social ills, which derive in larger measure from poverty and inequality. As they view it, just taxation must be based on the criterion of ability to pay.

Property Tax   (255)

A state or local ad valorem (according to value) levy on real or personal, tangible or intangible, property. The property tax reflects historic U.S. emphasis on property as a measure of personal wealth. Indeed, at the nation's founding, the framers permitted the states to provide for a property qualification as a condition of suffrage. Throughout history, the property tax has served as a major source of state and local revenue. However, in recent times, state governments have adopted alternative tax sources, while local governments have become reliant on the property tax. The property tax process consists of four steps: (1) assessment; (2) rate determination; (3) tax computation; and (4) collection. Property taxes are based on two main factors: the value of the property and the property tax rate. Property valuations are determined by an assessor, whose calculations are based on a unit called "millage." The tax rate is established by the taxing district, which decides the rate based on the amount of money the property tax must raise to pay for government services. *See also* ASSESSMENT, 237; PROPOSITION 13, 257; PROPERTY TAX: REAL PROPERTY, 256; REGRESSIVE TAX, 258.

Significance   The property tax has been described by its critics as one of the most abhorent taxes ever conceived. Still, it constitutes a major source of local revenue. In the late 1800s, personal wealth was figured in terms of real property (e.g., land and buildings). This assessment was relatively easy to render. Today, however, individuals possess many kinds of wealth, including both personal property and real property. Personal property consists of two types, tangible (e.g., furniture, jewelry, art) and intangible (e.g., bonds, stock, bank savings). In addition, personal property can easily be concealed—for instance, in a low-rent apartment. Moreover, the nature of real property has changed. It no longer consists primarily of homes, barns, and land, but of industrial facilities, large retail stores, and office complexes, which are often difficult to valuate. Increasingly, property ownership has been demonstrated to bear little relationship to ability to pay. The escalation of property values has, in many communities, created a false impression of personal wealth. Apart from these difficulties, the property tax has been criticized on several other grounds, chief of which is the question of equity. Major objections include: (1) There are wide variations in assessed values not only among taxing jurisdictions but within them. (2) A large amount of property does not appear on the tax rolls (e.g., church property, industrial exemptions, veteran allowances). (3) The property tax is regressive. Assessors will frequently value more expensive homes at a lower amount, relative to the market value, than less expensive residences, owing to the influence of wealth. In this regard, affluent families spend a lower percentage of their income on housing than poorer families. (4) The property tax discourages property improvements, as such improvements inevitably result in increased taxes. Despite these failings, the property tax continues to be a primary source of local revenue, as it constitutes a gainful and malleable tax that can be manipulated to generate additional revenue. Finally, local governments have few, if any other taxing options, as these have already been adopted by the federal and state governments.

Property Tax: Real Property (256)

An annual levy on the assessed valuation of real estate. The real property tax is a wealth tax. It takes property deemed immovable or permanent, such as land and land improvements. This includes farm, residential, commercial, and forest land. Improvements such as farm buildings, residences, business dwellings, and fences and sidewalks can also be taxed. The bulk of the tax is levied on improvements, while the tax base is roughly evenly split between residential and nonresidential real estate. Real property tax administration consists of three steps: assessment, rate setting, and collection. Assessment involves the discovery and determination of the value of the property to be taxed; rate setting establishes the percentage of the assessed valuation to be paid by the taxpayer; and collection typically occurs the year following the one in which the assessment was determined. Failure to pay taxes may result in the legal confiscation of the property taxed. *See also* ASSESSMENT, 237; PROPERTY TAX, 255.

Significance   The real property tax is employed by both state and local governments to generate revenue. Most states rely minimally on this tax, whereas local governments are far more dependent. The real property tax, coupled with the personal property tax, represents approximately 80 percent of local governments' tax base, and 90 percent of this revenue derives from the real property tax. Local governments often experience problems when they become overly dependent on this form of wealth taxation, as the value of real estate is not an accurate measure of wealth. Wealth is not so much determined by land, as it is by stocks, bonds, and other types of intangible personal property that often escape taxation. A low-income family is much more likely to have a greater proportion of its total wealth invested in real property than is a wealthier family. Since the tax rate is determined as a percentage of the assessed valuation, it taxes the lower-income family at the same rate as the wealthier one. It does not tax according to a person's ability to pay, thus making it a regressive tax, one that imposes a greater tax burden on the poor than on the wealthy. This criticism has provoked considerable debate. However, economists often point to a more serious problem surrounding the use of the property tax by state and local governments, namely, the disparity between different localities rather than between different households. Clearly, wealthier communities are more likely to have a greater tax base than poorer ones. The greater the tax base, the greater a community's ability to provide for more and better public services, such as public education. Clearly, superior schools are more likely to be found in wealthier communities than in poorer ones. This problem has generated major concern at the state level, particularly following the California State Supreme Court's landmark 1971 ruling in *Serrano v. Priest* (5 Cal.3d 584), which required the state to revise its school finance formula to disassociate a school's available resources from its property tax base.

Proposition 13   (257)

An initiative approved in California in 1978 that limits the cumulative property tax rate and the rate at which assessed values of property may increase. Proposition 13 (also known as the Jarvis-Gann initiative) had three main effects: (1) it reduced the maximum tax rate to 1 percent of the 1975–1976 assessed value of the property; (2) it limited future assessment increases to 2 percent per year, except when ownership changes; and (3) it prevented the state legislature from raising state taxes to offset the reduction in revenue, unless the new taxes were approved by a two-thirds majority vote. Voter support for Proposition 13 was fueled by a speculative real estate boom in California, which caused housing prices to double between 1973 and 1978. As real estate values soared, property taxes increased commensurately. At the same time, the California treasury boasted a $5 billion state surplus. Despite widespread opposition to ever-escalating property taxes, the state legislature failed to act. This set the stage for Los Angeles businessman Howard Jarvis, who, with Paul Gann, drafted a citizen-sponsored tax relief initiative. In short order, they collected 1.2 million signatures to qualify the measure for the June 1978 ballot. Following a heated campaign, the initiative passed by a two-to-one margin. Upon passage, property taxes were cut by over $7 billion, which represented a 57 percent relief for California homeowners. *See also* ASSESSMENT, 237; PROPERTY TAX, 255; REGRESSIVE TAX, 258.

Significance   Proposition 13 not only reduced the individual property tax burden for California homeowners, it also forced local governments to examine alternative tax sources or reduce expenditures. Despite predictions of doom and gloom, Proposition 13 did not precipitate the drastic cutbacks predicted by its opponents. Still, its impact was widely felt, both in California and elsewhere. In California, it resulted in a reduction in library hours, the curtailment of school enrichment programs and summer school, and diminished park maintenance. Proposition 13 proponents contend that it has increased governmental efficiency, created an improved business climate, and saved the average homeowner $1,000 a year. Opponents charge that it has crippled public services, devitalized governmental programs, lessened public works, and debilitated many people-oriented initiatives. Following the passage of Proposition 13, tax reformers qualified similar tax relief measures for the ballot in over 25 states. In most cases, Proposition 13–type initiatives have failed (e.g., Arizona, Michigan, Oregon, South Dakota, and Utah), owing, in part, to dissimilar conditions in these states—that lacked the California combination of inflated property values coupled with intense pressures to increase public services. One important exception was a 1980 Massachusetts initiative, Proposition 2 1/2, which was even more expansive, as it required numerous changes in state and local finance. Still, many state and local governments have enacted taxation and/or spending limitations since 1978. In their study *The Tax Revolt*, Alvin Rabushka and Pauline Ryan discovered that, during the 1978 and 1979 legislative sessions, 37 states restricted sales tax collections.[10] Income and sales tax reductions topped $4 billion. At the national level, President Ronald W. Reagan proposed a constitutional amendment that, if approved, would require a balanced national budget.

Regressive Tax   **(258)**
A levy that falls more heavily upon the poor than upon the rich, as measured by the ratio of tax to income. A regressive tax imposes a steeper burden on lower-income groups, which, because of the nature of the tax, are required to pay a larger percentage of their income. Conversely, a progressive tax is one that taxes individuals based upon their ability to pay. State and local governments make extensive use of regressive taxes, most notably, the property and sales taxes. For example, the property tax is regressive in that it ignores the changing economic circumstances of the individual property owner and the escalation of housing costs. Likewise, the sales tax is equally regressive. A flat tax, it employs the same rates for all customers, regardless of their personal income or the size of their purchases. The poor, however, must spend a larger proportion of their income on basic necessities (e.g., food, clothing, shelter, medicine), so that the sales tax constitutes a greater percentage of their income. In recognition of this fact, many states have sought to exempt such necessities from taxation. *See also* PROGRESSIVE TAX, 254; PROPERTY TAX, 255; SALES TAX, 260.

Significance   Regressive taxes inevitably raise the question of equity, that is, Who should pay, and how much? Regressive taxes ignore ability to pay. State and local tax policies, when compared to federal policies, are considerably more regressive. This derives, in large part, from their reliance on property and sales taxes. On the other hand, the federal government relies extensively on the income tax, which is a progressive tax—the poor are taxed minimally, while the rich can pay as much as 50 percent. Still, it must be remembered that state and local tax policies differ, and that there are wide variances in the types of taxes they impose and the rates they set. For example, in 1981, the Advisory Commission on Intergovernmental Relations surveyed the "tax effort" of each state, that is, the relationship between its tax collection and its total wealth.[11] Its objective was to determine the extent to which each state tapped its wealth as a source of tax revenue. The top-ranked states included Alaska, New York, and Massachusetts, while Nevada, Texas, and Wyoming ranked at the bottom end. More specifically, the Coalition of American Public Employees, in a 1979 study, analyzed the states on the basis of tax fairness.[12] Those states with the most "equitable" tax systems included Oregon, Wisconsin, California, and Minnesota, while the least equitable ones were Alabama, Mississippi, Wyoming, Tennessee, and Texas. Interestingly, public opinion fails to reflect the issue of equity. For instance, in 1981, the Advisory Commission on Intergovernmental Relations conducted a study in which it asked those polled, "Which do you think is the least fair tax?"[13] Of those questioned, 36 percent cited the federal income tax, 33 percent the local property tax, 14 percent the state sales tax, and 9 percent the state income tax. Obviously, public attitudes bear little relationship to progressivity or regressivity. Instead, research indicates that taxes that are the most visible or that appear to be the most discriminatory at a particular time are most likely to draw public criticism.

Revenue Bonds   (259)

Public bonds supported from the receipts earned from the particular project in which the funds were invested. Revenue bonds generate funds from self-liquidating projects, such as toll roads and bridges, convention centers, industrial parks, university dormitories, and city-owned athletic complexes. Usually, voter approval is not required to issue revenue bonds, and they are often used to increase a government's cumulative debt beyond constitutionally permissible limits. Interest on these bonds may be exempt from federal taxation, and frequently they earn slightly higher interest rates, as they are somewhat less secure than general obligation bonds (bonds backed by the full faith and credit of the issuing government). Revenue bonds are also referred to as "nonguaranteed" or "limited liability" bonds. These bonds may be long- or short-term. Approximately 90 percent of all state and local debt is long-term, of which about 50 to 65 percent is nonguaranteed. Theoretically, revenue bond interest and principal derive solely from the earnings of the particular project. These bonds are not serviced from the general revenues of state or local government, nor are they affected by constitutional or statutory limitations that apply to general obligation bonds. *See also* GENERAL OBLIGATION BONDS, 247; GENERAL REVENUE, 248; LOCAL DEBT LIMIT, 252; STATE DEBT LIMIT, 262.

Significance   Revenue bonds were initially created to finance income-producing projects. However, their use expanded dramatically in the 1930s, in response to efforts by the Public Works Administration (PWA) to encourage increased state and local construction of public works. At that time, existing state and local restrictions on government borrowing precluded additional construction. To circumvent the problem, the PWA proposed the issuance of nonguaranteed bonds, and it offered assistance to state and local governments in drafting legislation authorizing their use. The states responded with enthusiasm. In 1931, only 15 states permitted local governments to issue nonguaranteed bonds; by 1936, the number had escalated to 40. Today, all 50 states allow the use of nonguaranteed bonds. In 1949, full faith and credit debt constituted nearly 88 percent of all state and local long-term borrowing; as of 1984, that figure had fallen to 34 percent. Moreover, many municipalities have expanded the use of nonguaranteed bonds to include not only public facilities, but also college dormitories, golf courses, and swimming pools, among other projects. Despite their popularity, nonguaranteed bonds pose several potential problems: (1) Since they are issued for long-term periods, they serve to increase interest rates. (2) They skew the use of government resources, since they provide a ready financial device. (3) If they are used for non-self-financing projects, they inflate the budgets of state and local governments. (4) They disguise the financial practices of governments, which may encourage unwise practices. (5) If state and local governments were to default, their credit ratings would be seriously affected. Interestingly, government finance experts J. Richard Aronson and John L. Hilley have found that the increasing popularity of nonguaranteed bonds has produced a peculiar irony.[14] "In some measure," they note, "the use of nonguaranteed debt aims at avoiding constitutional or statutory limitations on borrowing. Thus, an effort to protect state and local governments against the dangers of borrowing has induced growth of a type of debt that is more dangerous than the debt that was restricted."[15]

Sales Tax   (260)
A levy on goods, figured as a percentage of the commodity's price. The state sales tax originated in the midst of the Great Depression, while the local sales tax did not become widespread until after World War II. The sales tax is the largest and most important source of state revenue; it is levied in all but three states (Oregon, New Hampshire, and Delaware). Today, over 5,000 municipalities employ a sales tax, despite its unpopularity with many local businesspersons, who fear its adverse affects on sales. Typically, the sales tax ranges from 2 to 7.5 percent. It applies to most retail items, but in certain cases, it is levied on wholesalers and manufacturers as well. Depending on the state, the sales tax may apply to all commodities, to specific categories, or to individual items. For example, most states exempt food, medicine, clothing, and other necessities. *See also* GENERAL REVENUE, 248; REGRESSIVE TAX, 258.

Significance   The sales tax boasts numerous advantages, both economic and political. First, it generates a fairly stable and dependable source of revenue, despite fluctuations in the economy. Second, it is a hidden tax, unlike the income tax or property tax, which must be paid in lump sums to the state and county and which are perceived as more painful. Third, it is levied on all citizens, without regard to income. Fourth, it is relatively simple and inexpensive to administer, since it imposes the responsibility on the retailer. Fifth, it effectively reaches a mobile population—commuters, tourists, and transients, who enjoy various governmental services, but who would ordinarily escape taxation. Sixth, it diversifies tax sources and provides relief to the already overburdened property owner. Seventh, it is one of the few taxes left to the states, as the federal government makes extensive use of the income tax, while county governments rely heavily on the property tax. On the other hand, the sales tax is not without it critics. Opponents contend that it is a regressive tax—that it places a disproportionate burden on low-income groups. They argue that the poor must spend a larger share of their income on consumer goods, while the affluent are able to devote more to savings and investing. Since the sales tax is a flat tax (a fixed tax based on the cost of the item and not on one's income or ability to pay), it penalizes the poor to a greater degree. Many states have attempted to solve this problem through tax credits and by exempting basic necessities. Thus, in these states, if one's income is used to purchase basic necessities of life, one pays little in the way of sales tax. These measures have served to shift the tax burden from the poor onto higher-income groups.

Severance Tax   (261)

A levy on natural resources extracted from the land. Severance taxes are employed by 34 states—mostly in the West, Southwest, and South—for revenue and conservation. Typically, they apply to such commodities as gas, timber, coal, and oil. Although widespread, severance taxes have proven most lucrative in energy-rich states, which boast large mineral reserves. In fiscal year 1982, severance tax revenues exceeded 20 percent of total tax income in eight states: Alaska, Louisiana, Montana, New Mexico, North Dakota, Oklahoma, Texas, and Wyoming. In these states, the severance tax has served as a great financial boon. For most states, severance taxes have failed to generate comparable sums. This has led Steven D. Gold, an authority on state and local finance, to opine, "Unevenly distributed mineral wealth has led to increasing fiscal disparities among the states."[16] In large part, severance tax receipts escalated as fuel prices soared. As a result, severance tax receipts increased nationally from $2.1 billion in 1977 to $4 billion in 1980. This enabled such states as Texas and

Wyoming to produce large budget surpluses of 20 to 30 percent in 1980. Present trends, however, portend a significant decrease in oil-generated revenues. *See also* GENERAL REVENUE, 248.

Significance   Severance taxes have fostered fierce public debate. For example, when Montana raised its severance tax on coal to 30 percent, its action was challenged in court as an unconstitutional restriction on interstate commerce. The United States Supreme Court disagreed and, in 1981, upheld the constitutionality of the severance tax. In response to this action, legislation was proposed in Congress to limit coal taxes to 12.5 percent. This action, in turn, led Iowa to propose a severance tax on soybean and corn exports. Since its inception, the severance tax has produced rancor and rivalry among the states, pitting the fuel-rich states against the rest of the country. Unlike many states, Alaska profited enormously for several years from the severance tax, so much so that it was able to rescind its income tax, offer cash grants to its citizens, and establish a permanent fund to ensure long-term revenue. Numerous solutions have been proposed to resolve disputes over severance taxes, but none has proven successful. The energy-consuming states continue to attack the severance tax as "legalized gouging" by the energy-producing states. In essence, the Supreme Court has affirmed the constitutionality of the severance tax, except where states have sought to exempt their own residents. For instance, Louisiana enacted a tax on natural gas drilled in the state but piped to other states. The Court declared this action unconstitutional, as it exempted Louisianans. On the other hand, it approved Montana's 30 percent coal tax, which was borne by Montanans as well as others. In addition, the Supreme Court has acknowledged the right of Congress to legislate on this issue. Despite the introduction of numerous severance limitation bills, none has yet passed.

State Debt Limit   **(262)**
A legal constraint placed on the state's ability to finance expenditures through either deficit spending or the issuance of bonds. State debt limits prevent states from imprudent overspending. However, if actual expenditures exceed actual revenues, the states have two main options: (1) the issuance of bonds and (2) borrowing from private markets (e.g., banks or loan institutions). Bonds are issued to secure additional capital for the construction of public projects, such as highways, office buildings, and parks. Private borrowing occurs when additional revenue is required to finance ongoing programs, including salaries and

supplies. When a state borrows money to finance expenditures, a deficit is said to occur in the state's budget. Likewise, the issuance of bonds indicates financial indebtedness. State debt limits are necessary to prevent the accumulation of large and burdensome debts. *See also* GENERAL OBLIGATION BONDS, 247; LOCAL DEBT LIMIT, 252; PROPERTY TAX, 255; REVENUE BONDS, 259.

Significance   State debt limits have precipitated the legal requirement that the governor submit a balanced budget to the legislature (e.g., in California). In Florida and New Jersey, state law requires a balanced appropriations act. In Maryland, Illinois, and Pennsylvania, both a balanced budget and a balanced appropriations act are required. These legal provisions encourage state budget officers to exercise restraint in estimating revenues and in budgeting additional money for ongoing and new programs. Conservative budget estimates frequently produce large surpluses in the state treasury. This was the case in California during the mid-to-late 1970s, when the state surplus rose to nearly $5 billion. This surplus served to stimulate public support for Proposition 13, a 1978 grass-roots initiative that placed a ceiling on property taxes. It also provided financial relief to local governments, which were adversely affected by Proposition 13's reduction in local revenues due to the property tax ceiling. Most states go to great lengths to avoid bonded indebtedness and deficit spending, which can generate severe short- and long-term financial problems. State governments lack the ability to influence or control money-market conditions, as does the federal government. This means that they must hope for favorable market conditions when they borrow money to finance expenditures.

State Lotteries   (263)
Gambling games in which numbered tickets are sold and a drawing is held for prizes, as a means of raising revenue. State lotteries attracted widespread support in the 1970s, owing to increased demands for public services, cutbacks in federal assistance, and citizen opposition to additional taxation. To provide these services, many states introduced legalized gambling as a way of generating additional revenue. During the past decade, the main sources of such funds have been pari-mutuel betting and lotteries. Nevada relies more heavily on legalized gambling than any other state, collecting over 40 percent of its revenue from gambling taxes. Today, 20 states plus the District of Columbia have lotteries. In 4 states, gambling is prohibited: Hawaii, Utah, Missouri, and Mississippi. Still, only 2 states—Nevada and New

Hampshire—raise over 10 percent of total state revenues through gambling. In 1983, lotteries produced less than 2 percent of these states' overall revenue per capita. However, lotteries are not the only way in which gambling revenue is or can be raised. Other methods include bingo, horse racing, jai alai, dog racing, off-track betting, numbers games, and sports wagers. *See also* EARMARKED REVENUES, 244; GENERAL REVENUE, 248; REGRESSIVE TAX, 258.

Significance   Although state lotteries have become increasingly popular in recent years, they are not a new creation. The Continental Congress initiated a lottery to raise funds for the Revolutionary War. The practice languished until 1964, when New Hampshire became the first state to revive the lottery as a budget-balancing device. Many state legislatures have joined the lottery refrain, as it enables them to raise revenue without raising taxes. Presently, state lotteries generate approximately $2 billion for the states involved. These funds are earmarked for various purposes. For example, Massachusetts returns its lottery funds to local governments; Pennsylvania spends it on programs for senior citizens; Colorado uses it for capital construction projects. Other states allocate it for education, while still others deposit it in the general fund to be used for a variety of purposes. Despite its perceived benefits, the lottery has been criticized on several grounds. Opponents contend: (1) that it constitutes a regressive tax (a tax in which the burden falls more heavily on the poor); (2) that its operational costs are inordinately high; (3) that it appears to encourage illegal gambling; (4) that it is an undependable and unstable source of revenue; (5) that it encourages graft and corruption; (6) that it represents an immoral practice; and (7) that it engenders inflated expectations and personal disappointment. Even so, many nonlottery states are weighing the advantages of legalized gambling, hoping that it will ease their tax burdens and provide needed relief to an already overtaxed citizenry.

User Fees   **(264)**
Charges levied on individuals who avail themselves of various public services, which are frequently earmarked to fund these services. User fees have become increasingly popular in recent years, owing to the loss of other revenue, the amount of revenue raised, and the ease of collection. Typical user fees include toll charges to use the New Jersey Turnpike or the San Francisco Golden Gate Bridge. Other user fees include charges to use public swimming pools or to play on public tennis courts. In addition, many municipalities are expanding their

use of user fees to apply to special assessments, such as sidewalks, street paving, fire protection, and other government services that benefit the individual property owner. In this regard, some municipalities are levying user fees on real estate developers, so that new residents, rather than the existing property owners, will be required to bear many of the costs of development. User fees have become commonplace, as local governments attempt to counteract the loss of badly needed revenues due to tax and expenditure limitation initiatives. As a result, many municipalities are applying user fees to public parks, museums, and hospitals, which derive part of their funds from such charges. *See also* GENERAL REVENUE, 248.

Significance   User fees pose problematic questions, as local governments seek to apply them to an increasing number of public services. Ultimately, one must ask, Which services should be funded by general taxation, and thus be made available free of charge to the public, and which should be paid for by the users of these services? It is difficult, if not impossible, to delineate the target group—to determine if the service will be used primarily by a well-defined group of individuals, or if it will be used by the general population. Generally, local governments have eschewed user fees where they create hardships for particular groups or result in high administrative costs. For example, public schools benefit most the children of families who attend them, rather than the general citizenry. Still, it is widely accepted that schools provide benefits to the entire community that go well beyond those enjoyed by the children themselves. As a result, local governments have opposed the use of user fees to subsidize public education. Moreover, most individuals would oppose user fees to pay for fire departments, where only those who had experienced fires were required to assume the costs. Even so, user fees can be justified on various grounds, including the fact that they promote efficiency and economy. If all public services are made available free of charge, it is highly likely that more service would be produced and consumed than is feasible or desirable. Overall, most taxpayers are content to pay small user fees, as was illustrated by a 1981 Advisory Commission on Intergovernmental Relations study, which found that 55 percent of those surveyed felt that user fees were the most effective way to generate revenues.[17] Clearly, user fees are the fastest growing source of municipal revenues. In one study, Robert Cline found that, from 1977 to 1983, user fees increased at an annual rate of 11.4 percent.[18] This compared to the 9.3 percent annual growth rate in the previous 20 years. The importance of user fees is most evident in their relation to local tax collection. For instance, in 1957, they produced 40 percent as much revenue as local taxes; in 1977, 45 percent as much; and by 1983, 64 percent as much. However, as Cline points out, there are wide variations among states in their reliance on user fees.[19] He attributes this to tradition, legal restrictions, and fiscal conditions. User fees are most prevalent in the Southeast, Southwest, and Far West, while they are less so in the Northeast.

11. Citizen Needs and Government Policy

Building Codes (265)

Regulations for administrative guidance of construction within a city or county. Building codes regulate the type of wood beams, distance between studs (wood framework), and the amount of pressure a structure must be able to withstand. They also regulate electrical capacity, heating equipment, and the insulation content of construction. Building codes are intended to ensure the safety of those using the structure. Inspectors check construction in progress to ensure that all fire, safety, sanitation, and material standards are met. The states' right to protect the health, welfare, safety, and morals of the people—the state police powers—is provided by the Tenth Amendment to the United States Constitution. *See also* LAND USE PLANS, 278.

Significance Building codes vary from state to state and region to region. The studding of a house must be much closer together in the northeastern United States than in the South. Houses in the Northeast must be able to sustain the great weight of snow and ice, which is unusual in the South. The amount of insulation in a building also varies from region to region. Building codes may require materials to be installed by specialists in electrical wiring or plumbing, and these requirements obviously increase the cost. Often the poor settle in older houses that no longer meet modern building code standards. They suffer from inadequate heating and electrical fire hazards, especially during harsh winters when frayed wires are overused. Builders may use cheap materials to reduce costs, and contractors sometimes bribe building inspectors to overlook the use of cheaper material. Plastic pipe, for example, is much less expensive to use than copper pipe, which lasts longer. Although many people are opposed

283

to governmental regulation, when a disaster occurs these same individuals may blame government for not requiring such health and safety devises as smoke alarms and wiring standards.

Civil Defense   (266)

The safety and security of the civilian population from enemy attack. Civil defense is the responsibility of the Federal Emergency Management Agency (FEMA), which advises the president in times of war or other national emergency. Civil defense includes all nonmilitary actions that can be taken to reduce harm from enemy military action of any kind. The FEMA has designated many structures as fallout shelters for protection against nuclear radioactivity. It was not until World War II that aerial attack on cities prompted organized civil defense planning. Some civil defense measures along the coast of the United States consisted of blackouts to reduce the risk of night bombing. In World War II citizens were trained in fire fighting, rescue, and first aid. With federal assistance, both state and local governments maintain rudimentary civil defense programs.

Significance   Civil defense is not so much a concern of people in the United States as of Europeans because the United States has not experienced war at home since 1865. The public regards civil defense as futile and believes it implies that war is inevitable; therefore volunteers are hard to recruit. Even in this nuclear age many U.S. citizens see war as remote and feel that their military and technological superiority is a sufficient safeguard. Those in favor of a stronger civil defense think it would save civilian lives for further mobilization and the continuation of war, but opponents claim that civil defense does not guarantee fewer deaths and casualties. There is also disagreement on how to run an effective civil defense program, if indeed one is possible. The awesome destructive powers of modern weapons and the complexities of crowded urban life make civil defense seem scarcely worth the effort.

Corrections   (267)

Attempts to rehabilitate criminals. Corrections involve three areas of activity: impoundment, probation, and parole. In the United States one-half of the convicted criminals are imprisoned, and the other half are released under supervision. Upon conviction, offenders are generally subject to a presentence background investigation. Medical, psychiatric, and psychological studies are presented to specialists on a classification committee, whose analysis will form the basis of the subject's assignment and treatment. Organizing treatment and then applying therapy is the basic approach in corrections. Preparation in prison for employment upon release has long been part of the rehabilitation process. The alternative to incarceration is probation, during which an offender must adhere to certain conditions, including supervision by probation officers. Parole is another form of corrections in which an inmate is freed under conditions that permit his or her reincarceration for misbehavior that violates parole rules. *See also* CRIMINAL JUSTICE, 269; PRISON, 280.

Significance   Correctional programs are the least visible and the most misunderstood segment of the criminal justice system. Rehabilitation is not taken seriously in our society except by the officials who are charged with its implementation. No one is sure which rehabilitation program will work to reduce recidivism (return to a life of crime). As a result, a trend toward stricter punishment is developing. Current opinion would reinstate the death penalty and impose longer, more rigid sentences to deter crime. Some criminals obviously should be incarcerated, but capital punishment remains a highly controversial issue in the United States. Some offenders could be rehabilitated if allowed to return to their community. As Robert S. Lorch, a noted political scientist, points out, "Nothing seems to reduce recidivism, neither the amount of money spent on corrections systems, nor sentencing policies, nor parole systems."[1] But since many criminals must legally be released to society someday, the public has come to see the need for effective rehabilitation programs.

Crime (268)

Commission of an act prohibited by criminal law. Crime is an offense against public law and can be classified as treason, a high crime; felony, an atrocious act; and misdemeanor, a lesser act. The term *crime* is derived from the Latin *crimen*, meaning "an accusation or complaint." In the United States statutory prohibitions vary from one jurisdiction to another and from time to time within the same jurisdiction. Adultery, sodomy, and gambling are forbidden in some states and tolerated in others. Traffic rules and regulations also vary in different states. The Federal Bureau of Investigation (FBI) lists the following offenses as crimes: criminal homicide, rape, robbery, aggravated assault, burglary, larceny, auto theft, other assaults, forgery and counterfeiting, embezzlement and fraud, dealing in stolen property, weapon carrying or possessing, prostitution and commercialized vice, sex offenses against family and children, sale and use of narcotics, violation of liquor laws, drunkenness, disorderly conduct, vagrancy, gambling, driving while intoxicated, violation of road and driving laws, parking offenses, and other traffic law violations, and violations of state and local laws. *See also* CRIMINAL LAW, 158; CRIMINAL PROCEDURES, 159.

Significance   Crime defines the idea of a public as opposed to a private wrong, and it is deemed socially dangerous and punishable by law. While statutes define crime, it remains for law enforcement officials (police and the courts) to enforce compliance. Crime was long considered the result of poverty and an antisocial economic system, for which the state was responsible, and it is still argued that, with the removal of poverty and ignorance, the greatest proportion of crime would disappear. However, some modern crimes are far more complex, including political protectionism, gangsterism, and terrorism. Authorities are powerless to act in some cases and may become a party to graft. Although the United States is a leader in scientific and technological development, the detection of crime has not advanced accordingly.

Criminal Justice   (269)

The administration of justice, which includes the structural organization of the law-enforcing mechanism, its principles, and the personnel in charge. Criminal justice includes the network of courts and tribunals that deal with criminal law and its enforcement. These involve (1) police; (2) courts—judge, prosecutor, and defender; (3) corrections—probation, confinement, and parole. The administration of criminal justice begins with the police and prosecutors, who arrest violators of law and bring them to court for trial. The trial opens before a judge or a judge and a jury. If the jury finds the defendant guilty, a judge will impose the penalty. When a person completes the sentence (probation, confinement, and parole), his or her debt to society for breaking the law has been paid. *See also* CORRECTIONS, 267; CRIME, 268.

Significance   Criminal justice is one of many institutional systems in our society. Law-abiding citizens who never enter the criminal justice system know little about it. There are drawbacks in the administration of criminal justice. Arrests are made by officers who are under little direct supervision. The suspect is brought for a preliminary hearing before a magistrate, often unlearned in the law. An indictment by a grand jury is essential at the federal level and is required for serious crimes in most states before the accused can be tried. The prosecutor determines whether the accused will be freed or held for trial. The jury determines guilt, the judge usually determines the sentence, and the power of clemency rests with the governor. The method described is disorganized and slow, and state and local courts are largely independent of each other, compounding the problem of dispensation of justice. To a large extent the criminal justice system provides advantages for affluent persons, who are able to hire the best legal assistance available. While indigent persons are usually defended by the public defender's office or by a lawyer assigned by the presiding judge, those who fall between the extremes of wealth and poverty may lose everything in a costly effort to defend themselves.

Energy Crisis (270)

Shortage of fuel oil, gasoline, and natural gas, exacerbated by an oil embargo. The energy crisis of 1973–1974 was caused by the Organization of Arab Petroleum Exporting Countries' (OAPEC) decision to limit its supply of oil to the world. The temporary supply disruptions forced oil prices to rise suddenly. The United States (with 6 percent of the world population) consumes one-third of the world's energy. This and the lack of an energy policy in the United States were at the base of the crisis. An energy crisis is not caused by lesser governments (state and local) but by the national government. Energy and other vital resources are controlled by the federal government, whose policies and programs affect citizens all over the country. For example, the 55 mile per hour speed limit to conserve energy was implemented by all states.

Significance   The energy crisis of 1973–1974 created temporary panic in the industrialized world, including the United States. The immediate effect of the crisis was that the price of oil soared from a few dollars a barrel to approximately $38 a barrel. At its height, Presidents Richard M. Nixon, Gerald R. Ford, and Jimmy Carter designed strategies to meet the energy crisis by seeking public cooperation to conserve energy (e.g., reduce driving, lower thermostats, and use less electricity). President Ronald W. Reagan's strategy has been to reduce government's role in energy by deregulating fuel prices and providing tax incentives to oil companies and energy corporations. Internal dissension within the Organization of Petroleum Exporting Countries (OPEC) and effective conservation, development of new sources of energy, and increased production by non-OPEC suppliers have resolved the crisis. The crisis could recur when non-OPEC suppliers exhaust their surplus, but for the time being, the crisis has been reversed, with the oil exporting countries of the world suffering severe economic dislocations as a result of the collapse of oil prices.

Environmental Impact Statement   (271)
A report to the Council on Environmental Quality demonstrating how a project will alter land, air, or water quality. Environmental impact statements are required by the National Environmental Policy Act of 1969 before any project can be built. The Environmental Protection Agency (EPA) holds public hearings concerning how a proposed project will affect the environment and the livesof the people who reside in the area. The Council on Environmental Quality (CEQ) attempts to ensure the safety of those affected. The CEQ and EPA are also charged with protecting the environment from any harmful development. Both the developer and the publicmay participate in the hearings. The developer discusses the economic and environmental benefits to the area, whereas the publicis concerned with economic growth and how the community'snatural well-being may fare. The primary purpose of the hearings is for the CEQto receive more input on which to base approvalor rejection. *See also* ENVIRONMENTALISTS, 272; ENVIRONMENTAL POLLUTION, 273.

Significance   An environmental impact statement is required for any major engineering project that may threaten an area's biological balance. Prior to 1960 there was no coherent federal program for this purpose. State environmental programs were usually decentralized throughout several state agencies and often proved inadequate. If environmental impact statements had been used prior to the 1960s, the Love Canal disaster in Niagara Falls might have been prevented. From 1947 to 1952 chemicals were dumped in this area; then in the late 1960s a housing development was built on top of the dumps. In 1978 heavy rains flooded the area and brought toxic chemicals into residential quarters. Families required relocation, and some children suffered congenital birth defects. Today, much of the protection of the environment has been left to the states, which spend billions of dollars to ensure clean air and water. However, states are cautious in enacting laws and enforcing them because of possible adverse economic effects. The states compete to attract jobs and industries, and the cost of environmental protection may drive prospective businesses and industries away and into states with less stringent laws.

Environmentalists   (272)

People who are concerned with preserving the benefits of nature. Environmentalists warn the public about ecological dangers and encourage governmental action to protect the environment. They have achieved mixed results. Environmentalists have a long tradition of political action. One of the first environmentalist groups was the Audubon Society (1905), which has broadened its scope beyond its original goal of protecting bird species from extinction. Similar groups with environmental concerns have grown substantially in membership. Common Cause, the people's lobby, has consistently supported the environmentalist position. Environmental Action sponsors Earth Day, and the Environmental Defense Fund files lawsuits and seeks injunctions against activities that may harm the environment. The Friends of the Earth organizes media and motion picture celebrities to help raise funds for environmental issues. Environmentalists have allies in the Environmental Protection Agency (EPA) and the Council on Environmental Quality but have few allies in the Department of Energy, which tends to reflect the interests of large oil and gas companies. *See also* ENVIRONMENTAL IMPACT STATE-MENT, 271; ENVIRONMENTAL POLLUTION, 273.

Significance   Environmentalists favor more government action, both state and national, to clean up the increasing pollution. They believe the nation should make a healthy environment its number one priority. Environmentalists are often opposed by powerful corporations and large unions, who argue that it will not do any good if we save the environment and destroy our economy. Environmentalists have used all forms of interest group activity to pressure government to combat pollution. Environmentalists now protest the use of nuclear energy; they prefer the development of solar energy as cleaner and safer.

Environmental Pollution   (273)

The contamination of the earth, its waters, or its atmosphere by noxious substances. Environmental pollution is created when we abuse the atmosphere, seas, rivers, and earth on which we live. This is a global problem. The term *environment* includes both natural and synthetic matter, and the term *pollution* is relative. One person's pollution is another person's purity, especially if it involves profit. Generally, pollution is anything that hinders life. If we breathe polluted air, we may die sooner; buried radioactive wastes may eventually poison the water we need to survive; and pesticides can poison the food supply or cause cancer. Man's technological progress has offset the balance in nature and cannot restore a new balance. Industrial production is at the root of modern society, but with increased productivity comes greater pollution. Environmental pollutants include products of combustion; human excreta; expired air; dusts; pathogenic organisms; vapors; gases; industrial solvents; extremes of temperature; agricultural fertilizers; infrared, ultraviolet, and even visible light; ionized radiation; radioisotopes; noise; ultrahigh-frequency sound; and microwave electromagnetic radiation. *See also* ENVIRONMENTAL IMPACT STATEMENT, 271; INDUSTRIAL POLLUTION, 275.

Significance   Environmental pollution is one of humanity's greatest concerns. Theoretically, few people are opposed to clean air, clean water, or the maintenance of nature, but there is a gap between theory and practice. The pollution problem remains. The simple fact that we live gives rise to environmental pollution by the release and buildup of metabolic excretions unless such materials are utilized by other organisms to balance the ecology. The modern problems of environmental pollution are essentially those of rapid human population growth and expanding technology. The danger is that, unless we are able to reverse the tide of environmental pollution and create a new balance, planet earth could succumb to man-made pollution.

Fire Department   (274)

A localized department that protects property and persons from fire and injury. Fire departments are administered by the municipalities, townships, towns, and special fire districts. State participation is usually confined to forest fires. Volunteer fire departments are almost extinct, replaced by organized, paid municipal ones. Fire departments have responsibilities in the area of fire prevention, too, waging educational campaigns to inform the public of fire hazards. The cities have modern and professional fire departments; the larger the city is, the more sophisticated is the equipment. Fire departments are also responsible for enforcing fire regulations by periodic inspections. Fire departments are sometimes administered together with police departments, and when joined, they are called the public safety or protection departments. *See also* BUILDING CODES, 265; POLICE DEPARTMENT, 279.

Significance   Fire departments do much routine work, but at times the work is quite hazardous and requires special training. Fire duty can involve extinguishing brush fires, rescuing people from burning places, resuscitating people, and dealing with the shock and terror of major fires. A good fire department operates on the assumption that the best way to fight a fire is to prevent it through citizen education and enforcement of fire regulations. Per capita fire losses in the United States are considered the highest in the world, although U.S. fire departments have the best fire fighting equipment. European countries, where fire damage is minimal, rely on prevention. There will always be fires, and fighting them will be necessary, but many U.S. cities have failed to prevent fires through the enforcement of building codes and other regulations. The organization of fire protection fits into no simple pattern and occurs strictly on a local level.

Industrial Pollution   (275)

The contamination of soil, air, water, and the environment by industrial substances and noises. Industrial pollution is fast becoming a major problem because our productive capacity has surpassed our ability to control the impact of that development. Productivity and profit have been our priorities. Industrial pollution destroys air, land, and water resources, and may adversely affect future generations. Strip mining for coal is an example of industrial pollution at the development stage. Environmentalists and the government now combat this form of pollution. The burning of soft coal to run plants has polluted air throughout the United States. Pesticides and chemicals are needed to grow food, but some become carcinogenic in man or other animals. Also, a pesticide may seem safe when used, but its long-range effects may not be known. *See also* ENVIRONMENTALISTS, 272; ENVIRONMENTAL POLLUTION, 273.

Significance   Industrial pollution is a major concern of the industrialized nations of the world. Newspapers and television dramatize industrial pollution, and this problem is now familiar to most people in the United States. Oil spills offshore attest to the ugliness of pollution. No town or village is safe from noxious fumes released by chemical truck accidents. It is a vicious cycle. We need the radioactive isotopes that industry produces to fight cancer, but later these isotopes must be properly disposed. Even then, their danger lingers for centuries. The question then arises, Why permit any of these pollutants to contaminate our living space? For such a simple question, the answer is complex. One answer is that a nation cannot develop as the United States has without industrialization, which in turn creates pollution. The crux of the problem is how to control industrial pollution. The authors cannot embark on the nuts and bolts of industrial pollution control, but it might be well to recognize that control of industrial pollution, like control of environmental pollution, is a critical factor in our struggle for survival.

Inner City   **(276)**
The core of the city—the area that includes the old central business district and the immediate area that surrounds the nucleus of the original city. The inner city has not changed as dramatically as the rest of the city. Usually its inhabitants are poor, minorities, and either unemployed, unemployable, or working at menial jobs. The core of the city became the central business district, and later the inner city. The development of large shopping malls outside the city with ample parking facilities devaluated the inner city. People and businesses moved away from the inner city as interstate highways became more accessible and industrial parks dotted the belt lines around cities. Remaining inner city residents could not supply an adequate tax base. Houses and businesses were abandoned, and traffic circumvented the area as much as possible. Only a few government offices, courts, lawyers' offices, and some insurance companies remained. The federal and state governments attempted urban renewal, but this has caused dislocation and even greater segregation of residents from inner city life. *See also* INTERSTATE HIGHWAY SYSTEM, 277.

Significance   Some inner cities are being revitalized by investors who see them as inexpensive land that can be developed. Some service-oriented businesses are returning but not production-oriented ones. The bicentennial celebration of America's independence (1976) activated some restoration of the nation's historic past and the area and neighborhoods surrounding Independence Hall in Philadelphia. In some areas expensive condominiums have replaced slums. Baltimore has restored its inner harbor, converting a deteriorating, crime-infested area to a minor scenic attraction and generating jobs, income, and housing. San Francisco has restored some areas of its inner city. Still, many problems linger. The process of *gentrification* (displacement of lower-income groups and minorities due to lack of urban reinvestment, resulting in continuing neighborhood deterioration and eventual forced abandonment) has caused the number of homeless people and vagrants to increase. As measured by numbers of people, there is little evidence of a nationwide back-to-the-city movement.

Interstate Highway System   (277)

A series of interlinking multilane roadways that expedite travel from one major population center and industrial base to another. Interstate highways were established by the Federal Highway Act of 1944. Today, the interstate highway system runs from Maine to Florida and from New York to California. Interstate highways connect every major city in the United States. Most interstate highways are freeways. However, where the interstate system duplicates turnpikes (mostly in the eastern United States—Pennsylvania, Delaware, New Jersey, Maryland, and Virginia), some fees are collected. Interstate highways are limited-access roads; that is, there are no crossroads and only prescribed entrances and exits. Interstate highways expedite the flow of commerce across the nation and generally avoid the congested central business districts. New industries, research parks, and communities spring up around the exits of interstate highways. The United States Constitution gives the federal government the right to construct interstate highways, in Article I, Section 8, Congress has the right to construct post roads for the delivery of mail. States have received federal aid for highways since the 1919 Federal Road Act, which was implemented by the Bureau of Public Roads. *See also* INNER CITY, 276.

Significance   Interstate highways have greatly fostered the development of the United States. These roadways have become lifelines of transportation and commerce. Almost everything that we eat, drink, or wear moves over interstate highways. The interstate highway system is a transnational network of roads that unites Americans. Interstate highways have transformed the urban areas of the United States, and the southwestern and western parts of the nation have grown in population and industrialization, partly because of the system. The interstate system presents a major subsidy to the trucking industry and has helped to destory the economic viability of the railroads. The interstate highway system is in need of repair—bridges demand reinforcement, and paving requires constant reconditioning. This road system has not been completed due to legal and political roadblocks.

Land Use Plans   (278)

Programs to formulate, develop, and revise the use of real estate.

Land use plans are designed to protect the environment, raise the aesthetic quality of life, assure residential and industrial development, provide recreation, and give order to the geographic management of the community. Most land use plans have been developed by state and local government units. Zoning is a common form of land use planning. Some areas are zoned for single dwelling units; others for commercial development. Land use plans are flexible, changing as the city changes. Population migrations cause changes in land use. Today, most cities are not planned but develop around new industry or malls. Reston, Virginia, and Columbia, Maryland, are planned and boast a diversified population base and educational system, among other features. *See also* BUILDING CODES, 265; INTERSTATE HIGHWAY SYSTEM, 277.

Significance   Land use plans are sorely needed today. With tremendous shifts of population, especially to the Sun Belt (an area of the South and Southeast) because of a favorable climate and relocation of industry, cities tend to develop rapidly. The city needs to ensure planned growth, sufficient water supply, adequate housing, new roads, sewage treatment facilities, and schools. Much land is owned by the states and each state may develop a management plan. Wisconsin passed an early Water Resources Act (1966) to save its Lake Michigan shoreline, and California and Florida have been leaders in trying to preserve the ecological balance of their states. A few states, like Alaska, Nevada, Utah, Idaho, and Oregon, where the federal government owns over 50 percent of the land, have developed land use plans. Today, most cities are not planned but develop around multiple nuclei, new industry, or a mall.

Police Department   (279)
The government agency charged with the maintenance of law and order, safety, morals, and the detection, prevention, and punishment of crimes. A police department is an organized agency at the state, county, or city level with power to investigate crime and arrest suspected violators. The police function is primarily of state and local concern. However, the Federal Bureau of Investigation (FBI), Internal Revenue Service (IRS), Secret Service, Bureau of Narcotics, and Postal Service enforce federal laws. Most of the 3,041 counties in the United States have police departments headed by a sheriff, whose duties vary. In some counties this official functions as sheriff, tax collector, coroner, supervisor of roads and highways, and process server. Generally, city police enforce municipal ordinances and

regulations and state statutes. Each state has police troopers or patrols for various investigative purposes. All police perform three major roles: enforce law, maintain order, and provide services. *See also* FIRE DEPARTMENT, 274.

Significance   Police forces are better equipped today and wield more power. Improved surveillance and the use of computerized criminal justice records are sometimes regarded as threats to personal privacy. Police fall into a quasi-military structure. The typical military symbols—uniforms, insignia, weapons, rank, and discipline—are visible characteristics. With federal financial assistance, state and local police maintain law and order and control crime for the semi-autonomous state and local governments. Unlike those of most countries, the U.S. police organizations are decentralized. Despite some corruption and inefficiency in police departments, a police officer is a welcome person in times of trouble.

Prison   **(280)**
A place to detain persons convicted of a crime or awaiting trial. Prisons are designed to punish and to rehabilitate. There are 323 federal and state prisons divided into three types: 110 maximum security, 110 medium security, and 103 minimum security. Federal prisoners are incarcerated in four types of penal institutions: prisons or penitentiaries, reformatories, correctional institutions, and prison camps. States maintain four similar types called prisons, reformatories, houses of correction, and prison farms. City and county jails serve as detention institutions or places of commitment, or both. In addition, there are federal and state institutions for juvenile offenders. There are about half a million prisoners in all prisons and reformatories in the United States. In the past, some 60 percent of the inmates were unskilled and semi-skilled laborers, and 80 percent were manual workers. More recent prisoners include professionals, businesspersons, government officials, and public leaders, such as congressmen. *See also* CORRECTIONS, 267; CRIMINAL JUSTICE, 269.

Significance   Prisons are generally poorly financed and over-crowded and lack educational, medical, and recreational facilities. These problems and the need for reform have been dramatically demonstrated in many recent prison uprisings. The most sensational of these riots was at the Attica State Correctional Facility in New York in 1971. Some observers question whether or not prisons in the United States constitute "cruel and unusual punishment."

Surprisingly, the prison system is largely a U.S. phenomenon. Prior to the eighteenth century, imprisonment was a method used to take retributive vengeance, designed to eliminate the offender or permanently stigmatize him or her. The new concept of a prison system, designed to rehabilitate inmates, was primarily the consequence of changed philosophies of human conduct. However, life in today's prison is demoralizing, dangerous, and alienating. Results indicate that the prison system has failed to transform criminals into good citizens. One main issue today is state prison overcrowding and the action of the federal courts to relieve it. In some states many prisoners have had to be prematurely released because of federal court orders to maintain humane conditions.

Public Education   (281)

Schooling funded by taxes and administered by state and local governments. Public education makes mental and physical training available free in the formative years. In Colonial days and the early days of the Republic education was the concern of churches and private individuals and groups, but the Tenth Amendment to the Constitution provided state-supported education. The states and local governments have assumed a major role in public elementary and secondary education and in many cases administer post-secondary institutions. At the post-secondary level, public education is offered at state universities, community colleges, and technical institutes. Each state has a department of education, the head of which is often called superintendent of public instruction, usually an elected office. Most states operate their school systems through districts controlled by locally chosen board members. The school district is independent of local government. School finances are closely tied in with city, county, state, and federal financing. Professional administrators and teachers are responsible for running schools and educational activities, but the state usually sets standard requirements for teachers, equipment, length of school terms, uniform courses of study, textbooks, and so on. *See also* EDUCATION, DEPARTMENT OF, 122.

Significance   Public education is the largest single enterprise of state and local authorities, even though the federal government has become increasingly active in the field. In establishing free public education, it is also necessary to provide an effective mechanism to administer it. This has been extremely difficult in many localities. Although private and parochial schools have continued to grow, the majority of U.S. children attend public schools. With the introduction of a public school system, education has become universal; all children under certain ages attend schools. Free public education, however, faces enormous problems. In addition to financing educational programs for about 60 million youngsters, public education must respond to the political needs of U.S. citizens. It is necessary to remove the remaining vestiges of segregation in public schools and to introduce innovations to meet the challenges of a supertechnological society.

Public Health Service (282)

Government-supported activity to prevent disease and promote mental and physical fitness. The public health service researches the causes and prevention of disease, issues health information to the public, and curbs communicable diseases. This service is available at all levels of government, but mainly from the U.S. Department of Health and Human Services (HHS). HHS studies the causes and prevention of disease, enforces quarantine laws at ports of entry, cooperates with state and local governments in public health programs, controls air and water pollution, and administers grants for hospitals and sewage treatment programs. Since the establishment of the first board of health in Massachusetts in 1869, state and local governments have also provided public health services. Their role was expanded dramatically by the Kerr-Mills Act of 1960, which established the Medicaid program and by the passage of the Medical Act of 1965, which provides additional medical services to the poor. *See also* HUMAN RESOURCES, DEPARTMENT OF, 128.

Significance   Public health service is involved with human welfare. Although public health is generally a state function, many health activities are performed by county governments. Despite advances in medical facilities, health and treatment of illness remain major problems in the United States. Although the United States has enough physicians, they are distributed unevenly across the country. Generally, the states and cities with the highest per capita income enjoy the best health care. Because the United States Constitution does not mention anything about health, the states invoke the police power to deal with health services. Current controversies before state and local health authorities include state hospitals for the chronically ill and home care for minor illnesses. The enormous expansion of health services has induced an elaborate system of health administration, but medical care costs put services beyond the reach of many U.S. citizens.

Public Housing   (283)
A federal government program to develop residential units (apartment and single dwelling) for poor people who cannot afford conventional housing. Public housing is primarily the responsibility of the Department of Housing and Urban Development (HUD). The 1937 United States Housing Act provided funding for slum clearance and low-rent housing projects. By 1964 the federal government was subsidizing 55,000 new units, and in 1970–1971 a high of 400,000 units was reached. The federal government has developed a concept called urban homesteading. The original Homestead Act enabled citizens to settle public lands in rural parts of the United States. Urban homesteading allows the federal government to purchase abandoned urban dwellings to be sold at a nominal cost, provided the new home owner will improve the property. Every major city has a housing authority that cooperates with HUD to assure clear title to a property, then acquires and improves it. The Federal Housing Administration (FHA) has developed subsidized mortgages at lower interest rates for prospective buyers. The Veterans Administration (VA) has helped armed service veterans to purchase homes with mortgage benefits and no down payment. The federal government has established a rent subsidy for the poor who live in government-approved apartments and houses. *See also* LAND USE PLANS, 278.

Significance   Public housing has failed to solve the needs of low-income people. It developed as a reaction to crisis, not as a planned activity to avert future problems. Life in public housing units tends to deprive one of privacy and marks the individual as inferior, not up to social standard. Loss of self-respect ensues. Furthermore, impoverished areas breed crime. Public housing, with a high population density, increases tensions and problems in the area. Single dwelling units are preferable to high-rise apartments, but they are very costly. Public housing also tends to be segregated by race or ethnicity, thus contributing to the problems of those who live there.

Public Utilities   (284)
Businesses, generally privately owned and operated, that perform essential services for people. In some cases, public utilities are owned and operated by local units of government, including cities, towns, counties, and special districts. Public utilities include, among others, the generation and distribution of electric power, water supply, transportation, pipelines, telephone and telegraph, radio, and television. They occupy an intermediate position between state and private

enterprise. The utility companies sell their services to the public at prices fixed by government commissions. Because utilities function as natural monopolies, these commissions grant franchises to companies to administer noncompetitive operations. There are two types of utility services. The service type of utility cannot store the service but must adjust to public demands by maintaining productive capacity as required. Electricity, telephone, telegraph, and transportation are service utilities. The other type is the product type, such as water, sanitation, and irrigation. The utility services are regulated (1) legislatively, by means of licensing; (2) judicially, by court decisions; and (3) executively, by the police powers of the government. The members of the utility commissions are popularly elected or appointed. *See also* URBAN PLANNING, 289.

Significance　　Most public utilities are not publicly owned but function as private enterprises. Whether an industry is a public utility, for which people have to allow use of their property, is determined by practical considerations. From an economic point of view the concept of a public utility is twofold—monopoly and necessity. When a government regulates an industry such as a public utility, both of these elements enter into its decision. While government confers a legal monopoly on business in a utility to a corporation, it also regulates prices. Government is also responsible to see that proper service is rendered to the community, and utility commissions conduct public hearings to formulate rules and determine rates. While competition may be wasteful of resources, experience sometimes has shown that lack of it results in inferior and more costly services. Recent deregulation of the gas and telephone industries show that, in the short run at least, competition tends to lower prices and to encourage industries to be more efficient.

School District (285)

A unit for the maintenance of public schools. School districts are fully responsible for public schools in 32 states, mostly responsible in 8 states, and partially responsible in 5 others. Alaska, Hawaii, Maryland, North Carolina, and Virginia have no independent school districts. School districts are usually governed by elected boards. The membership varies from 3 to 15, not usually compensated. The board has custody of school property, hires teachers, and maintains general supervision over schools. Nearly all states have boards of education with general authority over elementary and secondary education. The U.S. Census Bureau classifies school districts into two types:

dependent ones, which are part of a governmental unit, and independently run districts. Either type tends to be controlled by the same elite group that dominates other community activities. *See also* EDUCATION, DEPARTMENT OF, 122; SUPERINTENDENT OF PUBLIC INSTRUCTION, 287.

Significance   School district consolidation, especially of high schools, has increased dramatically. In recent years the number of these districts has declined appreciably, and the trend is continuing. Dwindling enrollments and skyrocketing costs have forced mergers into larger and more efficient systems. Still, there is no real uniformity in the structure of school districts. Only Delaware has a statewide school district. In New England, the town is the basic school district. In many southern states, the county is the basic unit for school districts. Financial inducements and breadth of program are the main reasons for consolidation, although it is not certain that centralization of school districts will save money. Some argue that, although the costs of education have not declined, they certainly would be much higher if the reduction in school districts had not taken place. By consolidating it is hoped that services will improve and confusion will be eliminated.

Social Welfare   (286)
Legislation and facilities designed to protect families and individuals who need help. Social welfare includes government and voluntary organizations that provide medical care, public health services, housing, community development, social adjustment, and facilities for recreation. Many programs are administered by federal, state, and local governments to assist the poor. Some federal programs include old age insurance, survivors' insurance, disability insurance, unemployment insurance, aid to the blind, food stamps, and Medicare. State and local programs include assistance supplementing federal aid to the elderly, the disabled, and the poor, and institutes for the destitute, lonely, and ailing. Some joint government programs are Medicaid, Aid to Families with Dependent Children, and public housing. The basic federal welfare program was legislated in 1935, and is called the Social Security Act. Social welfare programs are managed by the Department of Health and Human Services at the federal level and in the states by a department of human resources or a department of social welfare. *See also* HUMAN RESOURCES, DEPARTMENT OF, 128; UNEMPLOYMENT COMPENSATION, 288.

Significance   Social welfare programs are under severe criticism. Before the worldwide economic depression of the 1930s, social welfare programs looked toward a permanent class of paupers. However, the 1935 act looks toward restoration of families and individuals to a position as self-respecting and self-supporting members of society. The federal government determines the philosophy and structure of social welfare programs; the state and local governments implement most of them and determine eligibility. Qualification for welfare benefits is often arbitrary and differs among counties and states. The main explanation for disparity is that some localities are more affluent than others, but while affluence may be a partially satisfying explanation, political forces influencing welfare decisions cannot be ruled out. Many Democrats favor increased national responsibility for welfare programs, while Republicans would reduce benefits. Critics fear that the Democrats are attempting to create a permanent underclass, perpetually in need and dependent on government, particularly on Democrats.

Superintendent of Public Instruction   (287)

A state official responsible for supervising the public school system. The superintendent of public instruction, also known as commissioner of education in some states, is popularly elected in 18 states. In others he or she is either chosen by the state board of education or appointed by the governor. The main duties of this official are to oversee school district activities in teacher qualification, curriculum development, and school funding. In some states county government performs these services. Before public education, some Americans, like Thomas Jefferson, favored elementary education at public expense, but many others did not. The position of chief state officer was created with the 1850 approval of the first free school system in the nation in New York state. Today, public education is available in all states, largely run by superintendents of public instruction. *See also* EDUCATION, DEPARTMENT OF, 122; SCHOOL DISTRICT, 285.

Significance   The superintendent of public instruction runs one of the largest operations in state government. Considered in terms of current and recurring expenses and personnel, he or she holds a position of major responsibility. This office has developed from mainly clerical functions to provision of a vital service—educating citizens to participate in society and in national affairs. Taken together, the 50 state superintendents of public instruction in the country have the broad responsibility of educating some 60 million U.S. residents who attend public schools. These officials handle about $100 billion for the country's entire public education program. For

this reason many educators and social scientists insist the superintendent be professionally qualified and appointed by the state's chief
executive or the board of education. Consequently, the number of
elected superintendents has declined in recent years, but many
superintendents are still deeply involved in state and local politics
because of the increased demand for resources for education.

Unemployment Compensation   (288)

Benefits for jobless people, often called unemployment insurance.
Unemployment compensation is offered to unemployed workers
who, after a certain period of registration with the state employment
service, cannot find a suitable job. Both employers and employees pay
into the system, which is administered by the state. The federal
government levies an excise tax on the total payroll of all employers
of four or more persons. Ninety percent of this revenue is credited to
the states and the remainder used for administrative purposes. The
U.S. Department of the Treasury holds this revenue to be distributed
to states as needed. The 1935 Social Security Act provides for
payments for a limited period of time, and each state determines the
amount to be paid and for how long. The state plans differ in minor
details, but all conform to the same general specifications set by the
act. *See also* SOCIAL WELFARE, 286.

Significance   Unemployment compensation has been criticized for
a variety of reasons. Employers contend that the excise tax is an unfair
burden, and workers complain that the benefits are too low. While
these complaints have some basis in fact, undoubtedly the principal
threat to the security of the working population is joblessness. A
reasonable attempt was made in the 1930s to protect workers against
the effects of involuntary unemployment. The constitutionality of the
Social Security Act was upheld by the United States Supreme Court in
Steward Machine Co. v. Davis (301 U.S. 548: 1937). Despite fraudulent
attempts to gain benefits, the system is generally popular, and the
trend has been toward increasing the duration of benefits. Having
failed to solve the problem of unemployment, the United States and
other industrialized nations have ameliorated its effects. States vary in
their approaches to eligibility, and a major issue concerns whether
workers on strike are entitled to receive jobless benefits.

Urban Planning   (289)

A comprehensive and systematic study of present trends and future growth of cities. Urban planning embraces such areas as availability of land, resources, population growth, and socioeconomic and political factors. Planning is conducted on a permanent basis at all levels of government in the United States. At the local level much of the urban planning is conducted by a planning commission, which usually has five to nine members. It may consist of *ex officio* members, volunteers, or a combination of both. Members of the planning commission or board serve specific terms on a staggered basis, which contributes to their independence, since their terms need not coincide with those of mayors or council members. The powers and duties of the planning commission vary. Generally, it formulates planning proposals, holds hearings, promotes the public interest, and evaluates new proposals. Urban planning envelops zoning of property, streets, utilities, parks, recreation, housing, traffic, public health, and other social concerns. *See also* LAND USE PLANS, 278; ZONING, 290.

Significance   Urban planning is relatively new and carried on in almost all cities. A highly educated staff serves the commission, and political reality dictates that the city council usually follows its recommendations. The planners are subjected to pressure from special interest groups, and must also cope with shortages of resources. Modern planning recognizes the interrelationship between the physical and social environments, often focusing on growth and revitalization of urban neighborhoods. Urban planners are being urged nationally to find ways to facilitate favorable urban change. They must take three basic approaches to planning: first, stimulate the broadest understanding of emerging national growth and development trends and their local implications; second, identify development options and specific issues requiring public attention; and, third, define a local means to plan for urban change with private and public cooperation.

Zoning   (290)

Regulation of the use and occupation of property. Zoning is division of a city (or county) by statute or ordinance into districts and regulation of the use of land for commercial, industrial, and residential purposes. The principal types of zoning are: (1) exclusionary zoning, which sets stringent requirements for housing construction; (2) aesthetic zoning, which is designed to preserve the aesthetic qualities of an area; (3) cluster zoning, which limits residential density to a minimum lot size; (4) contract zoning, which is an agreement by the landowner to restrict physical development of the property;

(5) density zoning, which regulates open space and density of population; (6) spot zoning, which allows a particular lot to deviate from conformity with the area; (7) euclidean zoning, which sets forth use of certain areas in the ordinances; and (8) floating zoning, which allows an exception to the use of a district to permit building of shopping centers and apartments. Zoning had its origins in cities and has since spread to rural areas. *See also* BUILDING CODES, 265; LAND USE PLANS, 278; URBAN PLANNING, 289.

Significance   Zoning provides for orderly economic development and planned residential communities. State zoning safeguards the health, safety, and welfare of the community. The United States Supreme Court upheld zoning as a proper exercise of police power in *Euclid v. Amber Realty Co.*, (272 U.S. 365: 1926). Zoning also protects property values by designating residential areas by income groups. Social reformers have called this "zoning for race," as it separates large single-family home neighborhoods from low-income apartments and industrial establishments. They note that Houston, Texas developed as a major city without zoning and that no affluent neighborhoods have been disrupted by the poor. Other areas of the country, they say, can do likewise. They consider zoning an unnecessary restriction intended to keep various racial groups apart. It permits the suburban communities to maintain their distinct character and the homogeneity of the population.

NOTES

1. Federal and State Constitutions

1. James F. Barnes, Marshall Carter, and Max J. Skidmore, *The World of Politics: A Concise Introduction* (New York: St. Martin's, 1984), 84.
2. Ibid., 85.

2. Intergovernmental Relations

1. William H. Riker, *Federalism: Origin, Operation, Significance* (Boston: Little, Brown, 1964), 152–153.
2. Ibid.
3. Morton Grodzins, "The American Federal System," in *A Nation of States*, ed. by Robert A. Goldwin (Chicago: Rand McNally, 1964), 21–22.
4. Jeffrey R. Henig, *Public Policy and Federalism: Issues in State and Local Politics* (New York: St. Martin's, 1985), 16.
5. David B. Walker, *Toward a Functioning Federalsim* (Cambridge, Mass.: Winthrop Publishers, 1981), 46.
6. Edwin S. Corwin, "A Constitution of Powers and Modern Federalism," in *Essays in Constitutional Law*, ed. by Robert G. McCloskey (New York: Alfred A. Knopf, 1962), 188–189.
7. Walker, *Toward a Functioning Federalism*, 63–65.
8. Jack L. Walker, "The Diffusion of Innovations among the American States," *American Political Science Review* 63 (September 1969): 880–899.
9. Morton Grodzins, "The Federal System," in *American Government: Readings and Cases*, ed. by Peter Woll (Boston: Little, Brown, 1972), 125.
10. Stephen Goode, *The New Federalism: States Rights in American History* (New York: Franklin Watts, 1983), 17.
11. Ibid.
12. Walker, *Toward a Functioning Federalism*, 121.
13. Ibid., 114.

14. Terry Sanford, *Storm Over the States* (New York: McGraw-Hill, 1967), 80.

15. George E. Hale and Marian L. Palley, *The Politics of Federal Grants* (Washington, D.C.: Congressional Quarterly Press, 1981), 26.

16. Hale and Palley, *The Politics of Federal Grants*, 78.

17. Walker, *Toward a Functioning Federalism*, 186–187.

18. Hale and Palley, *The Politics of Federal Grants*, 166.

19. Rodney L. Mott, *Home Rule for American Cities* (Washington, D.C.: American Municipal Association, 1949), 11–12.

20. Parris N. Glendening and Mavis M. Reeves, *Pragmatic Federalism* (Pacific Palisades, Calif.: Palisades Publishers, 1977), 53.

3. Parties and Elections

1. Thomas R. Dye, *Politics in States and Communities* (Englewood Cliffs, N.J.: Prentice-Hall, 1985), 272.

2. Nelson W. Polsby and Aaron Wildavsky, *Presidential Elections* (New York: Scribner's, 1976), 35–59.

3. John F. Bibby, "Parties in State Politics," in *Politics in the American States: A Comparative Analysis,* ed. by Virginia Gray, Herbert Jacob, and Kenneth N. Vines (Boston: Little, Brown, 1983), 68–69.

4. Ibid., 99.

5. Malcolm E. Jewell and David M. Olson, *American State Political Parties and Elections* (Homewood, Ill.: Dorsey Press, 1982), 26.

6. Michael J. Ross, *State and Local Politics and Policy: Change and Reform* (Englewood Cliffs, N.J.: Prentice-Hall, 1987), 43.

7. Kevin P. Phillips, *Post-Conservative America* (New York: Random House, 1982), 222.

8. Howard L. Reiter, *Parties and Elections in Corporate America* (New York: St. Martin's, 1987), 285.

9. Ruth K. Scott and Ronald J. Hrebenar, *Parties in Crisis: Party Politics in America* (New York: John Wiley, 1979), 274.

10. Ibid., 274–275.

11. E. E. Schattschneider, *Party Government* (New York: Rinehart, 1942), 1.

12. Frank J. Sorauf, *Party Politics in America* (Boston: Little, Brown, 1980), 8–10.

13. Reiter, *Parties and Elections,* 159–160.

14. Harry Holloway and John George, *Public Opinion: Coalitions, Elites, and Masses* (New York: St. Martin's, 1986), 287.

15. M. Margaret Conway and Frank B. Feigert, "Motivation, Incentive Systems, and the Political Party Organization," *American Political Science Review* 57 (December 1968): 1165–1166.

16. John J. Harrigan, *Politics and Policy in States and Communities* (Boston: Little, Brown, 1984), 102–106.

4. The Legislative Branch

1. Citizens Conference on State Legislatures, *The Sometimes Governments: A Critical Study of the 50 American Legislatures* (New York: Bantam Books, 1971), 23–24.

2. Jeffrey M. Elliot and Sheikh R. Ali, *The Presidential-Congressional Political Dictionary* (Santa Barbara, Calif.: ABC-Clio, 1984), 250.

5. The Executive Branch

1. Robert S. Lorch, *State and Local Politics: The Great Entanglement* (Englewood Cliffs, N.J.: Prentice-Hall, 1983), 407.

2. Larry Sabato, *Goodbye to Good-Time Charlie: The American Governor Transformed, 1950–1970* (Lexington, Mass.: Lexington Books, 1978), 50–56.

3. Lorch, *State and Local Politics,* 155.

4. Ibid., 135.

7. Bureaucracy and Civil Service

1. Randall B. Ripley and Grace A. Franklin, *Bureaucracy and Policy Implementation* (Homewood, Ill.: Dorsey Press, 1982), 50–51.

2. Ibid., 51–52.

3. Phillip E. Present, *People and Public Administration: Case Studies and Perspectives* (Pacific Palisades, Calif.: Palisades Publishers, 1979), 97–99.

4. Saul Gellerman, *The Management of Human Resources* (Hinsdale, Ill.: Dryden Press, 1976), 1.

5. George J. Gordon, *Public Administration in America* (New York: St. Martin's, 1978), 263.

6. Joseph LaPalombara, *Interest Groups in Italian Politics* (Princeton, N.J.: Princeton University Press, 1963), 262.

7. B. Guy Peters, *The Politics of Bureaucracy: A Comparative Perspective* (New York: Longman, 1978), 150.

8. William L. Morrow, *Public Administration: Politics and the Political System* (New York: Random House, 1975), 170.

9. Ibid., 171.

10. Present, *People and Public Administration,* 133.

11. Rufus E. Miles, Jr., "Considerations for a President Bent on Reorganization," *Public Administration* 37 (March–April 1977): 158.

12. Taylor Branch, "Courage without Esteem: Profiles in Whistle-Blowing," in *The Culture of Bureaucracy,* ed. by Charles Peters and Michael Nelson (New York: Holt, Rinehart and Winston, 1978), 218.

8. Counties, Districts, and Towns and Townships

1. Herbert S. Duncombe, *Modern County Government* (Washington, D.C.: National Association of Counties, 1977), 8–12.

2. Michael J. Ross, *State and Local Politics and Policy: Change and Reform* (Englewood Cliffs, N.J.: Prentice-Hall, 1987), 171.

3. Joseph F. Zimmerman, *State and Local Government* (New York: Barnes & Noble, 1976), 143–144.

4. Robert B. Morgan and C. Edward Alexander, "A Survey of Local Prosecutors," *State Government* 47 (Winter 1974): 43.

5. Donald B. Hayman, "The County Manager," in *County Government in North Carolina*, ed. by Joseph S. Ferrell (Chapel Hill: University of North Carolina, 1979), 23.

6. Ann H. Elder and George C. Kiser, *Governing American States and Communities: Constraints and Opportunities* (Glenview, Ill.: Scott, Foresman, 1983), 243–244.

7. Michael Engel, *State and Local Politics: Fundamentals and Perspectives* (New York: St. Martin's, 1985), 238.

8. Ibid.

9. Cities and Metropolitan Areas

1. Thomas R. Dye, *Politics in States and Communities* (Englewood Cliffs, N.J.: Prentice-Hall, 1985), 350.

2. "Are Our Cities Dying?" *New York Times*, 2 May 1971.

3. Edward C. Banfield, *The Unheavenly City* (Boston: Little, Brown, 1970), 1.

4. Ibid.

5. Richard P. Nathan and Charles Adams, "Understanding Central City Hardship," *Political Science Quarterly* 91 (Spring 1976): 51–52.

6. Brett W. Hawkins, "Public Opinion and Metropolitan Reorganization in Nashville," *Journal of Politics* 28 (May 1966): 408–413.

7. Raymond L. Bancroft, "America's Mayors and Councilmen: Their Problems and Frustrations," *Nation's Cities* (April 1974), 20.

8. Jeptha J. Carrell, "The City Manager and His Council: Sources of Conflict," *Public Administration Review* 22 (December 1962): 204–207.

9. Dye, *Politics in States and Communities*, 312–313.

10. John P. Kotter and Paul R. Lawrence, *Mayors in Action: Five Approaches to Urban Governance* (New York: John Wiley, 1974), 249.

11. Douglas Yates, *The Ungovernable City* (Cambridge, Mass.: MIT Press, 1977), 165.

12. Jeffrey L. Pressman, "Preconditions of Mayoral Leadership," *American Political Science Review* 66 (June 1972): 511–524.

13. John J. Harrigan, *Politics and Policy in States and Communities* (Boston: Little, Brown, 1984), 144.

14. Dye, *Politics in States and Communities*, 316.

15. *Newsweek*, 13 March 1967, 38.

16. Dye, *Politics in States and Communities*, 373–374.

17. Harrigan, *Politics and Policy*, 184–185.

18. Nelson Wikstrom, *Councils of Government: A Study of Political Incrementalism* (Chicago: Nelson-Hall, 1977), 38.

19. John F. Dillon, *Commentaries on the Law of Municipal Corporations* (Boston: Little, Brown, 1911), 448.

20. Ibid.

21. Edward C. Banfield and James Q. Wilson, *City Politics* (Cambridge, Mass.: Harvard University Press, 1963), 65.

22. Robert L. Lineberry, "Reforming Metropolitan Governance: Requiem or Reality?" *Georgetown Law Journal* 58 (March–May 1970): 675–718.

23. *Report of the Advisory Commission on Civil Disorders* (New York: Bantam Books, 1968), 22.

10. Financing State and Local Government

1. Ann H. Elder and George C. Kiser, *Governing American States and Communities: Constraints and Opportunities* (Glenview, Ill.: Scott, Foresman, 1983), 141.

2. Thomas J. Anton, *The Politics of State Expenditures in Illinois* (Urbana: University of Illinois Press, 1966), 126–131.

3. Nicholas Henry, *Public Administration and Public Affairs* (Englewood Cliffs, N.J.: Prentice-Hall, 1975), 159–160.

4. Allen Schick, *Budget Innovation in the States* (Washington, D.C.: Brookings Institution, 1971), 103.

5. Aaron Wildavsky, *The Politics of the Budgetary Process* (Boston: Little, Brown, 1979), 203.

6. Ibid., 215–216.

7. Michael Engel, *State and Local Politics: Fundamentals and Perspectives* (New York: St. Martin's, 1985), 280.

8. Joseph A. Pechman and Benjamin A. Okner, *Who Bears the Tax Burden?* (Washington, D.C.: Brookings Institution, 1974), 326.

9. Joseph A. Pechman, *Who Paid the Taxes, 1966–85?* (Washington, D.C.: Brookings Institution, 1985), 60.

10. Alvin Rabushka and Pauline Ryan, *The Tax Revolt* (Stanford, Calif.: Hoover Institution, 1982), 1.

11. Engel, *State and Local Politics*, 280.

12. Ibid.

13. Advisory Commission on Intergovernmental Relations, *Significant Features of Fiscal Federalism, 1980–81* (Washington, D.C.: ACIR, 1981), 36.

14. J. Richard Aronson and John J. Hilley, *Financing State and Local Government* (Washington, D.C.: Brookings Institution, 1986), 179.

15. *Business Week*, 11 July 1983, 80–87.

16. Steven D. Gold, "Recent Development in State Finances," *National Tax Journal* (March 1983): 14.

17. Advisory Commission on Intergovernmental Relations, *Changing Public Attitudes on Government and Taxes* (Washington, D.C.: U.S. Government Printing Office, 1981), 38.

18. Robert Cline, *User Charges* (Washington, D.C.: Advisory Commission on Intergovernmental Relations, 1984), 10.

19. Ibid., 11.

11. Citizen Needs and Government Policy

1. Robert S. Lorch, *State and Local Politics: The Great Entanglement* (Englewood Cliffs, N.J.: Prentice-Hall, 1983), 407.

INDEX

In this index, references in **bold** type indicate the entry numbers where that particular term is defined within the text. Numbers in roman type refer to entries containing additional information about a term that the reader may wish to consult for further information, e.g., Delegated powers, **10**, 24.